27.50

RED SPY
QUEEN

RED SPY QUEEN

A Biography of ELIZABETH BENTLEY

Kathryn S. Olmsted

The University of North Carolina Press

Chapel Hill and London

Set in Charter, Champion, and Justlefthand types
by Tseng Information Systems, Inc.
Manufactured in the United States of America

The paper in this book meets the guidelines for
permanence and durability of the Committee on
Production Guidelines for Book Longevity of the
Council on Library Resources.

Library of Congress
Cataloging-in-Publication Data
Olmsted, Kathryn S.
Red spy queen : a biography of Elizabeth Bentley /
by Kathryn S. Olmsted.
p. cm.
Includes bibliographical references and index.
ISBN 0-8078-2739-8 (cloth : alk. paper)
1. Bentley, Elizabeth. 2. Women communists—United
States—Biography. 3. Communism—United States—
1917– 4. Intelligence service—Soviet Union.
5. Espionage—Soviet Union. 6. Informers—United
States—Biography. I. Title.
HX84.B384 O45 2002
327.1247073'092—dc21   2002002824

06 05 04 03 02   5 4 3 2 1

To

my mother, Joane,

and the memory of my father,

Alvin Olmsted

Contents

A section of illustrations follows page 80.

Preface

On an unseasonably chilly day in August 1945, a Connecticut Yankee named Elizabeth Bentley stole into an industrial building in New Haven that housed a field office of the Federal Bureau of Investigation. Looking anxiously over her shoulder for tails, she rode the elevator to a top floor, then slunk down the stairs. She took a deep breath and entered the small government office. Just two weeks earlier, the Second World War—and the grand alliance between the United States and the Soviet Union—had come to an end. Bentley was now thinking of ending her own, illegal alliance with Soviet intelligence.

When she finally began to tell her tale to the FBI, Bentley would name more than fifty Americans who she said had helped her spy for the Soviets. She would describe and identify the most powerful Soviet spymasters in the United States, as well as the American government officials who served as their agents. Her defection would effectively shut down Soviet espionage in the United States for a period of years.

She would also help trigger an earthquake in American politics. The Alger Hiss case, the Smith Act prosecutions of Communist Party leaders, and Senator Joe McCarthy's denunciations of State Department Reds all stemmed from Bentley's decision to walk into that forbidding FBI office. Her allegations seemed to provide hard evidence that the Soviets had undermined the American government—that there was, in McCarthy's words, a "conspiracy so immense" to destroy the United States from within.

Despite her importance, Bentley has been neglected by historians.[1] In part, this neglect has been due to the difficulty of assessing her truthfulness. Now, though, new documents coming out of Russian and American archives make it possible to verify the broad outlines of her story—and to disprove some of her exaggerations.

Bentley has also been overlooked because many observers regarded her as a pathetic or even laughable figure. Walter Goodman, for example, condescendingly described her as "the heroine of all the bad novels she had ever read," while Robert Carr, in a stunning underestimation of her abilities, called her a "sadly confused idealist who was used by persons shrewder and cleverer than herself."[2] A large-boned, self-confident brunette with a sharp nose and receding chin, she was called a spy queen, an old biddy, a beautiful young blonde, and a neurotic old maid. Her critics spread rumors of her promiscuity, her abortions, her bisexual tendencies, and her alcoholism. She was, as her onetime boyfriend and fellow witness Harvey Matusow says, "probably attacked more than the other witnesses of the period."[3] She seemed somehow unworthy of the type of serious historical analysis applied to intellectual, male defectors like Whittaker Chambers.

But Bentley's "spy queen" image makes her more, rather than less, historically interesting. There was something about her that touched the fears and fantasies of postwar Americans. Her media image revealed Americans' concerns about gender relations after the upheaval of the war. Her story became interwoven with the cultural, as well as the political, history of the Cold War at home.

Finally, some critics have viewed Bentley as a relatively unimportant puppet of the political right. She did, indeed, serve the interests of the right. But she was never anyone's dummy. She became J. Edgar Hoover's top informant—and also his chief headache. She helped to create the spy scare, then threatened to discredit it with her own wild allegations and personal indiscretions. The FBI always had to balance its desire to promote her conservative political message with its distaste for her liberal standards of personal behavior. Once, an angry witness denounced Elizabeth to the bureau as a lying slut. The FBI agents responded that "they knew she was a 'slut,' but that she could be telling the truth about other things."[4]

At times, she did tell the truth; at other times, she was a lying, manipulative opportunist. Throughout her life, she was a bundle of contradictions. She was an alcoholic daughter of a temperance crusader; a fan, at different times, of Mussolini, Stalin, the pope, and J. Edgar Hoover; a shrewd woman who outsmarted the NKGB and the FBI but who chose boyfriends who abused her. She was, as one FBI agent who knew her says, "a highly intelligent woman with a very unfortunate life."[5]

Above all, she was an intensely lonely woman searching for love and acceptance. Ordinarily, such a personal quest would not be historically significant. But Elizabeth Bentley's particular search led her to betray her country, betray her friends, and initiate one of the most destructive episodes in U.S. political history.

Acknowledgments

Many people helped to make this book possible. Among the numerous archivists who assisted me in finding obscure documents, I especially appreciate the efforts of Valerie Browne at Loyola University of Chicago; Joy Eldridge at the University of Sussex; Janie Morris at the Perkins Library at Duke University; Carol Leadenham at the Hoover Institution; David Haight at the Eisenhower Library; Richard Gelbke and Greg Plunges at the National Archives in New York; and Fred Romanski at the National Archives in Maryland. Krystyna von Henneberg, Paula Findlen, and Anne Bressler all helped me in the difficult task of finding research assistants in Italy, and I could not have asked for better assistants than Federica Fabrizzi in Rome and Erika Moseson in Florence. Veronica Wilson also proved to be a knowledgeable and discerning research assistant in Connecticut. Other scholars pointed me to new sources or gave me drafts of their own work. I would particularly like to thank Bruce Craig, Thomas Devine, John Earl Haynes, Gary May, Herbert Romerstein, Roger Sandilands, and Allen Weinstein. Hayden Peake, who provided me with documents and contacts from his own research on Bentley, was a model of scholarly generosity. My colleague Karen Halttunen read the chapters on gender with her trademark intelligence and insight.

I am very grateful to all of the people who graciously submitted to interviews about remote—and sometimes painful—episodes in their past or their relatives' past. Eleanore Lee provided tips, encouragement, and much information about her uncle, Duncan Lee. George Pancoast, Harvey Matusow, Robert Lamphere, Jack Danahy, John Turrill, Edward Buckley, and Don Jardine obligingly shared their memories of Bentley in interviews. Ishbel Lee, Joanna Budenz Gallegos, Nancy Applegate, Sheila Kurtz, Richard Green, and Howard Dejean answered key questions. At the Holy Trinity Episcopal Church in Middletown, the Reverend Margaret Minnick provided great help in researching Bentley's last years. Kenneth Boagni graciously opened up his Louisiana barn to my intrepid research assistant, Laura Midgett, to assist her search for documents on Bentley. Roger Turrill kindly agreed to send me the photograph of his cousin Elizabeth in his family photo album.

Because I began this project as an independent scholar, I faced many obstacles and incurred great debts. Roland Marchand, my late mentor, helped me obtain library privileges and offered unrelenting optimism and support. My editor, Chuck Grench, believed in this manuscript from the beginning. In Washington, my incredibly supportive friends May Liang and Jim Lintott fed, housed, and chauffeured me during my research trips. The Great Falls van pool provided transportation and lively conversation. My sister Ann Holmes critiqued multiple drafts of the manuscript and buoyed me with her enthusiasm. My mother, Joane, and my late father, Alvin Olmsted, sustained me as always with their encouragement and love. I owe my greatest debt to my husband, Bill Ainsworth, who not only edited the manuscript but also used his vacation time to watch our three young children, Julia, Sarah, and Isabella, while I went on research trips. I could not have written this book without him.

ACKNOWLEDGMENTS

RED SPY
QUEEN

The Sad & Lonely Girl

fter she had launched her career as a former "blonde spy queen," Elizabeth Bentley liked to emphasize her patriotic origins by claiming that one of her ancestors had signed the Declaration of Independence. It made a good story, but it was not true.

Her family certainly had impeccable New England credentials. Both of her parents could trace their families back to the early days of Connecticut, when sturdy English immigrants had carved out towns in the wilderness. Her mother's family, the Terrills or Turrills, as the name was variously spelled, had lived for generations in New Milford, a charming Connecticut town complete with white clapboard buildings and a Roger Sherman Hall on the town green. Favorite son Sherman was the Declaration signer whom Elizabeth credited with siring one of her ancestors. He had indeed lived in New Milford for eighteen years and fathered fifteen children. None of them, though, ever had a descendent named Elizabeth Bentley.[1]

Apparently, Elizabeth believed that a connection to Sherman would add to the shock value of her autobiography. The evil Communists, she implied, could corrupt even the children of the nation's founders. It was not the only time she would fudge the facts to create a better story.

Elizabeth's father, Charles Prentiss Bentley, was a dry-goods merchant originally from Morristown, New Jersey. After relocating to New Milford, he met and married a "strict but inspiring" local schoolteacher, May Charlotte Turrill. Charles and May both married rather late: the groom was thirty-seven, and the bride, at twenty-nine, was facing the specter of spinsterhood. Their wedding was held on April 10, 1907, at St. John's Episcopal Church.[2] Nine months later, on January 1, 1908, Elizabeth Terrill Bentley was born. Her parents never had another child.

Charles Bentley worked for many worthy causes in New Milford, including temperance reform. He was so committed to curbing alcohol abuse, in fact, that he helped found a temperance newspaper when the *New Milford Gazette* refused to print his group's antidrinking ad. For several years he served as the journal's business manager.[3]

The Bentleys and the Turrills, in short, were old-family Republicans and Episcopalians who enjoyed respect from their fellow small-town New Englanders. They were, in the words of the townspeople, "good, Christians, honest."[4]

They were also somewhat restless. Charles Bentley was a hapless businessman. "It seemed as if everything he tried failed," Elizabeth recalled later. He was a partner in a mill that burned down, then in a store that folded.[5] When his daughter turned seven, Charles began moving his family from state to state in a fruitless search for success. Elizabeth, who described herself as a "lonely, withdrawn child," attended public schools in four towns before her father finally settled into a position as a department store manager in Rochester, New York, in 1924.[6] Fellow executives praised him as "a very nice gentleman of the straight-laced New England type."[7] May Bentley taught eighth grade in Rochester, where she was remembered as a woman who generously gave food to the hungry. Elizabeth later portrayed her childhood home as "cluttered up with lonely people" whom her mother had invited for dinner.[8]

Elizabeth attended East High School in Rochester, where the high school yearbook jocularly described her as "strong, active and bright; always jolly and full of life."[9] She later told the local newspaper that the "nicest" memories of her life were from Rochester, where she filled her days with piano lessons, Girl Scouts, the Presbyterian Church, and basketball.[10] But former students surveyed years later had only dim and generally unfavorable memories of

THE SAD AND LONELY GIRL

the "not very popular" and "uncolorful" girl who had transferred in during her junior year.[11]

Elizabeth later explained that her "very, very strict" mother "didn't allow me to befriend girls of my age who were drinking, smoking and visiting nightclubs"—all popular activities for teens in the 1920s.[12] In later years, she seldom talked about her parents except to describe her upbringing as "overly stern" and old-fashioned.[13] Whatever her relationship with her parents may have been during her childhood, she spent most of her adulthood trying to find love and acceptance.

In 1926, eighteen-year-old Elizabeth won a scholarship to Vassar College, the oldest and most elite women's college in the United States. There, this sheltered young woman met emancipated students who did all the things her mother abhorred. Many Vassar "girls" rouged their cheeks, shortened their skirts, swilled their gin, smoked their Lucky Strikes, and "petted" with their boyfriends.[14]

During her undergraduate years, Elizabeth was just an observer of these changes in women's roles and sexual mores. The cloak of loneliness she had donned in high school still clung to her at Vassar. She was a tall girl—over five feet nine—with a large build, long neck, and shy smile. She was growing into the kind of woman that some people would term "somewhat attractive," but more critical observers would call plain. At Vassar, Elizabeth seemed uncomfortable among her rich, prestige-conscious classmates. She made few friends and took solitary bird walks at 5:00 A.M.[15] One former classmate, Elizabeth Bliss, described her as a "kind of a sad sack, plain, dull, very teacherlike. She didn't have a single boyfriend, if I recall correctly, a pathetic person really. Everyone that knew her just called her Bentley. She was a sad and lonely girl."[16] Nor did she distinguish herself academically: she was an indifferent student, earning a C plus average.[17] One of her aunts described her as "a brainy girl who spent too much time on world affairs and not enough on living."[18]

Elizabeth later claimed that the views of "world affairs" she found at Vassar turned her into a political radical. Indeed, she said, Vassar "had gotten me to the point where I was a complete pushover for communism."[19] Certainly, Vassar had a reputation in the late 1920s for independent thinking. Once the depression hit, many Vassar students began to feel guilty about their comfortable lives at an exclusive school during a time of such privation.[20] The college hosted a chapter of the League for Industrial Democracy, a student organization with socialistic ideals, which Elizabeth joined briefly.[21]

Moreover, Vassar had on its faculty one of the most influential leftists in American higher education at that time, the director Hallie Flanagan. Elizabeth later greatly stressed the influence of her one drama course with Flanagan. The director, who was just starting to build her reputation as head of the Vassar Experimental Theatre, overflowed with enthusiasm for the Communist government in Russia. In 1930, shortly after she taught Elizabeth, she took some Vassar students to Leningrad and burbled in her journal, "Oh, I was right. Russia is what I thought it was, only infinitely more. It is a country of free men, it is a land of workers. They exist to help others."[22] Later in the 1930s, Flanagan oversaw the Federal Theater Project, the only federally supported theater in American history. The left-wing content of some of the plays it put on prompted a subpoena from the House Committee on Un-American Activities in 1938.

Knowing that Flanagan's name was well known to Red hunters, in her later testimony Elizabeth dwelt on the pernicious way Flanagan in particular and Vassar in general had affected her ideological development. However, in reality Hallie Flanagan was no more Elizabeth's political mother than Roger Sherman was her ancestral father. While admiring of the Soviets, Flanagan only produced two left-wing plays while Elizabeth was at Vassar.[23] Hundreds of young women passed through her classes without joining the Party. Indeed, Flanagan herself was never a Party member.

Most important, though, Elizabeth would not join the Party until five years after she had left Vassar's supposedly subversive influence. In the meantime, her political journey would take her on a detour hardly endorsed by Flanagan: down the path of Italian fascism.

One year before she was graduated from Vassar, Elizabeth was devastated by the unexpected and early death of her mother.[24] Emotionally adrift, she spent her small inheritance on three trips to Europe in the next four years. Her first grand tour came immediately after graduation in 1930. Before the trip, she was "shy and a virgin," she later told the Soviets. But on board ship, she was attracted to a British engineer and enjoyed her first romance.[25]

On her return, her Vassar degree in English, Italian, and French helped her win a teaching job at the exclusive Foxcroft preparatory and finishing school for girls in Middleburg, Virginia. She spent the next two years alternately teaching languages to Virginia's wealthiest daughters and attending school herself: one summer studying at the University of Perugia in Italy, and another at Middlebury College in Vermont. Her employers judged her to be a "very competent teacher."[26]

In 1932, she quit her job to attend graduate school full time at Columbia University. This was a relatively unusual choice for a woman at the time: women made up less than 20 percent of the doctoral students in the 1930s.[27] As she matured, she became more confident with men. In Perugia, she had an affair with an older Hungarian officer. At Columbia, she fell in love with an Arab student and moved in with him.[28] They planned to marry, but in 1933 she broke her engagement when she won a coveted fellowship to the University of Florence.

Before she left for Italy, her sixty-three-year-old father fell gravely ill. In April, he died of arteriosclerosis in a Connecticut convalescent home.[29] Orphaned at twenty-five, Elizabeth tried to ward off despair with continuous activity and amusement.

In the land of *la dolce vita,* she threw off the shackles of her strict upbringing. The Vassar girl who "didn't have a single boyfriend" suddenly had a different one every week. She slept with older men and younger men, single men and married men, soldiers and teachers, Italians and expatriates.[30] She lived the high life, even though as a financial aid recipient she could not afford it.[31] She borrowed money frequently from her friends and did not always repay it. Breaking the last of her parents' rules, she also drank to excess. Elizabeth would be an alcoholic throughout her life, but her public displays of drunken behavior began in Florence. At a New Year's Eve party in the home of Joseph Lombardo, a fellow exchange student, she challenged other women "to pull down your pants and have your partner take you right here on the floor."[32] Friends and acquaintances from this period in her life later characterized her as a "leech," a "bum," a "lush," and, inevitably, a "slut."[33] Not surprisingly, considering her enthusiasm for spontaneous sex in the years before oral contraceptives, there were rumors that she had had some illegal abortions.[34]

She never admitted her drinking problem to anyone, and she certainly never explained what drove her to the bottle.[35] It is possible, though, that she was self-medicating for depression and anxiety. "She used alcoholism to ease her pain," says one of her later boyfriends, Harvey Matusow, "and she had a lot of pain." Matusow suspects that she was manic-depressive.[36]

Throughout her life, she would have "blue periods" when she would weep and beg for help. She would often drink so much during these bouts of depression that she would be unable to leave her home for weeks at a time. She had different euphemisms for these episodes: sometimes she said she suffered from a "virus," or the "grippe," or the "black influenza." But her doctors and her friends suspected that her health problems were the result of too much alcohol.[37]

Elizabeth also developed her lifelong taste for political extremism in Florence. Like many Americans at the time, she was impressed by the Mussolini regime's order and efficiency. In 1934, the year Cole Porter wrote the popular lyric "You're the tops; you're Musso-li-ni," she joined the local group of college fascists. She was so active in the Gruppo Universitate Fascisti, in fact, that she began neglecting her studies.[38]

She did not need to study, however, once she started an affair

THE SAD AND LONELY GIRL

with her faculty adviser. Mario Casella was a prominent literary critic more than twenty years her senior. The recipient of literary awards and the author of several books, Casella taught classes in courtly romance literature.[39] He appears to have been charmed by his new American student and lover, for he assigned his assistant to write her master's thesis for her. Elizabeth did the research for the analysis of a fourteenth-century poem, but the assistant wrote the paper for her.[40]

Elizabeth's decision to claim credit for a master's thesis written by someone else was a case of monumental academic dishonesty. If her ruse had been discovered, she could have been kicked out of the university and stripped of her degree. But she relished taking risks; she loved breaking the rules and deceiving the authorities. Throughout her life, she seemed to believe that other people's regulations and laws did not apply to her. If egotism is a central ingredient for treason, as Rebecca West has said, then Elizabeth Bentley had it in abundance.[41]

Casella not only helped her get her graduate degree, but he also turned her against fascism. A critic of the Mussolini regime, Casella was on a special "watch list" of the Italian secret police.[42] Elizabeth's later claims of antifascist activism in Italy appear to stem from her romantic liaison with this anti-Mussolini professor.

Her lover's assistant could write her thesis, but he could not take her exams for her. In May, the University of Florence notified her that she had failed one of her courses and was in danger of being expelled. She had already been suspended twice, once for violating the university's ban on smoking. When she received the notice of possible expulsion, Elizabeth sank into depression. In despair, she swallowed some poison. She received medical help in time, and the U.S. consul in Florence hushed up the whole affair.[43]

She returned to New York that summer with an addiction to alcohol, considerable sexual experience, and a talent for deception. Tucked away in her luggage was a pilfered master's thesis with her name already typed on the title page. Her lover's assistant had written an impressive dissertation. It would not fool her professors, who knew immediately that "it was not hers and could not have been hers." But, as she had expected, it was simply too much work for them to contest it. She would get her degree.[44]

New York City in 1934 was a forbidding place for a recent graduate hoping to start a new life. As her ship entered the harbor, Elizabeth knew her job prospects were dismal. "Standing there on the deck, I felt alone and frightened," she remembered later.[45]

The scene that greeted her was bleak. Along Riverside Drive, close to Columbia, a line of tarpaper shacks, packing crates, and oil barrels served as makeshift "homes." New Yorkers who had no place else to go huddled in these "Hoovervilles" by night and raked through the dumps for food during the day. That winter, 40 percent of the city's workers were unemployed. Many New Yorkers fortunate enough to live under real roofs began to question an economic system that produced such tragedy. As New York writer (and later Communist) Hope Hale Davis wrote, "[S]omething was wrong with a day that began with buying a five-cent apple from an unemployed architect who stood shivering at the entrance to my building."[46]

Stuck in the ranks of these jobless professionals, Elizabeth grew increasingly angry about her situation. "All those years of academic study have been wasted," she concluded.[47] After months of fruitless job searching, she lowered her expectations and enrolled in business courses at Columbia. There, she thought, she could learn shorthand and typing and ultimately land a secretarial job. She took an apartment near the university. Her choice of accommodations turned out to be significant, for down the hall lived a woman who was unusually friendly to the lonely, unemployed Vassar graduate with a drinking problem. Her name was Lee Fuhr, and she was a Communist.

Actually, according to her FBI file, her name was Lini Moerkirk Fuhr. She had been born three years before Elizabeth in Paterson, New Jersey, into very different economic circumstances. A child of Dutch immigrants, she had spent her youth as a factory worker. Paterson was the site of a famous, violent strike in 1913, and the

THE SAD AND LONELY GIRL

city was known for its oppressed workers and radical politics. Despite her poverty, Fuhr had managed to improve herself through education, obtaining a nursing license and working toward a bachelor's degree in public health.[48]

Lee was a widow trying to balance her last year of undergraduate education at Columbia with raising her four-year-old daughter. She reached out to the solitary woman down the hall, and Elizabeth was more than happy to return the friendship. Soon, Elizabeth decided that Lee was "one of the most unselfish people I had ever known."[49]

Elizabeth quickly learned that Lee was vehemently antifascist. Conveniently enough, so was Elizabeth—or at least she had been for the past few months. She excised the profascist period from her life and implied that she had been an active opponent of fascism throughout her year in Florence. The story of Elizabeth Bentley, intrepid enemy of Mussolini, was born.

Lee was fascinated by Elizabeth's tales of the horrors of Italian fascism and invited her new friend to tell her stories to others in New York's antifascist community. In a short period of time, Elizabeth found herself at the center of a group of politically active, idealistic intellectuals who regarded her as an "expert" on Italian fascism and a heroine of sorts for "opposing" it.

Lee took Elizabeth to meetings of the American League against War and Fascism, a Communist-front group designed to expand and unify Americans' opposition to fascism in Europe. The members of the local chapter, mostly students and teachers at Columbia, paid Elizabeth great respect, and she blossomed in her new identity. "Surprisingly enough," she later wrote, "from then on my life took on a new zest. I seemed to have cast off the old feeling of listlessness and despair."[50] She met a new "circle of friends" and a new lover, a worker from Greece. She belonged, at last.

Soon, however, she discovered that her friends were nervous about discussing their politics. When Elizabeth jokingly mentioned the Communist Party at a meeting with other antifascists, the group fell silent. Lee loved to educate Elizabeth by pointing out the problems caused by capitalism, but she always hesitated to spell out the implications of her views. Finally, one day, after Elizabeth eagerly asked how the "new society" could be achieved in the United States, Lee confided that she belonged to the Party.[51]

At first Elizabeth was surprised by Lee's confession: she had always thought Communists were "the down-and-outers" she saw around Union Square. Even as she adjusted herself to Lee's true political beliefs, she did not want to join the Party. But as word of her reluctance spread among her new friends, she found that they became increasingly distant with her. One March afternoon, staring at the barren trees on Riverside Drive, craving companionship, Elizabeth decided to stop vacillating. She hurried over to Lee's apartment and asked for a membership application.[52]

Elizabeth had hesitated because she knew that joining the Party was not an act to be taken lightly. Not only were Communists ostracized, but the Party itself demanded total commitment. Elizabeth, for example, had to attend four meetings a week. At various times she served as her unit's financial secretary, agitprop director, and organizational director. She had to attend classes in Marxism-Leninism at the Party's Workers School, circulate petitions, throw parties for new recruits, attend rallies and marches, and even brave the occasional police baton. Many American members lasted only a few months or years, given these requirements. But, for the lonely woman from New England, the endless meetings were a small price to pay for the true comradeship the Party offered.

Elizabeth joined a movement in transition. For years the Party had been a small, largely foreign-born sect in America. After the Communists took power in Russia in 1917, left-wing admirers of the Bolsheviks in the United States had bolted from the Socialist Party and formed two small Communist parties. These parties faced daunting obstacles during their early years. Their membership, small to begin with, was sliced by 80 percent thanks to the anti-Communist drive launched in 1919 by the U.S. Department of Justice. Led by Attorney General A. Mitchell Palmer, a staunch anti-Communist with presidential ambitions, federal officials routinely arrested American Communists, held them without trial or counsel, and deported those who were foreign-born.

The first Red Scare ended in 1921, and the surviving Communists stumbled out from the underground to merge into one legal entity, the Communist Party of the United States of America. But the government persecution had a lasting effect. During the Red Scare, Communists had been forced to lie about their politics and even change their names. They lived in fear of government repression—and government infiltration. Party members grew increasingly paranoid about potential informers within their midst.

The stock market crash of 1929 and the subsequent depression could have provided Communism with its greatest recruiting opportunity. Here, after all, was proof that Marx had been right about the inherent contradictions of capitalism. But the Party did not take advantage of this opportunity for a few years. Following the dictates laid down by Soviet leaders, American Communists continued to shun alliances with liberals and even other leftists in the United States, reserving their harshest criticism for Norman Thomas, the leader of American Socialists.

Then the Party began to change. As fascism cast its shadow across Europe in 1934, the Communist International, or Comintern, in Moscow began to rethink its strident opposition to others on the left. International Communist leaders began their slow, halting progress toward a "Popular Front" with other antifascists. In August 1935, under orders from Moscow, the CPUSA tentatively began to make common cause with liberals.[53] The period of the Popular Front, which lasted from 1935 to 1939, was the most successful time for Communists in American history. Thousands of Americans like Elizabeth joined in the mid-1930s, bringing the Party to its peak in membership and influence; many more sympathized without actually signing membership cards. By 1936, for the first time, most Party members were native-born.[54]

The Party of the mid-1930s had several attractions for college graduates like Elizabeth. To Americans disgusted by the failures of capitalism, the Communists seemed to offer the most accurate roadmap to the future. Communist writer John Dos Passos derided Socialism as "near beer," and many American intellectuals agreed. A number of the most talented writers, artists, and philosophers in Europe and the United States began to gravitate toward the Communist Party, which seemed to be the only group taking action to prevent depressions and to stop Nazi expansionism.[55]

The CPUSA's theories on gender and sexuality also increased its appeal to young, educated, sexually emancipated women like Elizabeth. Theoretically, the Party advocated the end of discrimination against women in the marketplace and in the bedroom. Leaders condemned unequal pay along with the sexual double standard. Especially in their early years, Communists were known for their bohemian attitudes toward sex, and Party leaders had numerous affairs. Elizabeth clearly enjoyed this aspect of Party culture: she frequently invited visiting Communists from other cities to stay in her apartment, and sometimes invited them to sleep with her as well.[56]

Of course, the Party did not always deliver on its rhetorical commitments to gender equality. In general, American Communists in this era believed that male chauvinism was a "bourgeois concern," not nearly as important as racism or poverty. By the mid-1930s, Party leaders also toned down their rhetoric about sexual experimentation, hoping to broaden their appeal to culturally conservative American workers.

Nevertheless, despite its limits, the CPUSA still advanced a much more progressive and broad-minded view of women and of sex than other political parties in the United States. Women like Elizabeth had the opportunity to learn organizational and leadership skills while discovering an empowering ideology. Even if American Communist leaders seemed hesitant about ending sexism, feminists in the Party could always look for inspiration in the Soviet Union. There, they believed, the Bolsheviks had achieved true gender equality.[57]

Indeed, the Soviet Union, with its booming economy and just society, provided a model for every aspect of life, the Communists believed. At least, that was the image projected by the official Soviet press reports. In a world plagued with unemployment, Columbia student James Wechsler remembered, "[T]he Russians (we were told) had everybody working. If there were occasional reports of trouble in paradise, they could be discounted as the evil imaginings of the 'capitalist press.'"[58]

For many Americans like Elizabeth, the contrast between this "paradise" and the shattered American economy proved that Karl Marx had been right. "We felt that the world was moving very, very fast," remembered Jack Olsen, a Young Communist League organizer in California. "People joked about expecting the revolution in two or three years, but there was a feeling that this *was* a revolutionary period. No question that in our lifetime we'd see socialism."[59]

"History"—with a capital "H"—is repeatedly invoked by former Communists to explain their reasons for joining the Party. "That was the tremendous thing about those times. The sense of *history* that you lived with daily. The sense of remaking the world," one former Communist told author Vivian Gornick. Others used almost the same words: "A new world was coming—and I wanted to be part of it"; "We literally felt we were making history"; "We felt . . . like we had our hands on 'the throttle of history,' as we used to say. That's an extraordinary feeling."[60]

Elizabeth enjoyed this extraordinary feeling, and threw herself wholeheartedly into Communist activities. But it was a struggle to balance her Party obligations with her studies. In the fall of 1935, she once again began studying at Columbia, this time in the sociology department. She believed it would be easier to get a good government job with a doctorate in that field. She needed a loan, however, to continue her studies, and she was shocked when she discovered in October, two months into the semester, that the Italian department had vetoed her application.

Elizabeth immediately saw a potential for a political protest against the loan denial. Columbia's Italian department was notorious among New York leftists. The preceding spring, the *Nation* had proclaimed that "avowed fascists" controlled both the department itself and the Italian cultural center, the Casa Italiana.[61] In the fall of 1935, when the department denied the loan, New York antifascists were especially sensitive to fascist outrages because Mussolini had just invaded Ethiopia.

Given the timing of the loan denial—and the notoriety of those who denied it—Elizabeth seized the opportunity to gain stature in the eyes of her newfound leftist friends. She told the Columbia campus newspaper, the *Spectator*, that the loan had been denied because of her antifascist activities in Italy. Since these alleged activities are not documented in any other source, though, this explanation is extremely unlikely. A more probable reason was either her current membership in the American League against War and Fascism or her adviser's belief that she had not written her master's thesis. The dean's office explained that administrators approved loans after deciding "whether or not they were students of whom Columbia could be proud."[62]

Whatever the reasons for the denial, Elizabeth could not have hoped for a better response to her protests. Not only did the *Spectator* place the article on page 1, but the staff also wrote an editorial condemning the loan denial. "Every indication was that hers was a case of discrimination on account of her political views," the paper intoned the next day. The editors went on to suggest that the Italian department was "the nucleus of Mussolini's propaganda machine in this country."[63] Three days later, a near-riot occurred outside the Casa Italiana when fascist sympathizers assaulted a small group of antifascist protesters angry over two events: the appearance of the Italian consul and the denial of Elizabeth's loan.[64]

The battle in front of the Casa Italiana was just one of many antifascist protests at American colleges that year. It was an era when Columbia students held a torchlight parade for Angelo Herndon, a black Communist arrested for leading a march in Georgia. It was an era when the *Yale Daily News* editor could compliment the joie de vivre of Soviet youth and contrast it with the "harsh discipline and militarism" of Germany and Italy.[65] It was an era when

THE SAD AND LONELY GIRL

a young book reviewer at Columbia could snidely attack Socialist leader Norman Thomas from the left for his "pious slip-slop about war."[66] In this atmosphere, the twenty-seven-year-old Communist who had been denied a student loan for her "antifascist activities" in Italy was nothing short of a celebrity.

As Elizabeth struggled to survive the Great Depression with a succession of short-term jobs, she devoted all of her spare time to Party work. Some of the work was quite straightforward: distributing literature, for example, and collecting dues. But other aspects of her Party life grew more burdensome—and more bizarre.

Elizabeth first met Juliet Stuart Poyntz, one of the most intriguing and mysterious Communist spies in America, shortly after she joined the Party. Pauline Rogers, an official with the American League against War and Fascism, introduced the two women at a Childs restaurant in Manhattan. Elizabeth learned that this heavy-set, poorly dressed, middle-aged woman was—allegedly—organizing underground cells of revolutionaries in Italy. Known as "Mrs. Glazer" during this period of her life because of her brief marriage to a German, Poyntz wanted to discuss Italy with Elizabeth and learn Italian from her. Mrs. Glazer, it turned out, did not speak the language of the country she was attempting to organize.[67]

At least that's what Elizabeth was told. She did not know that her "student" had actually been one of the leading lights of the Communist Party in the 1920s. Like Bentley, Poyntz was a native-born Communist whose highbrow accent and Barnard-and-Oxford pedigree pleased leaders who were looking to put a more American face on the Party. A stirring speaker, Poyntz had been the first director of the Workers School in New York and a Communist congressional candidate. In 1934, though, she suddenly stopped her well-publicized involvement with the Party.[68]

Party insiders knew what it often meant when a formerly prominent member dropped out of public activities: the "dropout" had joined the underground. Ever since the first Red Scare, the CPUSA had maintained a secret department. This clandestine arm of the

Party was not well organized in the 1920s, but by the 1930s it had become a significant force.

The underground served many purposes. It regulated the activities of Party members, and it recruited, trained, and fielded potential spies. Sometimes these spies would infiltrate party "enemies" such as rival radical groups or fascist organizations. Sometimes they would collect information from sympathetic journalists. And sometimes, if they had government jobs, these agents would steal official documents that might be useful to the Party.[69] These underground members had a complicated relationship with Soviet intelligence agents. Officially, they worked for the American party. But often they would share the information they gathered with their counterparts in Moscow.

Indeed, Poyntz began working for Soviet intelligence in 1934.[70] Her duties included spotting and recruiting future agents—particularly women.[71] Elizabeth, with her Vassar degree and her alleged antifascist credentials, was a leading prospect. Poyntz, however, was an incompetent recruiter. She had three lengthy meetings with Elizabeth without even beginning to discuss antifascism or disclose her true purposes. New to the Party, Elizabeth still had no idea that this woman wanted something from her other than Italian lessons. Moreover, she was put off by Poyntz's rambling and abusive tirades.

According to Elizabeth's autobiography, she was also shocked by Poyntz's lack of traditional moral values. During their fourth meeting, Poyntz suddenly erupted in fury when Elizabeth declined a second drink. As a Communist underground agent in Italy, she shrieked, Elizabeth would have to drink heavily and sleep with many men to help the cause. The movement did not need a delicate "hot-house flower."[72]

Elizabeth's autobiography is filled with improbable moments like this. She consistently portrays herself as an innocent schoolgirl who was appalled by the Communists' flouting of traditional sexual mores. However, given her history of alcohol use and sexual adventures, it seems unlikely that Poyntz would find her wanting in this area.

But Poyntz certainly did something to antagonize and terrify her would-be recruit. Elizabeth was especially upset when Poyntz introduced her to a slick, rather intimidating foreigner—"Mr. Smith"—who promised her financial help for school and seemed to expect sexual favors in return.[73] "Mr. Smith" was actually a Russian agent who used his position to recruit, then assault, American women.[74]

As an ardent and idealistic Communist, Elizabeth decided that "Glazer" must be an imposter and a counterrevolutionary. She was sure that the Party would never allow such an unpleasant person to hold an important job. Determined to expose the infiltrator, Elizabeth and a male friend charged over to Poyntz's apartment and accused her of being a fraud and a spy.

They were shocked at her response. "Her face went chalk white and the rouge stood out in blobs," Elizabeth later wrote. "I don't think I have ever seen such naked terror in anyone's eyes in my life." Elizabeth glimpsed the figure of a man hiding in the next room, and wondered if he might have anything to do with her fear.[75]

Two days later, Poyntz stormed over to Elizabeth's apartment with Pauline Rogers, the woman who had initially introduced them. After loudly denouncing Elizabeth as a subversive, she paused and stared directly into her eyes. "Just remember one thing," she said, "if ever you meddle in my affairs again, I'll see that you're taken care of. You'll be put six feet under and you won't come back to do any more talking!"[76]

In the end, though, it was Poyntz who was put six feet under. Shortly after she threatened Elizabeth's life, she visited Moscow and grew disillusioned with the Communist cause. According to ex-Communist Benjamin Gitlow, "She saw how men and women with whom she had worked, men and women she knew were loyal to the Soviet Union and to Stalin, were sent to their doom."[77] After she returned to New York, there were rumors that she planned to write about her years in the underground.

In June 1937, Poyntz took a phone call at her hotel from a former lover. She put on her hat and coat and walked out into the night.

In her room, her clothes were neatly folded, her passport was in her drawer, and a candle was burning. She was never seen again. One of her friends, the anarchist Carlo Tresca, investigated her disappearance and concluded that her old lover had lured her out to be kidnapped and killed.[78]

Many years later, Elizabeth would remember Poyntz's fate and learn important lessons from it. The long arm of Stalin's enforcers, it seemed, reached even to the residential hotel rooms of lonely, single women in New York.

Juliet Poyntz's fury—and even her subsequent disappearance— did not end Elizabeth's contacts with Soviet intelligence, however. She was too good a prospect for the Soviets to ignore. She had no foreign accent, no police record, and no family to hinder her in "special" work. Over the next two years, Soviet spies met intermittently with her but did not activate her as an agent.[79]

Actually, as in all the major developments in her life, Elizabeth made her own decision to become a Soviet spy. In effect, she activated herself. She later claimed that she just happened to get a job at a fascist propaganda agency, thanks to a tip from the Columbia placement office. But she told the Soviets a much different story. After she had tried unsuccessfully to get a job at the Romanian consulate, she "managed to join" Mussolini's propaganda bureau, called the Italian Library of Information.[80] Excited by the opportunity to spy on and sabotage the fascists, she rushed down to the "inner sanctum of United States communism," as ex-Communist James Wechsler called it: the ninth floor of the CPUSA headquarters on East Thirteenth Street.[81]

At the Party offices, Elizabeth was directed to an Italian Communist with the improbable alias of "F. Brown." He assigned her to a contact who seemed bored by her reports. When she protested, he promised to introduce her to someone more important.[82]

On October 15, 1938, Elizabeth and "Comrade Brown" walked to the corner of Eighth Street and University Place to meet her new controller.[83] A short, sturdy man in his mid-forties "appeared seemingly out of nowhere," Elizabeth remembered later. He was well built, with dazzling blue eyes and red hair. He spoke English well, but with an Eastern European accent. His name, he said, was "Timmy."[84]

Elizabeth did not know that she was meeting one of the Soviets' most important intelligence agents in the United States. She did know very quickly, however, that she had met the love of her life.

[2]
Vitally Important Work

The man Elizabeth Bentley met on a street corner in 1938 was an authentic Bolshevik agitator. He had been born an outsider, a Jew in the anti-Semitic Russian empire. His family was rather wealthy, but, like many Jews in Russia, they were attracted by the Communist promise to overthrow the bloody Russian dictatorship. At the age of eight, he braved the secret police by distributing illegal Communist literature. When he was a teenager, the police threw him in prison for his Bolshevik activities. One day, the guards dragged him into the courtyard with other revolutionaries to be shot. He escaped by falling to the ground and playing dead for two days.

His early brush with death confirmed Jacob Raisin's determination to overthrow the repressive czar. After his release from prison, he continued his underground work. The police arrested him again for running a radical printing house and sent him into Siberian exile. He spent two years at hard labor before managing to escape to Japan. Eventually, with help from other Communists, Raisin arrived in the United States and became a citizen. His sisters and parents also came to America. Continuing his radical agitation in his new home, Raisin became one of the founding members of the U.S. Communist Party.[1] The stocky, sandy-haired ideologue was deeply involved in Party factional disputes and organizational efforts. By the early 1920s, he was helping to organize workers and to write, edit, publish, and distribute Communist newspapers. The fledgling Bureau of Investigation began to follow his activities as early as 1922. Because of the government's suppression of radicals, Raisin had already adopted an alias. He took the name Golos, the Russian word for "voice."[2]

As a survivor of Siberian labor camps and a botched mass execution, Golos was fanatically loyal to the Communist cause. He would maintain that loyalty in the United States. When the Party directed him to claim that he was married so that a woman in his unit could get a passport, he complied. He never officially married her, but they lived together for some time. He was distressed when she later bore a son against his wishes. In 1925, when the Kuzbas industrial colony in the Soviet Union asked for his assistance, Golos eagerly asked the Party bosses for permission to go to Siberia and help rebuild Soviet industry. He stayed for two years. When he returned to the United States, he was ready to do anything the Party required.[3]

Stationed in New York, Golos undertook his first secret job for the Party: getting passports for Soviet spies and other Communists who wanted to enter the country undetected. He bribed government workers and officials at foreign consulates to provide him with fake passports and birth certificates. At the same time, his "cover"—his ostensible job—was the directorship of World Tourists, a travel agency that sent packages and arranged trips to the Soviet Union.[4] By 1930, secret Soviet intelligence cables already referred to him as "our reliable man in the U.S."[5]

In 1934, Golos expanded his power and responsibilities within the Party when he became the head of its Central Control Commission. Anthony Cave Brown has compared the commission with the Spanish Inquisition: "As with Tomas de Torquemada and Isabella I of Spain, so with Golos and Stalin," he writes.[6] Golos's job, in short, was to make sure that all Party members toed the Stalinist line. Violators were hauled before his secretive tribunal—Golos himself hid behind a screen—and were forced to recant their unorthodox positions. If their answers were not satisfactory, they were expelled from the Party. Only true Party insiders had even heard of the Control Commission, and they were terrified of it.[7]

The mid-1930s were an especially active time for Stalinist ideological enforcers because of the political battles convulsing the international Communist movement. Since Lenin's death in 1924, Stalin had been struggling to consolidate his power and vanquish his rivals. His greatest threat came from Leon Trotsky, the man Lenin had hoped would succeed him. Stalin first expelled Trotsky from the Communist Party, then banished him from the Soviet Union. While Trotsky advocated "permanent revolution" from his bases in Turkey, France, and finally Mexico, Soviet Stalinists began purging and even killing Communists accused of following him. In the United States, the Control Commission kept the Party ideologically pure by expelling suspected "Trotskyites," the derisive term used by Stalinists.

Golos also arranged the ultimate Trotskyite liquidation: the assassination of Trotsky himself. At the time he met Elizabeth, Golos was already helping Mexican Stalinists to plot the great revolutionary's murder. He carefully planned the infiltration of Trotsky's Mexico City compound with the hope of getting close enough to kill him.

In addition to his roles as the Party's chief travel agent, document forger, and ideological enforcer, Golos was also a Communist spy. His espionage responsibilities were somewhat modest at the start. In 1937, Soviet intelligence officials asked him to recruit American sailors to serve as couriers for secret documents.[8] Although the Soviet spy chiefs realized that it might be foolhardy to use an active Communist as an agent, they decided to use him anyway. By the 1940s, the true professionals who took over the NKGB would regret the shortsightedness of this policy.[9]

Following Soviet directives, Golos slowly expanded his passport network to include Canada and served as a liaison between the CPUSA and Soviet intelligence. As he sank deeper into the underground, he cultivated a quiet voice, a "tiptoe walk," and a "stealthy manner."[10]

He also began to work with American Communists who had secrets to share. The leader of the Party, Earl Browder, put Golos in touch with members who had learned information that they thought the Party should know. In time, these members would include Communists who worked for the U.S. government, but in the

VITALLY IMPORTANT WORK

beginning most were employed in private business. Like Elizabeth, if they thought they had learned something exciting at work, they wanted to tell the Party. Golos would listen to their reports, look at their documents, and pass the information along to Browder. He also shared some of the most interesting tidbits with Soviet intelligence officials, though he did not tell them his sources' names.[11]

In 1938, when Elizabeth met him, the forty-eight-year-old, beefy redhead was "among the cleverest, most mysterious, and most powerful" Communist spies in the United States, according to Anthony Cave Brown.[12] He was also unencumbered by a family. Three years earlier, Golos had arranged for his common-law wife, Celia, and their son, Milton, to go to Moscow. The marriage had apparently never been happy. In any event, Celia and Milton Golos did not return to the United States.[13] Golos also had very little contact with his siblings. Although two of his sisters had also come to New York, they were "as distant as though they lived in different countries," one of them explained.[14]

Like any good spy, Golos did not stand out in a crowd. A heavyset, rather nondescript man in a bad suit and scuffed shoes, he did not make a favorable first impression on Elizabeth. At five feet two inches, he was seven inches shorter than the strapping young woman he hoped to use as a source. She eyed with disapproval his tattered felt hat and shabby car. After he dropped off "Comrade Brown," the Party leader who had introduced them, he and Elizabeth headed for a downtown restaurant to discuss her case. She did not have high expectations for the meeting.

Yet as she talked with the man known as "Timmy" over dinner, she discovered that she had underestimated him. He seemed intelligent and thoughtful. Soon she found herself telling him the story of her life, including her disappointing earlier contacts with the Soviet underground. As she warmed to him, "Timmy" seemed to grow better looking. He was no longer short and squat but "powerfully built"; he was not colorless but had "startlingly blue" eyes that stared straight into hers.

After a two-hour dinner, this intriguing man took her for a long drive. She had opened up to him over dinner about her personal travails; now he began to tell her of his ideological journey. "He told me," she wrote later, "of the misery and suffering he had seen in Europe, and of the greed and selfishness of a few that had made these conditions possible." He talked of the hardships Communists faced as they battled greedy capitalists all over the world. Not everyone could withstand these hardships, he warned. Somewhat cryptically, he compared the Communist movement to an over-crowded buggy going up a steep road. Some people couldn't hold on tight enough, and they fell off. That, he said, had happened to "Mrs. Glazer."[15]

Elizabeth was understandably alarmed by the analogy. What exactly did he mean? "I felt as if someone had hit me in the pit of the stomach," she remembered later. Though she was intimidated, she felt flattered by the attention that this powerful Communist was giving her.

He also gave orders. "You are no longer an ordinary Commu-nist but a member of the underground," he told her. "You must cut yourself off completely from all your old Communist friends." The goal, he said, was to convince Italian fascists in New York that she sympathized with them. Her friends might regard her as a traitor, but "the Party would not ask this sacrifice of you if it were not *vitally important*."

Suddenly, the documents that had so bored her earlier contact were "vitally important" to the Party. Elizabeth sat in shock as her new spymaster gave her instructions on how to report to him in the future.[16] Before meeting Timmy, Elizabeth had been an under-employed, lonely, would-be informer. Now she was playing a vital role in the movement that would change the world.

For several weeks, Elizabeth and Timmy repeated their meet-ing routine. They would have dinner together in obscure restau-rants, then drive around in his car. She would deliver documents and oral reports on the fascists at the "Library of Information." He taught her what to look for and, just as important, what to ignore. He was especially annoyed by her "amateurish attempts to listen at closed doors and search wastebaskets."[17]

She was not the heroine in a mystery novel, he informed her sternly. She should impress her Italian bosses with her trustworthiness so that they would feel free to disclose their plans to her. These plans, she believed at this point, were "vitally important" to the American Communist Party. She did not know yet that she was also working for the Soviets.

As the meetings and spycraft tutorials continued, Elizabeth developed a definite crush on her instructor. She could not find enough favorable adjectives to describe him: kind, generous, humane, intelligent, hard working, loyal, sincere. In short, she believed he was the "ideal Communist."[18] He was not exactly available. He had a common-law wife and a child in Russia. At the time Elizabeth met him, he was living with another woman who was quite obviously in love with him.[19] But Golos's commitments did not bother his new recruit. Indeed, within a month of meeting him, Elizabeth decided that she was in love with her case officer. In her autobiography, she described their first kiss. According to her, it was a moment straight from a bad romance novel.

One night after dinner, they came out of a restaurant to find his car stuck in the snow. Together they pushed the car free, then clambered inside it, panting. As he gallantly offered to shake the snow off of her soggy hat, their hands touched. Their eyes locked. Suddenly, they fell into a clinch. As they drove away, she floated "into an ecstasy that seemed to have no beginning and no end." They drove all night, then sat, hand in hand, watching the sun rise over New York.[20]

Did it really happen like that, or, years later, did Elizabeth invent a B-movie scene to replace a more prosaic mutual decision by two lonely adults to jump into bed? Reviewers at the time and historians later have been suspicious of the "schoolgirlish" tone of the love scenes allegedly shared by an experienced thirty-year-old woman and her middle-aged, married lover. Once again, Elizabeth seems to have rewritten her life story to make it fit into the gender norms of the 1950s.

The new lovers decided to keep their relationship a secret. Golos explained that his bosses would take a dim view of the affair:

it was hardly good tradecraft to have a fling with a source. More-over, they both liked the idea of deceiving their superiors. Like his new girlfriend, Golos had little use for other people's rules. He was devoted to Stalin, of course, but he was impatient with Soviet bureaucracy. Throughout his espionage career, he hoarded infor-mation, quarreled with his superiors, and ignored their orders. He believed that he could be more effective by making his own rules. His bosses, in turn, viewed him as dangerously insubordinate— and careless.

This would be the longest, and most intense, relationship of Elizabeth's life. Golos was, she said many times, the only man she ever loved, and he shared at least a deep affection for her. They would stay together until his death five years later. In the mean-time, he would teach her all the skills she needed to become a full-fledged Soviet spy.

Elizabeth's assignment at the fascist library did not last long; a few months after meeting Timmy, she was fired from her job. She later claimed that her boss had discovered an antifascist article she had written for the *Columbia Spectator*.[21] This is not true because she never wrote any articles for the *Spectator*, but she had been the *subject* of the *Spectator* article on the denial of her loan. Ap-parently her supervisor had discovered the article, or else he had learned about her participation in leftist activities from another source. In any event, her secret life as a mole within New York fas-cism was over. Her life as an underground Communist was not, however. Instead of going back to the public side of the Party, Elizabeth continued to work for Timmy and for Soviet intelligence in other ways.

During these early months with Timmy, Elizabeth learned how to detect and evade surveillance, make secure phone calls, con-tact agents through third parties, and set up meetings on street corners. She learned how to determine if enemy agents had dis-covered secret documents in her possession. "If I had to leave the apartment, I was careful to put them in my black trunk and tie a

VITALLY IMPORTANT WORK

thin black thread around it so that I would know if they had been tampered with in my absence," she wrote later.[22]

She earned money during the day by doing odd jobs. At night, she would research topics that Timmy had assigned her. She delved into the Mexican elections for him and obeyed his somewhat mysterious command to write a long report on the life of former president Herbert Hoover.[23]

Timmy taught her to serve as a "mail drop"—a person who received mail for an agent who did not want to be traced. She found letters in her mailbox addressed to her and postmarked in Canada. She also went to Brooklyn to pick up letters with Mexican postmarks from a woman named Rose Arenal. All these letters she turned over to Timmy without question or comment.

Perhaps her most rewarding assignment was to help her boyfriend entertain some of the Canadians and Mexicans who wrote the letters. She found the head of the Canadian Communist Party, Tim Buck, to be charming and likable. The Mexicans, on the other hand, were rather forbidding and mysterious. One was a "tall, dark, fierce-eyed" young man named Leopolo Arenal, the brother-in-law of the woman who served as a mail drop in Brooklyn; another was Arenal's wife; a third was a fat painter. All the while, she had no idea that she was dining with key agents of the Russian secret police, some of whom were carefully plotting Trotsky's assassination.[24] Instead, she believed that she was helping the Party maintain links with foreign Communists.

Elizabeth fairly glowed with satisfaction and self-importance. A few years earlier, she had been an unemployed, unattached, virtually friendless young woman. Now she had a powerful, caring lover who was training her to play a critical role in the coming worldwide revolution. Though she supported Communist ideals, hers was a case of personal, rather than ideological, devotion to the Cause. Indeed, she later told a grand jury that she read little Communist literature and understood even less. "If you ever tried to read Marx, you will understand what I mean," she confided to the jurors. "I used to read one page ten times and give up."[25]

This indifference to ideology helped Elizabeth to overcome her disgust with the Nazi-Soviet Pact. The news broke at the end of August 1939. Joseph Stalin, the leader of the country that she presumed to be the most enlightened in the world, had made a pact with the devil himself. For thousands of American Communists, the nonaggression pact served to highlight the hypocrisy of the Soviet regime. Thousands of Party members deserted its ranks.[26] Most were recent recruits like Elizabeth who had joined in the era when Communism was supposed to be the strongest bulwark against fascism.

But Elizabeth was not an ordinary Popular Front Communist. For one thing, antifascism, despite her later claims to the contrary, was obviously not an overriding issue for a woman who was a former fascist herself. For another, Timmy and her new role as his assistant gave her reasons to stick with the Party that went far beyond ideology.

She quickly accepted her lover's explanation for the pact. As the Party said, Hitler would undoubtedly attack the USSR if not for the agreement, and the capitalist nations would cheer him on. The motherland of Communism must be preserved at all cost. In any event, the alliance was merely a "stalling move" until the Soviets had the resources to combat the Germans, he explained.[27] Satisfied, Elizabeth would not question the beneficence and wisdom of Comrade Stalin again—at least while Golos was still alive.

The pact, however, held a very different message for another veteran of Soviet espionage in America. It convinced him to blaze the trail that Elizabeth would follow. Together, he and Elizabeth would destroy Soviet espionage in the United States and help to create the second Red Scare.

Many adjectives can be used to describe Jay Vivian Chambers, also known as David Breen, Charles Adams, Lloyd Cantwell, "Carl," and, most famously, Whittaker Chambers: he was brilliant, disturbed, idealistic, dysfunctional. At Columbia, which he attended in the 1920s, his professors recognized him as a talented writer and an outstanding intellect—but also as a rogue. He went

VITALLY IMPORTANT WORK

on destructive drinking binges; he let his teeth decay into blackened stumps; he struggled to overcome his homosexual tendencies by launching numerous affairs with women; and he wrote a play about Jesus Christ that the university's administrators found blasphemous. At first suspended, he was then barred from ever attending Columbia again.[28]

Like Elizabeth, Chambers was a lonely soul searching for something he could not find in his family, religion, or education. He finally discovered what he was looking for one day when he picked up a pamphlet by Lenin. It all became clear to him. As his biographer, Sam Tanenhaus, has noted, "[H]e had at last found his church."[29]

Chambers joined the Party in 1925, a native-born WASP in a largely immigrant and Jewish organization, and he swiftly advanced through the ranks. Beginning as a reporter for the *Daily Worker*, he eventually became known as one of the Party's most effective propagandists. Ironically, though, just as his literary career was taking off, the Party decided it had a new job for him.

In 1932, on the orders of the leadership, Chambers dropped out of the open Party and went "underground." He became a full-time, salaried agent of the Soviet secret police. He worked for Soviet military intelligence, the GRU, in New York for two years before moving to the Washington area and landing his first important assignment.[30]

Chambers's job, he claimed later, was to cultivate the members of a group of Marxists who worked in various New Deal agencies. He ordered the most promising of these Communist bureaucrats to penetrate high government offices and give him secret documents.[31] His most significant contact, Chambers later claimed, was an employee of the Agricultural Adjustment Administration who later worked at the State Department. His name was Alger Hiss.[32]

But Chambers soon began to have doubts about his secret work. In the Soviet Union, Stalin began to see plots against his leadership everywhere. In 1936, a series of sensational trials of "Old Bolsheviks"—the leaders of the revolution—began in Moscow. Most confessed their "crimes" against the people and were executed. Over the next two years, probably more than a million Soviet Communists—including military leaders, most high party officials, and many intelligence agents—were exiled to labor camps or put to death.

The Soviet dictator could reach his enemies in Western Europe and the United States as well. In 1937, Ignatz Reiss, a high-ranking Soviet spy in Switzerland who had broken with Stalin, was kidnapped and killed near Lausanne; that same year, General Walter Krivitsky, a top Soviet military intelligence agent, defected in Paris and fled for his life. Most upsetting to Chambers was the disappearance of a fellow American, Juliet Stuart Poyntz.[33]

Indeed, even a valued agent like Golos was in danger from the Stalinist purges. The Soviets, according to Allen Weinstein and Alexander Vassiliev, debated for two years "whether to recall, arrest, or execute Jacob Golos, based less on concrete evidence of disloyalty than on the pervasive paranoia in Moscow at the time."[34] Security officials demanded that Golos come to Moscow because he had associated with known Trotskyists and had helped create the "absolutely inadmissible situation that, in fact, he knows more than the station chief" in New York.[35] Two imaginative NKGB operatives in Moscow charged him with simultaneously working for the Mensheviks, the Trotskyists, and the FBI.[36] Golos survived the purges, however, by refusing to leave the United States until the waves of hysteria in Russia had abated.

Chambers, too, repeatedly deflected and ignored orders to travel to Moscow. He then took some additional steps to ensure his survival. In desperation, he began to prepare a "life preserver" —something tangible that would convince the Soviets that they could not afford to kill him.

As he made his regular collections from his sources, Chambers began holding some documents back. The papers ended up in a large manila envelope hidden in Baltimore. In April 1938, when Chambers packed his family into his car and went into hiding, he stashed his envelope of evidence in a safe place.[37]

At this point in his defection, Chambers had no plans for going

VITALLY IMPORTANT WORK

to the U.S. government; he did not want to inform on his friends. Over time, however, he began to reconsider the matter, especially after he befriended the celebrated defector Walter Krivitsky.

The last straw for Chambers was the announcement of the Nazi-Soviet Pact. Not only was Chambers horrified by Stalin's symbolic embrace of Hitler, but Krivitsky also warned him that the Nazis would now use his former spy ring.[38] Finally, Chambers agreed to meet with someone from the government. He wanted to talk to President Roosevelt himself, but reluctantly accepted an appointment with Assistant Secretary of State Adolf A. Berle, a fierce anti-Communist who served as Roosevelt's intelligence adviser.

On September 2, 1939, as the Nazis invaded Poland with Red Army approval, Chambers flew to Washington to meet with Berle at his stately home. Over the course of two hours, Chambers named eighteen current and former government employees as spies or "fellow travelers."[39] Most of the alleged spies, however, occupied relatively minor posts or were already widely suspected of being Communists. The real surprise came with the last two names: the brothers Donald and Alger Hiss, well-regarded mid-level officials in Berle's own department.[40]

After Chambers left, Berle confided to his diary that he planned to "take a few simple measures."[41] But he was not unduly disturbed: Chambers, in his view, had been tentative and unclear and might even be suffering from some "neurosis."[42] Moreover, he had no corroboration. Chambers had decided not to produce his valuable envelope—yet. Years later, Berle would explain that "you didn't go to the President with reports that were relatively so unsubstantial as that. There was nothing offered by Mr. Chambers to back up his story."[43]

Berle filed his notes and took very little action for a year and a half. Then, on February 10, 1941, Walter Krivitsky's body was found in a Washington hotel. The police ruled the death a suicide, but many observers speculated that Soviet intelligence had silenced a man they viewed as a traitor. Alarmed, Berle contacted the FBI twice, telling an agent that the Soviets might try to kill

Chambers next. The agent was not convinced. According to an FBI memo, "This matter was not followed up and the memorandum concerning it was merely filed."[44]

The FBI, in short, had evidence that a Soviet spy ring was operating within the U.S. government as early as March 1941. Yet the bureau just noted and filed away this information. Chambers's story would continue to receive a low priority at the FBI until November 1945, when Elizabeth would come in from the cold and corroborate the strange defector's story.

Unlike Chambers, Elizabeth succeeded in rationalizing and accepting the Stalinist purges and the Hitler-Stalin Pact. Timmy's argument that the Soviets remained antifascist at heart seemed persuasive, especially after Elizabeth received her next assignment.

Timmy directed her to try again to spy on New York fascists. He wanted her to infiltrate the staff of a right-wing newspaper publisher, Richard Waldo of the McClure syndicate, to determine if he was a fascist agent. Elizabeth obediently took a job as Waldo's secretary, but she reported to her disappointed lover that she found no evidence that her boss had fascist connections.[45]

Although she failed to discover any fascist conspiracies, Elizabeth did unexpectedly uncover one of Timmy's deepest secrets. After more than a year of sharing "an ecstasy that seemed to have no beginning and no end," as she had put it, "Timmy" had still not told his beloved his real name. He scorned most of the standards of the underground, but this one rule—the prohibition against revealing his name—he would not break.

When Elizabeth did finally learn Golos's true identity, it was not because he confessed it to her in a fit of candor and devotion. Instead, it was simply a case of his trademark sloppiness and inattention to detail.

One day while sharing lunch on a park bench, Timmy asked her if she wanted some extra theater tickets he had obtained through his "publicity" work. She eagerly agreed. When he handed her the tickets, though, she noticed what she thought was the word "GOLD" printed on them. She handed them back to him, saying he

VITALLY IMPORTANT WORK

must have mistakenly given her the tickets intended for someone named Gold.

She was stunned by his reaction. "His face went very white and his eyes became wary," she said. He grabbed the tickets from her hand and told her coldly that he had to return to work.

Some time later, as they sat together in a Lower East Side restaurant, she started to address him as "Timmy."

"Why do you keep pretending you don't know my real name?" he interrupted angrily. "You've known it ever since I gave you those tickets."

Puzzled at first, she suddenly understood. She asked if his name was Gold. "You know perfectly well I am Jacob Golos," he shot back.[46]

Elizabeth was still somewhat confused. She did not know that Jacob Golos was the head of the Party's feared Central Control Commission. She did not know, until he told her, that he was the director of World Tourists, the Soviets' official travel agency in the United States. And she certainly did not know that he was a top agent of the Soviet secret police.

Elizabeth's story was consistent on this point. In both her secret statement to the FBI in 1945 and her highly embellished autobiography in 1951, she claimed that she was shocked by Golos's admission. In other words, after more than a year of virtually living with the man, she was surprised to learn that he had another name and a secret identity. If true, her story does not speak well of the depth of their relationship or of her powers of observation.

At the time, Elizabeth just quietly accepted her lover's name change and began to address him as "Yasha," the Russian diminutive for Jacob. Now that she knew his true name, however, she could begin to piece together the mystery of his past—and his present.

One clue to Yasha's identity was the U.S. government's intense interest in him. Not long after he told her his real name, Golos explained that the Justice Department was investigating him. He told her never to come to his office or call him there.

Soon, as Golos had feared, the Justice Department slapped him with a subpoena, commanded him to produce all his files, and raided his office. Unfortunately for his comrades, he had failed to destroy crucial documents at World Tourists, even though he knew that he was being watched.

Some of those documents proved that Party leader Browder had traveled on a false passport. Based on this evidence, officials arrested Browder on charges of passport fraud and successfully prosecuted and imprisoned him. Golos was horrified. "Earl is my friend," he told Elizabeth. "It is *my* carelessness that is going to send him to jail."[47]

Golos himself was in danger of going to prison for failing to register as a foreign agent. A special grand jury in Washington called him to testify about the foreign connections of World Tourists. To the relief of Party leaders, Golos was unwavering in his denials of any links to the USSR.

But the investigation took its toll. "His red hair was becoming grayer and sparser," Elizabeth remembered, "his blue eyes seemed to have no more fire in them, his face became habitually white and taut." He began to complain of chest pains. Elizabeth grew gravely worried about him.[48] Although he never told her, the Soviets were ordering him to flee to Moscow. He flatly refused.[49]

Meanwhile, the U.S. government investigated other Communist-affiliated organizations for operating as foreign agents. According to Elizabeth, prosecutors agreed to drop the whole investigation in return for a guilty plea from Golos.[50] As he explained bitterly to Elizabeth, Party leaders wanted him to be the "sacrificial goat."

"I never thought," he said angrily, "that I would live to see the day when I would have to plead guilty in a bourgeois court."[51]

Golos received a $500 fine, four months' probation, and an order to register as a foreign agent.[52] The punishment was extremely light, as John Earl Haynes and Harvey Klehr have noted, and typical of the "anemic" U.S. government response to Soviet espionage at the time.[53]

Yet even though he avoided jail, Golos was now officially iden-

VITALLY IMPORTANT WORK

tified as an agent of the Russian government. Other Communists would have nothing to do with him. "The rats are deserting the sinking ship," he said wearily to Elizabeth.[54]

Obviously, Golos could not continue running his spy network as he had in the past. The FBI was closing in. He had to make key changes in the way he operated. First, he needed to set up a new cover business, separate from World Tourists, and find someone to run it. Next, he would need to train an assistant to take over his duties as courier and case officer.[55] In both cases, he turned to the woman he loved.

[3]
Clever Girl

s a Yankee who had proven that she would do anything for her "Yasha," Elizabeth was the natural candidate to take over her lover's spy duties. For two years, she had eavesdropped on suspected fascists. Now, Golos needed someone to meet with his sources, collect their documents, calm their fears, and flatter their egos. He began training Elizabeth to receive documents from highly placed agents—and to debrief and control them as well.

Her first assignment in her new role as courier, secret agent, and Girl Friday was to handle an irascible and annoying industrial scientist. Abe Brothman, a New York engineer, had designed a mixing machine for chemicals. He periodically met with Golos to pass along blueprints for this invention and other new industrial processes. The blueprints were Brothman's personal property, so he hardly qualified as a major spy at this point in his career. Golos's long-term plan, though, was to develop the engineer as a future source of industrial secrets.[1]

Because of his girth and waddle, Elizabeth dubbed Brothman "the Penguin." Beginning in the spring of 1940, she began to meet with him regularly. They would rendezvous on the street, then proceed to dinner. In the course of the dinner, Brothman would hand her an envelope full of blueprints.[2]

Elizabeth found the work boring and her contact difficult. So she was pleased in the fall of 1940 when Golos told her that he was "somewhat discouraged" with the Penguin and the quality of his information. The Soviets were planning to turn him over to someone else.[3]

Brothman's new controller was a Philadelphia chemist, spy, and pathological liar named Harry Gold. Gold had such a talent for espionage that the Soviets used him as a courier for several sources. Some, like Brothman, would become skilled industrial spies; others, like Sergeant David Greenglass, who was stationed in the machine shop in Los Alamos, had access to top-secret military information. Gold's most important contact, though, was the Russians' prized spy, British atomic scientist Klaus Fuchs.

In 1945, when Elizabeth gave Brothman's name to the FBI, she would help agents uncover the trail that led from Brothman to Gold to David Greenglass—and eventually to Julius Rosenberg.[4] When Julius and his wife, Ethel, were later tried for the "crime of the century," Elizabeth Bentley would be a key witness for the prosecution.

After she was relieved of the burden of meeting Brothman, Elizabeth took on other responsibilities for Golos and the Soviets. Now that World Tourists had been exposed as an espionage front, Golos needed to set up a new company. On paper, it would be a privately owned firm that shipped packages to Russia. In fact, however, it would perform the same duties for the Communist Party as World Tourists had done: make money, forge passports, and provide cover for spying.

The new company, called the U.S. Service and Shipping Corporation, needed a respectable front man. The Party found one in John Hazard Reynolds, a Social Register millionaire and Communist sympathizer. "His slightly arrogant manner and his accent said loudly Park Avenue, the Racket Club, and the Plaza," Elizabeth said later.[5] He agreed to serve as president and put up $5,000 in capital. One of the Party's top money managers and fundraisers, Lem Harris, arranged for a secret $15,000 donation from the Party to help launch the operation.

Golos doubted, however, that Reynolds was capable of running the company. "He's the sort of person who likes to sit behind a desk and look important," he told Elizabeth. To avoid potential problems, the Party decided to hire someone else to run the firm.

Reynolds, however, sniffed with horror at the Party's list of potential managers. A "complete snob," according to Golos, Reynolds declined to work with anyone who did not have the "proper background."[6] Most men in the Communist Party either lacked that background or could not be trusted to run such a delicate operation.

But Golos did know one Communist who had the requisite birth and educational credentials and who had proven her trustworthiness beyond doubt. He asked Elizabeth to persuade Reynolds to give her the job. She agreed enthusiastically. After two meetings, the aristocratic Communist asked her to be vice president of his new shipping firm.[7] She now held two jobs vital to Soviet intelligence: handling sources and managing an espionage front.

Elizabeth was never paid to be a spy, but she was more than amply compensated for her work with the shipping firm. Her salary increased from $200 to $800 a month during her years with the company, which was, as one investigator later noted, "damn good dough" for the time.[8] In addition to her salary, Elizabeth also enjoyed a generous expense account, which she was not reluctant to use. She was finally able to give herself the things she thought she deserved: vacations in the Caribbean, lunches at fancy hotels, regular treatments at spas.

If it was a good living, though, it was also a dangerous one. She soon learned that her new bosses included murder in their list of standard business practices. One afternoon in 1940, she sat at a lunch counter, idly glancing over the newspaper. Suddenly, she "froze" in her seat.[9] A short article reported that Mexican police had found the body of Leon Trotsky's American guard, who had been missing ever since gunmen had botched an assassination attempt against Trotsky a month earlier. The police had arrested a pair of brothers, Luis and Leopolo Arenal—her charming dinner companions of months earlier.[10]

She immediately phoned Golos and set up a meeting. His response to the news was somewhat enigmatic. "That's the trouble with dealing with those hot-headed Mexicans," he told her. "They go off and act on impulse." Years later, Elizabeth claimed that she did not understand her soul mate: she thought he was condemning the assassination itself and not merely the way that the killers had bungled it. She was "weak with relief," she said, to realize that she was not in league with assassins.[11]

Perhaps she was. Or perhaps she understood Golos all too clearly—as she understood the necessity of liquidating all Trotskyist threats to the revolution. In any event, neither the death of the bodyguard nor the murder of Trotsky himself months later lessened her devotion to her lover and her cause.

A year after she had discovered the true name of her mysterious lover, Elizabeth now knew much more about the nature and extent of his secret activities. She knew that he dealt in forged passports; she knew that he met with men who gave him secret documents; she knew that he had some connection to assassination plots. Still, she claimed, she did not fully understand that he was a Russian spy. Finally, the last piece of the puzzle fell into place.

In the fall of 1940, as the House Un-American Activities Committee began to investigate his failure to register as a foreign agent, Golos decided that it was time to destroy his files. He showed up one winter evening at Elizabeth's apartment with a large package. "He said he had a lot of material that he should not have around," Elizabeth remembered later, "and since I was the only one he knew who had a fireplace he asked if it would be all right if he destroyed the material in my fireplace."[12] As she helped him toss pamphlets, passports, and letters into the fire, one document made her pause.

She later told the FBI that she found in his papers "either an identification card or credentials" with Golos's picture and the letters "OGPU" in gold type.[13] This was the old acronym for the dreaded Soviet secret police.

"What's this?" she asked him.[14]

In her book, years later, she claimed that he responded with a lie. It was a police officer's identification card, he said casually; it enabled him to get free bus and train rides in Russia.[15]

But Elizabeth gave a different account of this event in her top-secret statement to the FBI in 1945 and to a grand jury in 1948. Rather than emphasizing her innocence and ignorance, as she did in her autobiography, Elizabeth gave her FBI interrogators a much more credible—and more damning—account of Golos's response to her discovery. When she asked him about her discovery, "his replies indicated that he was connected in some manner with the Soviet Secret Police."[16]

Now there could be no more doubts. From that moment on, she admitted, she was "definitely sure that he was in some way connected with Russian Intelligence."[17]

The FBI was sure of this as well.

On January 18, 1941, bureau agents were tailing an espionage suspect, a secretive Russian named Gaik Ovakimian. They observed him meet Golos, a convicted Soviet agent, on a Manhattan street. Over the next few weeks, the agents saw Golos meet Ovakimian several times, and even watched the two men exchange documents.

The meetings intrigued FBI officials who were trying to uncover Soviet spy networks in America. The bureau had not shown much interest in Soviet espionage before the Nazi-Soviet Pact, but in 1940 agents began to piece together a picture of Russian intelligence in this country. They quickly identified Ovakimian, a Soviet who nominally worked for the Soviet trading firm, Amtorg, as a possible spy. Although they did not know it at the time, Ovakimian was actually the head of Soviet espionage in the United States from 1933 to 1941.[18]

Based on his numerous meetings with Ovakimian, Golos fell under bureau suspicion as well. The FBI began sporadically tailing Golos and filing reports on his movements from the winter of 1941 until September of that year. Agents observed him going to the offices of the U.S. Service and Shipping Corporation, where Elizabeth worked, and an apartment at 58 Barrow Street, where she lived. It became apparent that Golos, though he kept a hotel room elsewhere, was living with this woman. The agents wondered if she might be a Soviet spy as well. On May 23, 1941, shortly after they arrested and deported Ovakimian, bureau agents began tailing her.

Elizabeth grew terrified that she might be arrested at any time. She tried desperately to ensure that the tails never witnessed her meeting with important contacts. Very quickly, she "developed an incredible number of ruses" for shaking a tail, including sneaking out of fire exits, abruptly changing direction, and boldly walking up to her pursuer and asking him for directions.[19]

Her tactics worked. The FBI found nothing interesting in her activities. The surveillance was stopped on August 20, 1941, after just a few months.[20]

Ironically, the FBI stopped watching Elizabeth just as her espionage career was taking off. Moving beyond her simple dinners with Brothman, the apprentice spy began to supervise Soviet moles in sensitive American institutions—and even within the U.S. government itself.

Golos had several reasons to turn to Elizabeth for more help. He had, after all, been publicly identified as a Soviet agent—not exactly an ideal situation for a spy. Moreover, his health, which had been fragile since the ordeal of his indictment, continued to deteriorate. His pace slowed, his face lost its color, and he was tortured by sharp pains in his left side. A doctor diagnosed arteriosclerosis and advised him to take better care of himself.[21] Elizabeth afforded a simple solution: by taking over more of Yasha's spy duties, she could protect the security of the spy network while prolonging his life.

In the spring of 1941, Elizabeth began to travel regularly to Washington to meet with agents there. Her first contact was a young, single woman her own age. In Mary Price, Elizabeth finally found a friend in the underground.

Mary's ancestors had been prosperous slaveholders. By the time Mary was born in 1909, however, her parents had "slipped into a genteel poverty," according to a family historian.[22] One of Mary's older sisters, Mildred, was exposed to new, progressive ideas when she moved to New York to work for the Young Women's Christian Association.[23] Mildred strongly influenced young Mary, and the two sisters gradually became involved in radical politics. They took a tour of the Soviet Union in the mid-1930s and were impressed by its prosperity and efficiency.[24] According to Elizabeth and newly released cables, Mary acted on her enthusiasm for the Communist cause by joining the Party.[25]

Shortly after her tour of the USSR, Mary stumbled across a fortuitous job opening. A friend of a friend told her that America's preeminent political columnist, Walter Lippmann, was looking for a secretary.[26] Mary got the job. She quickly decided that the Party could use some of the high-level gossip she overheard in Lippmann's office. Party officials put her in touch with Golos, and Golos told her to see Elizabeth.

The two women took each other's measure at a dinner meeting in New York. Elizabeth looked at Mary's black curls, winning smile, and stylish clothes and judged her to be "attractive but not pretty" and quite self-possessed.[27] The two women had much in common, including membership in an "old American family." Mary's southern background "made her perfect for undercover work," Yasha explained.[28] Few "old family" southerners belonged to the Party. They agreed that Elizabeth would travel to Washington once a month to pick up Mary's files.

Elizabeth's first weekend as a spy courier in the nation's capital was thrilling. Since Lippmann was out of town, she and her new recruit went through his files and made copies of the material they found interesting, such as gossip on Anglo-American relations and future war plans.[29] "For two days we typed madly until our backs ached," Elizabeth wrote later. She slipped the copies into her briefcase and brought them to New York, where Yasha pronounced the material to be "excellent."[30] It is doubtful, though, that the information generated much excitement in Moscow. Lippmann, after all, was a journalist, and his files were hardly top-secret.

At about the same time, Golos introduced Elizabeth to another agent, Bob Miller. A former press aide for the Spanish antifascists, Miller was a journalist when Elizabeth first met him. At first, he simply turned over copies of his own Latin American newsletter to her. Soon, though, he got a job with the Office of the Coordinator of Inter-American Affairs, and he began giving her government documents.[31]

These secretive activities suddenly became much more urgent in June 1941 when Hitler attacked the Soviet Union. The only Communist government in the world was now fighting for its life. "Over there our comrades are being ruthlessly slaughtered," Golos told Elizabeth. "Over here we must work night and day, without any thought of rest, until the Fascist beasts have been wiped out."[32]

To accomplish this goal, Golos needed more highly placed sources than Miller and Price. In August 1941, he informed Elizabeth that he already had some. He was now supervising an agent network in Washington that relayed "secret and confidential information" from the U.S. government back to the USSR.[33] But he was not up to the task of handling this group. Instead, he asked Elizabeth to take over for him.

She fully realized the significance of this move. Now she would be responsible for far more than collecting gossip: she would be controlling an entire ring of agents, some of whom had access to the White House itself. She would be moving from the margins of Soviet espionage in America to the strategic center. She found, though, that she was not afraid. "I had made my choice," she wrote later, "and I would stick to it."[34]

Elizabeth's choice was to become a spy for Golos, the Communist Party, and the Soviets, all at the same time. Her espionage career would always be marked by tension—and confusion—among these competing authorities.

On the one hand, she worked for Yasha and the Communist Party. Most of her sources had approached CPUSA leader Earl Browder and suggested that they could spy for the Party. Some of them believed that their information went *only* to the Party. Golos also worked hard to maintain his autonomy from the Soviets by refusing to tell them his sources' names and by giving Browder a peek at the most relevant information before he sent it to Moscow.

But he did, of course, ultimately send the intelligence to Moscow. In other words, Elizabeth was working for an American political party *and* a foreign government. The Soviets gave her a code name: *umnitsa,* loosely translated as "clever girl" or "Miss Wise." They also assigned her a Russian case officer, whom she met for the first time in the fall of 1941.

This representative of the most powerful secret service in the world did not exactly inspire confidence. Elizabeth first saw her controller, code-named "John," in front of a drugstore. She had been told to wait for a man carrying a copy of *Life* magazine.[35]

Her heart sank as she watched a nervous young man carrying the magazine approach her at the designated time. A thin, pale man of "typically slavic appearance," he wore "badly fitting clothes of obviously European make."[36] He had a perpetually "tense, frightened air" and was prone to nervous starts and trembling hands.[37] If he had carried a sign saying "RUSSIAN SPY" he could not have been more obvious.

He did not seem especially skilled at his craft. Soon after he met Elizabeth, he called her at work—a huge risk for an agent assumed to be under surveillance by the FBI. He then compounded the mistake by asking for "Miss Wise" at her workplace and becoming quite belligerent when the receptionist insisted that no such person worked there. Elizabeth protested furiously to Yasha that "John" was endangering them both.[38]

Despite her objections, however, "John" remained her designated contact. Because he "seemed quite unable to detect when he was under surveillance," they agreed to meet in darkened newsreel theaters. She would enter a theater at a precise time, sit at an agreed spot, and put an attaché case full of documents at her feet. He would then enter the theater, sit down next to her, and place an identical case next to hers. They would nonchalantly pick up each other's attaché case and leave the theater separately.[39]

Though Elizabeth may have regarded him as a hopelessly callow youth, "John" would later be remembered as "one of the heroes of Russian intelligence," according to Christopher Andrew and Vasili Mitrokhin.[40] His real name was Anatoli Antonovich Yatskov, and he was the Soviet agent in charge of stealing scientific information from the atomic bomb project in New Mexico.[41]

John was the first in a series of Soviet controllers whom Elizabeth regarded as insensitive, arrogant, and rather stupid. Her Russian supervisors, in turn, viewed Golos and his new assistant as criminally lax and unprofessional. For a time, the professionals tolerated the American amateurs. Later, though, they would insist on recovering some of the authority that they had ceded to Golos and his protégée.

The mysterious attaché cases were packed with more and more documents as Elizabeth expanded her network of agents. In August 1941, she began supervising the group of government spies. Prosecutors and historians would call it the "Silvermaster group," and it would become one of the most productive Soviet espionage operations in the United States.

The leader of the group was Nathan Gregory Silvermaster, a native Ukrainian and a lifelong Bolshevik activist. Before World War I, Silvermaster had moved to the United States. He then earned a Ph.D. in economics at the University of California at Berkeley and became an American citizen. He also became an underground Communist. According to Golos, Silvermaster hid Communist leader Earl Browder in his apartment during the San Francisco general strike of 1934.

In 1935, Silvermaster got a job with the Resettlement Administration, a division of the Agriculture Department charged with helping migrant farmworkers, and moved to Washington.[42] By 1940, according to information uncovered in Moscow by Allen Weinstein and Alexander Vassiliev, he was spying for Golos.[43]

Silvermaster's wife, Helen, helped him spy. Unlike many of the Russian émigrés who spied for Elizabeth, she was neither Jewish nor poor. Her father had actually been a baron in the old country, but he was called the "Red Baron" for his support of the Bolsheviks. A devoted Communist, Helen Silvermaster still had "an indefinable air of quality in her tone of voice and in the way she held her head" that betrayed her aristocratic origins.[44]

To complicate the Silvermaster ménage, a sallow man in his mid-thirties, "Lud" Ullmann, lived with the couple. When Elizabeth met him, Lud worked at the Treasury Department. Later, with the help of a fellow spy, he would win a coveted job at the Pentagon. At first, Elizabeth was not clear about the relationship among the three members of the Silvermaster household. It soon became evident, however, that Ullmann was having an affair with his host's wife.[45]

Elizabeth's job as Golos's assistant was to win the émigré couple's trust, but that was not as easy as it seemed. At their first meeting, Helen Silvermaster ushered her into their tasteful, spacious living room and chatted pleasantly for an hour. Yet Elizabeth sensed that the Russian woman was suspicious of her. Later, Helen protested to Golos that Elizabeth must be an undercover agent for the FBI. Angry with Elizabeth for "creating such an impression of distrust" and with Helen for her "idiocy," Golos told the Silvermasters that they had no choice. Helen and her husband reluctantly accepted Elizabeth as their new contact.[46]

Every two weeks, Elizabeth would travel to Washington to pick up documents from the Silvermasters, collect their Party dues, and deliver Communist literature. Soon the flow of documents grew so large that Ullmann, an amateur photographer, set up a darkroom in their basement. Elizabeth usually collected at least two or three rolls of microfilmed secret documents, and one time received as many as forty. She would stuff all the film and documents into a knitting bag or other innocent feminine accessory, then take it back to New York on the train.

The knitting bag soon bulged with critical documents from the U.S. government. Shortly after the Nazi invasion of Russia, Silvermaster stole secret estimates of German military strength. Later, when the United States extended its policy of Lend-Lease to the USSR, he gave Elizabeth secret memos about the program.[47]

Silvermaster also passed along White House gossip, such as the rumors of frosty relations between the president and his secretary of state, Cordell Hull, and the arguments within the cabinet over financial aid to the Soviets.[48]

After the Japanese attack on Pearl Harbor in December 1941, the USSR became an official American ally in the war effort. But American policymakers were wary of the Soviets and kept many secrets from them. The Silvermasters believed that they were only doing what the U.S. government should be doing on its own: sharing intelligence with its ally.

The Soviets were not happy with the quality of Silvermaster's material. Intelligence bosses in Moscow cabled the station chief in New York that his documents were "in essence an incidental motley collection of information." The Soviets sought to provide more direction for their amateurish American agents. When were the Americans and British going to open a second front? Who supported and who opposed a second front? And what were they doing to detect and stop Soviet espionage in America? [49]

In short, as the Russian intelligence chiefs impatiently wrote their American agents, Moscow wanted "to penetrate into those places where policy is born and developed, where discussions and debates take place, where policy is completed." [50]

And just who was doing this penetration for the Soviet leaders? Obviously, Silvermaster, a mid-level economist, could not gather by himself all the information the Soviets wanted. Nor did Ullmann have access to much high-level data. But Bentley discovered that many other Communists and sympathizers in Washington—some with direct access to the president himself—passed information to Silvermaster and thus ultimately to Moscow. [51]

Several government economists were part of the "Silvermaster group." Most of them she never met. But Greg and Lud, her two stalwart members of the group, would tell her about their friends who helped them. For example, two advisers to Treasury Secretary Henry Morgenthau, Solomon Adler and Frank Coe, were secret Communists who supplied information about Treasury policy. Sonia Gold, a Treasury employee, and her husband, Bela, who worked for the Foreign Economic Administration, also gave documents to Greg. [52] In addition, Silvermaster told Elizabeth that a Treasury economist named William Taylor fed him some secret information about China. Taylor was a minor source, but he would later prove to be a formidable foe for Elizabeth when she went public with her allegations.

One of the most active and difficult members of the group was a Treasury statistician named George Silverman. This bright, mercurial Harvard graduate had been involved in the Communist underground since the mid-1930s, when he had known Whittaker Chambers. A heavy, broad-shouldered man with "thick glasses and untidy hair," he seemed brilliant but odd to his coworkers.[53] Some of his fellow Communists thought he was offensive, indiscreet, and insufferably dogmatic.[54] He was also terrified of being caught: he saw "FBI men behind every bush," Elizabeth said.[55] Yet he was a key member of the underground.[56]

For many years, Silverman had toiled away in obscure New Deal agencies like the Railroad Retirement Board, but in 1942 he won a transfer to the Pentagon. Soon afterward, he was able to arrange for Ullmann to join him there. Together they pilfered information on aircraft production, tank production, airplane deployment, and technological improvements to military hardware.[57]

Silverman and Ullmann were probably Elizabeth's most significant sources because they stole military secrets—albeit, of course, on behalf of a wartime ally, not an enemy. But Elizabeth's bosses in Moscow still wanted insight into American policymaking. Fortunately for them, Greg Silvermaster happened to be friends with two powerful men: the chief economist in the White House and the chief economist in the Treasury Department.

Lauchlin Currie and Harry Dexter White were by far the most prominent men accused of espionage by Elizabeth. Currie, a Canadian-born economist, had joined the Roosevelt administration in 1939 as the president's economic affairs adviser. A brilliant thinker who anticipated the arguments of John Maynard Keynes, he was "an intriguing, eclectic mixture of economic liberal and economic planner," according to his biographer.[58]

Currie met Silvermaster in 1940 when the two worked together to investigate a labor problem. They already had a good friend in common: George Silverman. Soon, Currie and Silvermaster also became fast friends. Along with Harry White, Currie defended Silvermaster when the FBI launched a loyalty investigation of him in 1942. Currie's intervention helped Silvermaster to survive the inquiry and keep his government job. "I found (Silvermaster) able, well-read, and an ardent New Dealer," Currie wrote later.[59]

Silvermaster was also, of course, a Soviet spy. Did Currie understand this? Did he know that George Silverman was also a Soviet agent? Did he know that anything he said to Silverman and Silvermaster went straight to Moscow? Elizabeth claimed that he did.

One day, she said, Currie rushed over to Silverman's office and breathlessly informed him that the United States was about to break the Soviet code.[60] It is unclear exactly what Currie meant by this. He might have been talking about the U.S. Army's still-unsuccessful attempt to decode Soviet telegrams, later known as the Venona project. Or he might have been referring to American efforts to read a partially burned Soviet codebook found on a battlefield in Europe.[61]

Currie later admitted that he had, in fact, told the Soviets about American code-breaking efforts. He confided to another "senior government official" that he wanted to prevent "the sowing of seeds of distrust between allies."[62] Showing the egotism typical of Elizabeth's sources, he liked the idea of conducting his own private diplomacy. He was not a Communist, and he did not consider himself a spy. But by selectively and consciously giving information to friends he knew worked for the Soviets, he was ultimately providing ammunition to men who would work to destroy his liberal ideals after the war.[63]

Harry Dexter White also wanted to do what he could to improve the relationship between the great powers. White was a most unlikely Communist spy. As the primary architect of the twin institutions of postwar international capitalism, the International Monetary Fund and the World Bank, he would later help stabilize global capitalism.

But White, according to Elizabeth, also chose to give some of his government's secret documents to a Communist nation.[64] He was good friends with Silvermaster, Ullmann, and Silverman, and he eagerly assisted them in their espionage, she claimed. Whittaker Chambers later supported her allegations, saying that White had given him some confidential information about U.S. policy in the Far East back in the 1930s.[65] In a definitive study of the allegations against White, Bruce Craig has concluded that Elizabeth's general charge against him was correct. White passed "oral information, perhaps written summaries, and possibly even sensitive documents" to the Soviets, Craig writes.[66]

Yet, like Currie, White did not see himself as a traitor or a spy. According to Craig, he could justify giving this intelligence to the Soviets because he assumed that "the information he was providing did not harm American interests." He was merely giving them "his personal opinions and observations on the future course of American politics."[67] By helping his friend Silvermaster, he hoped to advance the cause of Soviet-American cooperation and of progressivism throughout the world. He could not know that, with Elizabeth's help, his actions would help to ruin progressive causes and his own career.

Elizabeth also had contact with other agents outside the Silvermaster group. These were her "singleton" spies: they worked on their own and reported directly to her. A few were dedicated Stalinists like Greg Silvermaster. Most, however, were romantic idealists like Harry White, inadvertently helping to write an American tragedy.

The Stalinists, not surprisingly, were easier to handle. One of Elizabeth's coolest sources was Maurice Halperin, a devout Communist in the top-secret heart of U.S. foreign intelligence, the Office of Strategic Services.[68] A former political scientist at the University of Oklahoma, Halperin had been forced to resign from the university because of his rumored Communist sympathies. But he found his radical beliefs no hindrance in applying to the oss. When he was appointed the chief Latin American specialist within the research and analysis section, Halperin approached a Communist journalist, Bruce Minton of the *New Masses,* and signaled that he was ready to spy for the Party. Minton alerted Golos, who assigned the analyst to Elizabeth.[69]

In Mary Price's apartment, Halperin would meet Elizabeth periodically and hand over classified documents that had come across his desk. He had access to diplomatic cables covering the entire globe, not just Latin America: reports on Communist guerrillas in the Balkans, the French resistance, the Polish government in exile, and German opponents of Hitler. Elizabeth enjoyed meeting with Halperin because he struck her as a "well-balanced, stable person" who did not "have a nerve in his body."[70]

But most of her singleton spies were entirely different. Naive and enthusiastic, they wanted to help the brave Russians beat the Nazi war machine. They also wanted to defeat what they saw as the bizarre and counterproductive secretiveness of their own government. In contrast to true believers like Halperin, though, they worried about getting caught.

Duncan Lee, for example, did not relish leading a double life. Distantly related to General Robert E. Lee, Duncan had grown up in a pious and proper family. His parents were missionaries in China, where Lee had spent the first twelve years of his life. As a Rhodes scholar, he had discovered the radical left in the "highly politicized" atmosphere of Oxford in the late 1930s. "Everyone was acutely aware of the Depression in Britain—the unemployment, the grinding poverty and the despair," he recalled later. The threat of Nazi Germany greatly worried him, while he saw hope for the world in the "vast economic and social experiment" in the Soviet Union.[71]

After graduating from Yale Law School, Lee won a job at the prestigious Wall Street firm of Donovan Leisure.[72] His boss at the firm, William Donovan, was named head of what became the OSS in 1941, and the next year he asked the promising Rhodes scholar from Virginia to be his personal assistant.

While working on Wall Street, Lee had tried "to satisfy the prick of my social conscience" by volunteering his time to the Russian War Relief association and to the China Aid Council, which sent packages to war-torn China.[73] Through the China Aid Council, he made the fateful acquaintance of Mary Price.

Mary's sister, Mildred, was the executive secretary of the China Aid Council and moved in the same social circles as Duncan Lee. One night in 1942, Mary Price met the studious-looking young gentleman radical at a party. The two southerners immediately recognized that they had much in common. When Mary learned that this handsome, progressive lawyer was about to become William Donovan's adviser in Washington, she alerted Yasha and Elizabeth.

Intrigued, Golos responded that Mary should cultivate him as an agent. She did so eagerly and filed reports based on conversations with him. She implied that he realized that he was working as a spy, though Lee later insisted he did not. Golos was disappointed in the quality of the material: the right-hand man of the U.S. spy chief should surely be able to contribute more interesting news. Golos needed someone more seasoned and reliable to handle Lee. He chose Elizabeth.[74]

She found the great-great-grandnephew of the Confederate commander to be a reluctant spy. She claimed he was "a rather weak individual" who was "nervous and emotionally upset" because he was petrified of possible FBI surveillance and "troubled with a severe conflict of ideas."[75] He briefed her orally, never giving her actual documents. Elizabeth had to promise him that she would not write down his information—a promise that she had no qualms breaking.

Lee gave her valuable information in two categories: foreign intelligence and internal spy hunts within the oss. He verbally described oss activities in Europe, including a top-secret program to parachute agents into Hungary and negotiate a separate peace with the fascist government there.[76] He also helped the Soviets to protect their other sources. After examining the oss security files, he told her that two of her agents—including Halperin—were under suspicion. The Soviets ordered the agents to be more cautious.[77]

Because Duncan Lee was such a concerned, intelligent, and admirable man in so many ways, his children have steadfastly maintained that Elizabeth lied about him.[78] They charge that she lied about him to her Soviet spymasters and later to the FBI and Congress. This interpretation assumes that Elizabeth and Golos perpetrated a massive and complex fraud against their Soviet superiors by systematically taking documents from other sources and claiming that they came from Lee. Some of the documents in question, though, were much more likely to come from Lee than from any other OSS source.[79] A simpler, more logical interpretation of the Venona cables is to take them at face value and acknowledge that they confirm Elizabeth's story. That does not mean Lee was "some kind of Cold War demon," as his children describe his critics' characterization of him.[80] During World War II, many other hardworking, well-meaning native sons helped Elizabeth pass intelligence to Uncle Joe.

William Remington was another of those native sons. Ironically, Remington was an insignificant source for Elizabeth, but he would become her most important opponent in her later, ex-Communist career. Like Lee, Remington was a handsome, Ivy League graduate with a bright future ahead of him in government service. The "typical clean-cut American lad," as Elizabeth later described him, had first become interested in Communism while still in high school during the early years of the depression.[81] Later, while at Dartmouth, he became an activist in the Young Communist League.[82] He believed that the Soviets had the solution to the depression. "I thought Russia a great experiment: they were making great progress toward improvement of living standards and I liked what the Russians were proposing for collective security against Nazism and Fascism," he later testified.[83] Remington was not just an armchair Communist: he took time off from college to work as a union organizer in Tennessee, where he was beaten by antiunion thugs.

In 1942, after passing a rather superficial loyalty examination, Remington won an appointment to a critical wartime agency, the War Production Board. Remington and his wife, Ann, longed to reestablish contact with the Party in Washington, but they knew that open membership would hurt Bill's career. As a solution, some Party friends introduced them to a mysterious, redheaded man with an Eastern European accent. "John," as Golos called himself, in turn introduced them to his young assistant, "Helen."

Over the next two years, Elizabeth met Bill Remington several times, usually at designated spots in downtown Washington. At the meetings, he gave her classified information on aircraft production and testing. He also passed along "inside information" on his bosses and any material he thought might be of use to the Russians, such as a "vague" formula for making synthetic rubber.[84]

Remington was hardly a steely eyed Bolshevik. "[C]ertainly he was one of the most frightened people with whom I have ever had to deal," Elizabeth remembered later. After a few months, he began avoiding her and refused to return her calls. He and his wife insisted on joining Communist front organizations—apparently in the hope that this would lessen Remington's value as a spy. His unsympathetic courier contemptuously dismissed him as "a small boy trying to avoid mowing the lawn or cleaning out the furnace when he would much rather go fishing."[85]

Elizabeth wanted to dump Remington as a source, especially since his information was rather marginal. But Yasha insisted that he helped corroborate documents from other spies. "And, besides," he told Elizabeth, "there is still the possibility that we can push him into a really good position."[86]

Why did these intelligent, privileged men and women choose to spy for a foreign country? Elizabeth, ironically, was much less of an idealist than her sources. She had only the vaguest grasp of Communist doctrine, which of course made it all the easier for her to abandon it later. For her, spying offered the chance to take risks and break the rules, all while earning a good income. Most important, her supervisor loved her and kept her bed warm at night.

Her sources, though, were motivated by ideology. Some, like Silvermaster and Halperin, were dedicated Stalinists. They were prepared to pay any price to bring about a Soviet America.

Most, however, were sensitive, impressionable Americans who believed that they were contributing to world peace.[87] Elizabeth's sources tended to be idealistic, recent college graduates who were appalled by the poverty of the depression, the menace of Hitler, and the racism and greed they saw in American society. More than a bit self-righteous, they believed that their judgment was better than that of their employers and their government. They believed that their superior intellect or empathy gave them the right to decide when to share top-secret information.

None of Elizabeth's contacts spied for money; indeed, the Party members paid for the privilege of being Communists with their monthly dues. As John Abt, a labor lawyer who helped Elizabeth, wrote later, "In a material sense, I stood only to lose by being a Communist." But, he continued, "in a human sense, I was greatly enriched. The Party was involved, and consequently I was involved, in every struggle for decency and social progress for a half century."[88]

In their view, unregulated capitalism was a warped, corrupt system, forcing professionals to sell apples to survive, children to eat out of trash cans, and government officials to destroy food while millions were starving. "In that period of passionate conviction," wrote Hope Hale Davis, "I could not understand anyone's being merely a theoretical Marxist."[89] The times demanded action, and her loyalty—and the loyalty of other Americans who agreed to spy—was to Socialism and Humanity, not to the United States. Another American who spied for the Soviets, physicist Theodore Hall, later explained what he saw as the relative nature of treason. "If you care very much for the well-being of the people of your country and you take a step with the intention of keeping them from a horrible catastrophe, that is not disloyalty. The experiences of Auschwitz and the Gulag and Vietnam remind us that blind obedience to authority is not always a good kind of loyalty."[90]

Moreover, during the war, the Soviet Union was, after all, a U.S. ally. Members of the Silvermaster group were dismayed by the official distrust of the Russians in Washington. They were hoping to play a small role in bridging the distance between America and its mysterious wartime ally; they wanted to arrange a rapproche-ment between the future superpowers. As it turned out, of course, they were terribly misguided. They risked death and imprison-ment not for world peace but for a totalitarian dictatorship.

Although Elizabeth was handling more than a dozen agents for Golos by the middle of 1942, he still personally controlled many more that she knew little or nothing about. She had a glimpse into one of his other secret groups, however, one summer night in New York City.

As they drove through the Lower East Side on their way to din-ner, Golos stopped the car. He had to meet a contact, he said. She watched him walk toward someone standing on a street cor-ner. She saw the man only briefly, but later remembered that he was tall and thin and wore glasses. The man was a member of a group of engineers who were sending military information to the Soviets, Golos later told her.

Golos had given Elizabeth's phone number to the thin man. He would call her when he needed to get in touch with the Soviets, Yasha said. And indeed, the man did call Elizabeth a few times before Golos's death.

Beyond his sketchy appearance, Elizabeth knew only one thing about the spy. His first name was "Julius."[91]

A Serious & Dangerous Burden

o Elizabeth, the mysterious "Julius" was just a distant figure on a street corner and a voice on the telephone. But most of Yasha's shadowy sources became more distinct to her over time. As her lover's health deteriorated in 1942 and 1943, Elizabeth took over more and more of his sources. She was no longer just an apprentice; she was a powerful agent in her own right.

These new assignments were not always exciting. In 1943, for example, Golos told her to start handling a dull, middle-aged, Communist journalist. One of Golos's oldest friends, Louis Budenz had joined the Party in 1935 after many years as a labor organizer and activist. Because he had been close to some Trotskyists, Golos asked Budenz to spy on his former friends. Soon the journalist was helping the NKGB to find the people who would befriend and then kill Trotsky in Mexico. Later, after the assassination, Golos asked Budenz to pass along gossip he learned as a journalist. The two men met intermittently for years before Yasha told his old friend that his assistant would henceforth handle the meetings.[1]

Budenz would tell Elizabeth what he learned in his reporting, such as rumors of partisan activity in Yugoslavia.[2] She was bored by his intelligence. The information was not "particularly significant," Golos agreed, but he wanted her to continue the meetings.[3] Showing his usual disdain for proper tradecraft, Golos told Elizabeth her source's true name, and she guessed that Budenz knew hers as well.[4] In Golos's incestuous espionage world, one defector could potentially expose the entire network. At the time, Elizabeth had no idea that this insignificant source would later help inspire the most momentous decision of her life.

Golos also gave Elizabeth another "singleton" source who showed much more promise—and who was a lot more fun. Helen Tenney was a New York heiress who enjoyed parties, alcohol, and the attentions of men. Like Elizabeth, Helen was an emotionally unstable woman who found companionship and meaning in the Communist Party.

After a Party journalist introduced Golos to Tenney, he urged her to apply for a job in the OSS. She had earlier worked for an OSS contractor. He was pleasantly surprised when she landed a job in the Spanish division. This meant that she could spy on the ultimate enemies, Trotskyists, who were struggling with Stalinists as well as fascists in Spain.[5]

Pretty and accomplished, Tenney attracted a number of suitors. One of her Communist colleagues proposed to her "repeatedly."[6] Soon Elizabeth would worry that the Soviets planned to use her as a "honey trap" to lure men into confessing secrets in return for sex. She also worried about Helen's mental stability—a valid concern, as it turned out.

But in 1943, as Elizabeth took over Helen from Golos, the tangled, tortured tale of their friendship lay mostly in the future. For the time being, the two unhappy women found their calling by helping spirit secrets out of America for the men in Moscow they believed were making a better world.

Throughout his long career as a Soviet agent, Jacob Golos tried to remain independent from those men in Moscow. He taught Elizabeth the importance of American control of American sources. The two of them came to regard their autonomy as crucial to the success of Soviet intelligence in America.

During the 1930s, when the FBI paid little attention to Soviet spies, the NKGB tolerated Golos's willfulness. After the Nazi-Soviet Pact in 1939, however, the FBI belatedly woke up to the potential dangers of Soviet espionage. With J. Edgar Hoover's G-men breathing down their necks, the Soviets lost patience with Golos's unorthodox practices. As John Earl Haynes and Harvey Klehr have noted, the Soviets decided that their agents needed "a higher professional standard of tradecraft" if their network was to survive.[7]

As part of this effort to professionalize the intelligence service, Moscow in 1943 ordered Golos to turn over all his sources and agents — including Elizabeth — to its control. A Soviet, rather than an American, would now supervise his spies.[8]

Golos strenuously resisted the pressure he was getting from Moscow. As a naturalized citizen who had been in the United States for more than two decades, he believed he was "the only man in the organization who was able to deal with Americans."[9] Many of his agents had no idea that they were working for Moscow, he said. He was certain that his skittish, idealistic sources would panic if a burly NKGB agent just off the boat tried to handle them. William Remington was already trying to withdraw from espionage; Mary Price, who suffered from poor health, seemed exhausted by her underground work.

Trying desperately to maintain his control, Golos traveled to Washington to complain to the station chief there. But he could not change his superiors' minds. Their decision to take control of Elizabeth was "the last straw," she later explained to the Soviets.[10] He began to make "cryptic comments" to his lover about how much had changed in Soviet intelligence. "I don't understand what's happening," he told her. "It's all so different from what it used to be."[11] The years of autonomy were over.

In the last few months of his life, Golos complained to Elizabeth that the new Russian operatives were "young and inexperienced, didn't work hard, and were not careful."[12] He was particularly worried that the Soviets would exploit his valued sources, especially Greg Silvermaster and Mary Price.[13]

Despite the protestations of her lover, Elizabeth had no choice but to obey her superiors in Moscow. In mid-1943, she began turning over her biweekly trove of Silvermaster documents to a new Russian controller directly. Yasha was out of the loop.

Or so it seemed. Secretly, however, Elizabeth took the material to Golos for his inspection before she passed it on to the Soviets.[14]

The wily American couple would not be pushed aside quite so easily as that.

As he burned with hostility and frustration about the challenges to his authority, Golos struggled to overcome the weakness of his heart. "I knew now that Yasha was a dying man and that the end might come at any moment—it was only by some miracle of will power he was still alive," Elizabeth wrote later.[15] Terrified that he might die alone, Yasha stayed with Elizabeth every night. But they still did not get married. She told some people later that as Communists they disdained "bourgeois" marriage; she told others that he proposed to her but could not marry her because he was already married to Celia in Russia.[16]

By the fall of 1943, the lifelong revolutionary began to question whether the grand struggle against injustice had been hijacked by gangsters. "He said he fought for Communism and now he was beginning to wonder," Elizabeth told the FBI later.[17] In November, the Soviets finally gave their problem agent an ultimatum: he could give them his sources—or he could get out of their organization. They gave him three days to decide.

He never had a chance to make that choice. On the last day of his life, Thanksgiving Day, 1943, Elizabeth tried to distract her troubled lover with dinner and a movie. But she grew alarmed by his labored breathing and took him home to her apartment. Slowly, painfully, he climbed the stairs, stumbled into her apartment, and collapsed on the couch. Desperate to reassure herself that everything was normal, Elizabeth turned on the radio and began washing out her stockings in the sink. Suddenly, the music made her pause. It was jazz, the bête noire of Yasha and all good Stalinists. But instead of expressing his annoyance, Yasha merely closed his eyes and drifted off. Shaking off her increasing anxiety, Elizabeth got ready for bed, lay down beside him, and fell asleep.

She was awakened by "horrible choking sounds" coming from her lover. She tried frantically to wake him, then pinched his jaw to force brandy down his throat. Finally, she grabbed the phone and called for an ambulance. She murmured reassurances as she waited for help to arrive. It would come too late.

Two medical technicians coldly declared Yasha to be "D.O.A." Even though Elizabeth had seen him die—and had indeed been expecting him to die—the clinical pronouncement came as a shock. She sank into a chair and began to sob.

But she did not have much time to grieve. As she listened to the drivers argue about whether they should move their ambulance out of a No Parking zone, she realized that Yasha's demise in her apartment could present a serious problem for her. She speculated nervously about the contents of his pockets. (A careless agent to the end, he carried the coded telephone numbers of his sources even as he knew he was dying.) Thinking quickly, Elizabeth urged the drivers to move the ambulance before the police arrived.

When they protested that they could not leave her alone with the body, she resorted to a ruse that would serve her many times in the future: she played the dumb girlfriend. "Oh, please don't worry about me," she told them, deliberately misunderstanding their concern. "I can manage to stay alone for a few minutes."

Reassured that this dim woman would not tamper with the corpse, they left the apartment. She quickly bolted the door, emptied Yasha's front pockets (she could not reach the back ones), dumped the contents into her own purse, then unlocked the door and sat demurely in the place where they had left her.

Elizabeth continued to feign ignorance when two "large, friendly" Irish policemen arrived. She smoothly explained away the odd circumstances of this death. She worked with this man, she said, but she hardly knew him. He had been walking through her neighborhood earlier that evening when he had suffered some chest pains. He recognized her apartment building and came in for help. She could tell them very little about him except his hotel address. The police soon discovered that "Golos" was an alias, yet they failed to conduct a thorough investigation of his death—or of the dense young woman who was with him when he died.

That night, Elizabeth was too grief-stricken to focus on the reasons for Yasha's death. In the months to come, though, she would go over his last days in her head and come to a terrible conclusion. The Soviets, she believed, had killed him. With their new rules and their unyielding insistence on his subordination to their system, they had put too much pressure on his heart. For a while she managed to control her anger, but she would not control it forever.

As she waited for an undertaker to arrive, she bent down and kissed Yasha's forehead for the last time.[18] Once again, she would have to search for love and acceptance. She would not find them again.

Before dawn the next day, Elizabeth hurried to Yasha's office, opened his safe, and grabbed the documents inside. Carrying out her dead lover's instructions, she rushed home and burned the papers in her fireplace. Then, still in shock, she set up an immediate meeting with the head of the Party, Earl Browder.

Browder had recently finished his latest prison term, which had been forced on him by Golos's failure to destroy key documents. But he still remained a good friend of Yasha's, having known him since the Party's early days. Yasha, in turn, had grudgingly regarded Browder as a "good guy"—the one Communist leader who was "worth anything at all."[19]

Like Elizabeth, Earl Russell Browder was a native-born American radical. With his reassuring Kansas twang, Browder struggled to put a "native face" on the Party when he became general secretary in 1934.[20] The Popular Front era brought him "years of euphoria." During this era, the Party insisted that "Communism is Twentieth-Century Americanism."[21] Indeed, his commitment to Americanization would eventually cost him his leadership position.

Yet Browder's belief in moderating the Party did not lessen his admiration for the Soviet Union and its supreme ruler. An agile bureaucrat, he had astutely backed Stalin before it was imperative to do so. Stalin had rewarded Browder by helping him advance through the ranks of the CP, and Browder, in turn, had responded with slavish devotion.[22] The Soviets found his dedication

A SERIOUS AND DANGEROUS BURDEN

useful. ~~They wanted him to head the Party when he served their~~ purposes; in 1945, when he no longer did, they would arrange to have him expelled.

On the morning after Golos's death, however, Elizabeth knew only that Browder was the leader of the Party and that he had been Yasha's friend. She told him how Yasha had died, then gave him the $1,200 that she had found in his safe.[23] Carelessly stuffing the money in his pocket, Browder surprised her with a question.

"You're taking Golos's place, aren't you?" he asked.

Elizabeth was not quite sure what this meant but decided to pretend that she did. "Of course, Earl," she replied. Satisfied, Browder told her that he did not want the Silvermaster group or Mary Price to be handled by the Russians.

Elizabeth was pleased yet confused by Browder's enigmatic comments. Why was he so distrustful of their Soviet comrades? And why was he so deferential to her? Was it because "Golos's place"—which she was apparently assuming—was a very important one?[24]

Browder wanted her to continue helping him keep some American control over American spies. The Soviets, of course, did not. The Russians had already resolved to curtail Golos's autonomy. Now, with his death, that process would be even easier. They moved quickly to notify his successor that they would not tolerate any more willful behavior from their regional managers.

Although Elizabeth did not know it at the time, the young Russian now in charge of her had an impressive pedigree with the Soviet secret services. His real name was Iskhak Abdulovich Akhmerov, but he also went by Michael Green, Michael Adamec, and Bill Greinke. Elizabeth just knew him as "Bill." He was the leading NKGB "illegal," or spy without diplomatic cover, in the United States.[25]

Akhmerov had arrived in New York in 1934 as a struggling foreign "student" at Columbia. He gradually blended into New York society and established an identity as a prosperous furrier. As coordinator of Russia's spy networks in the United States, he met Whittaker Chambers, who, like Elizabeth, knew him as "Bill."

Eventually Akhmerov fell in love with Earl Browder's niece, Helen Lowry, who became his wife and partner in espionage.[26] Elizabeth knew her as "Catherine" and quickly developed a profound dislike for her.

Both Bill and Catherine were young, tall, and slender, and they shared a taste for the high life. Catherine favored tailored jackets with ruffled blouses, while Bill was a "dandy" who sported jaunty Panama hats and white seersucker suits.[27] Bill viewed himself as quite the ladies' man, and he liked to leer at women when his wife was not around. Above all, though, Bill was a professional NKGB agent, with all the hardness and cruelty that such a position required. From now on, Elizabeth was in the big leagues.

On November 29, the day after Golos's Marxist memorial service, Bill and Catherine treated Elizabeth to a lavish dinner at an expensive restaurant. Yasha had always viewed such luxuries as unseemly for People's Revolutionaries, and Elizabeth regarded the meal with disdain. Once they had finished off the caviar, oyster cocktails, and lobster, Bill came to the point.

"We want Mary and we want her immediately," he insisted. "We've put up with enough nonsense on this subject."

Elizabeth was frightened but struggled to remain calm. She explained that Earl did not want her to give Price to the Russians.

"Who the hell's Earl? You take your orders from us," Bill replied. He was tired of the insubordination shown by "that traitor Golos," and he was not going to put up with it anymore.

Furious with his characterization of her self-sacrificing lover as a "traitor," Elizabeth fought to control her emotions. Privately, she regarded the Russians as "nasty, arrogant" men who were "experts in the art of back-stabbing," and she vowed to protect her sources from them.[28] But outwardly she remained calm and assured Bill that she just needed more time "to work on Earl."

She was pleased when Bill dropped his combative tone; she believed that she had snowed him.[29] Indeed, she had. In a cable home to Moscow, Akhmerov wrote that he found Bentley to be amateurish, difficult, and overly influenced by Golos. But he grudgingly admitted that "she made a good impression on me."

Smart, "sober-minded," and sincere, she was someone he could work with, he said.[30]

He was not the best judge of character. She was, of course, neither sincere nor sober most of the time, and though she was smart, she would use her intelligence in ways that did not benefit him. Akhmerov would soon yearn for the days when his biggest problem had been "that traitor Golos."

Elizabeth responded to the Soviets' orders to turn over her sources by simply ignoring them and continuing to expand her own spy network. Shortly after 1944 began, Browder told her that he had another group of agents ready to deliver information to her. Their current handler, attorney John Abt, was an organizer of labor's political action committee, the CIO-PAC, and could no longer risk any involvement in espionage.[31] Although Golos had planned to take over the spy ring, he died before he could. Browder wanted Elizabeth to be the group's new courier and controller.[32]

In March 1944, Elizabeth had her first meeting with the "Perlo group." On a rainy afternoon in his Manhattan apartment, Abt introduced her to Charlie Kramer, Edward Fitzgerald, Harry Magdoff, and Victor Perlo.[33] She soon learned that there were five more sources who shared information with the group.

The four members of the group she met that day held various jobs in the government: three of them worked for the War Production Board, while Kramer was a staff member of Senator Harley Kilgore's Subcommittee on War Mobilization. Perlo was their undisputed leader.

Perlo's parents had been Russian Jews who had fled to the United States, and the young statistician had an almost reverential awe for the new leaders of his ancestral homeland. One Communist acquaintance remembered him as a dogmatic Leninist who condemned "fuzzy-minded liberals" for promoting inadequate reforms that only delayed the moment when the workers would seize power.[34] At his first meeting with Elizabeth, Perlo asked her anxiously, "Is Joe getting the stuff safely?" At nearly every meeting he would ask if Stalin had personally seen the documents.[35] (In 1992, after the collapse of the country for which he had sacrificed so much, Victor Perlo would denounce Mikhail Gorbachev's "opportunistic petty-bourgeois capitulation to capitalism" and pine for the days of Stalinist order.)[36] His enthusiasm for "Uncle Joe" caused headaches for his fellow agents. For example, he insisted upon publicly accosting fellow spy George Silverman and demanding if he had "anything for Joe." But despite his reputation as a "bull in a china shop," Perlo was indispensable to his spymasters.[37] According to his later Soviet controller, it would be "next to impossible" to organize the group without him. Perlo "settles everything," the agent wrote. "He is undoubtedly the most active one in the group."[38]

At the War Production Board, Perlo gathered information on aircraft production. Magdoff and Fitzgerald also contributed data on industrial production from the WPB, while other members of the group transmitted intelligence from the OSS, the Treasury Department, and the United Nations Relief and Rehabilitation Administration.[39] Kramer added information from congressional investigations of multinational corporations.[40] When the Soviets impatiently ordered him to give them fewer tales of capitalist perfidy and more intelligence about U.S. foreign policy, he lost his enthusiasm for helping them.[41] Like Remington, Price, and other idealists caught in Elizabeth's web, Kramer discovered that the men in Moscow who wanted his documents were not the romantic People's Warriors he wanted them to be.

Elizabeth's connection with the Perlo group very nearly led to her arrest and exposure. Just one month after she began meeting with Perlo, the FBI learned that it had good reason to begin tailing him. In April 1944, President Roosevelt received a letter naming Victor Perlo and several other Bentley sources as Soviet spies.[42]

The FBI determined that the letter had been written by Perlo's recently divorced wife, Katherine Wills Perlo. A diagnosed schizophrenic, Katherine had lost a bitter battle for custody of their daughter. When agents confronted her, she confirmed the contents of her letter.[43]

A SERIOUS AND DANGEROUS BURDEN

But the Perlo letter did not ignite the enthusiasm of the bureau the way Elizabeth's confession later would. There were no urgent telegrams in the middle of the night; no one assigned dozens of agents to follow and bug the people named in the letter. Possibly, the men of the FBI discounted the tale of an unstable, vengeful ex-wife. Or perhaps the tale of Russian espionage did not seem so sinister in 1944, when the brave Soviet allies were battling the Nazis. In any event, Katherine Perlo failed in her quest to destroy her ex-husband, and Elizabeth survived to spy another day.

At about the same time as she took over the Perlo group, Akhmerov finally forced Elizabeth to allow him to meet Greg Silvermaster. It was even worse than she had feared. "Bill plied Greg with drinks and told him what a wonderful person he was," she remembered later. "It was a nauseating performance, unworthy of a true revolutionary."[44] When Akhmerov insisted on a second meeting in New York, Elizabeth flatly refused. Greg would not be able to travel until the end of the summer, she said.

Akhmerov was still not sure what to make of his difficult American agent. "She, as a rule, carries out my instructions gladly and reports everything about our people to me," he wrote to Moscow. "However, her behavior changes when I ask her to organize a meeting with [Silvermaster]." He came to a reluctant conclusion. "Sometimes," he observed, "by her remarks, I can feel that at heart, she doesn't like us."[45]

As she struggled with her antipathy for her Russian supervisors and her despair over Yasha's death, Elizabeth began to drink excessively. She had had a drinking problem ever since her days in Florence, but now her neighbors began to notice that she drank all the time. Her health suffered as a result. She began to get frequent "colds" or "flus" that prevented her from going to work, but her doctor thought she was just hungover.[46] When she did go to work, she alarmed her boss, John Reynolds, with her biting comments and "extreme bitterness."[47]

Although she was just in her mid-thirties, the isolation of an espionage career made it difficult for her to meet men. She had enjoyed an active sex life up to this point in her life, and she resented her solitude now. She repeatedly complained to the Russians about her "lack of a male friend to satisfy her natural needs."[48]

Nor did she confine herself to male friends. Elizabeth had had countless affairs with men in the past, and she would continue to have male lovers in the future. Harvey Matusow, one of those lovers, says that he enjoyed a "good, heterosexual sexual relationship" with her.[49] But during this prolonged period of sexual deprivation after Yasha's death, she explored the idea of intimate relations with women. Two women claimed that they were the victims of unwanted sexual overtures from Elizabeth at this time. Mary Price told an interviewer in 1976 that she had rebuffed "homosexual advances" from Elizabeth.[50] In addition, a female worker at the U.S. Service and Shipping Corporation complained to the Soviets that Elizabeth had sexually harassed her and proposed "an intimate liaison with her."[51] Apparently, American society's proscriptions against homosexuality were among the many rules that Elizabeth was willing to break.

Her evident depression, her constant complaints, and her increasing reliance on alcohol for solace should have sounded some alarms in Moscow. Indeed, Akhmerov's supervisor in Russia, Pavel Fitin, did write to Akhmerov that he was worried by Elizabeth's "unbalanced state and inconstancy."[52]

But even as he reported on Elizabeth's problems, Akhmerov seemed unable to understand their significance. After noting her obvious bitterness, her refusal to follow orders, and her mood swings, Akhmerov rushed to reassure Moscow that she was "one hundred percent our woman." With a "tactful attitude, friendly treatment, and firm businesslike relations," he wrote, "it is possible to correct her behavior."[53]

That "firm" treatment included a refusal to let her retain control of Greg Silvermaster and his sources. Since Elizabeth would not listen to Akhmerov himself, the shrewd NKGB agent found other ways to get what he wanted. He asked Moscow to put pressure on Browder; Browder, in turn, could force Bentley to give up

A SERIOUS AND DANGEROUS BURDEN

her sources. Finally, in early June 1944, his machinations paid off. Bowing to Moscow's demands, Browder agreed to give the Silvermaster group to the NKGB.[54]

In her numerous retellings of her story, Elizabeth always highlighted Browder's capitulation as a turning point in her life. "I discovered then that Earl Browder was just a puppet, that somebody pulled the strings in Moscow," she explained.[55] That revelation, she implied, was the beginning of the end of her romance with American Communism.

But the moment was not really as fraught with ideological importance as she later implied. Given her activities for the past six years, it must not have come as a shock to her that the Soviets "pulled the strings" of the CPUSA. What upset her was the realization that the Soviets also had the power to pull *her* strings. Elizabeth had never been keen on following orders, whether it was her father's rules on alcohol or a university's ban on smoking. The NKGB's power play infuriated a woman who did not like other people to tell her what to do—and who did not seem to fully understand her own relative weakness. She resolved to find a way to get even.

She did not go straight to the FBI, though. Indeed, more than a year would pass before she took that momentous step. But after she lost her battle to keep the Silvermaster group, Elizabeth began a clever, manipulative, passive-aggressive campaign to hurt the people who had hurt her.

First, she tried to confuse and deceive the Russians by telling them what they wanted to hear. In the summer of 1944, after months of foot-dragging, obstructionism, and thinly concealed disdain for all things Russian, Bentley transformed herself into a model agent. She surprised her Soviet controller with a much more "obedient" frame of mind when she met with him in late June.

Akhmerov eagerly communicated to Moscow his delight over the change in his problem agent. "Now she tells me that her life is connected with us, that she doesn't have any other interests besides her work, and that she loves our country more than anything else," he reported. In fact, he said, she wanted to become a Soviet citizen![56]

Inspired by her newfound courtesy, the hardened NKGB agent reacted with fraternal concern. He decided that all Elizabeth really needed was a good man. "I would like to resolve [her] personal problem," he wrote Moscow. "If I could, I would give her in marriage to one of our operatives. If there is no one [here], why not send somebody from home?"

His supervisor responded with caution. "The question of a husband for her must be thought over," he wrote.[57]

In the meantime, the Soviets tried to cement Elizabeth's loyalty to them with gifts that were easier to obtain. One summer evening in 1944, Akhmerov offered her a monthly salary to enable her "to live more comfortably." He started with an offer of $50 a month and eventually raised it to $300.

Elizabeth reacted angrily. "What kind of a racket is this where they pay you for doing your duty?" she asked.

Akhmerov temporarily dropped the offer of money. Later, however, he would suggest that Elizabeth might like a Persian lamb coat or an air-conditioner.[58]

While she placated her bosses, Elizabeth also began to lie to them. She set out on a deliberate campaign to discredit her own sources. If they had inappropriate friends, she informed Moscow immediately. If they were involved in the open Party, she emphasized their public connections and dangers of exposure. If they had personal problems, she hinted that they were heading for mental breakdowns.

Two of her stories were particularly dramatic. She began with the man who had betrayed her, Yasha's old friend Earl. In October 1944, Elizabeth told the NKGB that Browder had committed the sin of criticizing the Soviets. He had called her espionage work "dirty blackmail," she claimed, and urged Americans to distance themselves from the Soviets. She reported that he whined about the Soviets' failure to appreciate him.[59]

The next month, Elizabeth informed on her friend Mary Price.

A SERIOUS AND DANGEROUS BURDEN

She told Moscow that Mary and Duncan Lee were having an affair. Lee's wife, Ishbel, had objected tearfully to the romance, but the affair continued anyway. Since Ishbel knew about Duncan's secret work, his cover was obviously endangered by the indiscretion. Elizabeth recommended that the Soviets drop Lee as a source.[60]

However, Ishbel Lee (now Ishbel Petrie), the only one of the principals in this alleged domestic conflict who is still alive, vehemently denies that the affair—or her angry denunciation of it—ever took place.[61]

Why did Elizabeth tell these tales to the Soviets? Years later, in her autobiography, she would claim that she lied to discredit her friends as agents and thus "save" them from the Russians. "I would slant the information I had on them to such a degree that they would look like poor risks to the Russian Secret Police, who perhaps would drop them," she wrote.[62] She was particularly worried about Mary Price, who was anxious and ill. In other words, Elizabeth admitted that she lied about her friends—but only for the best of motives. It was her first step out of the Soviet service.

It is true that she was angry over the way the Soviets had treated her, and she did undoubtedly want to save her friends from the same anguish. But her motives were not entirely as simple and altruistic as she suggested later. It is hard to see, for example, how Earl Browder gained anything from a poisoned relationship with the Russians. Instead, her purpose in that case seems to have been pure revenge. As for the alleged affair, Duncan Lee's widow doubts that Elizabeth's motive was as "benign" as she claimed in her autobiography. "In all probability," she speculates, "Bentley was looking to enhance her own credibility with the Soviets by showing that she could garner this intimate tidbit."[63] For her part, Mary Price believed that Elizabeth's hostility might stem from her rejection of her homosexual advances.[64]

Elizabeth had in fact many reasons to lie about her sources to the Soviets. She wanted to settle scores; she wanted to help her friends; she wanted to help herself by impressing her bosses. Most of all, though, she just wanted to lie to the tyrannical managers who had taken away her autonomy and who, she believed, had killed her Yasha. If they took most of her sources away from her, well, then, she would just give false reports about the ones she had left.

As the end of World War II and its grand alliance approached, one of the top Soviet agents in the United States was an unstable, alienated, mendacious American who drank too much and was doing all she could to sabotage her own agent network. She was not, in short, the perfect spy.

On September 14, 1944, the most powerful hurricane in six years slammed into the dunes of Cape Hatteras and slashed up the coast. In New York City, commuters confronted a lethal obstacle course of flooded subways and downed electrical wires.[65] Through the swirling wind and sheets of rain, Elizabeth shoved her way into packed trains headed to Washington. It was her last meeting with the Silvermaster group.

At the Silvermasters' home, she looked solemnly over their last documents, then shared a silent dinner with her subdued friends. She finally said her good-byes, and reminded them that they would begin regular meetings with "Bill" in two weeks.[66] They knew it was the end of an era. There would be no more jovial parties, no more knitting bags bulging with memos. The professionals were taking over.

While Akhmerov moved to Washington to take over the Silvermaster network, the Soviets assigned a new Manhattan contact to Elizabeth. She met him in early October 1944, in front of a drugstore on Park Avenue. In a scenario straight out of pulp fiction, she carried a copy of *Life* magazine and wore a red flower. As she scanned the street, she was startled by a voice behind her. It was her new boss, "Jack."

In stark contrast with Akhmerov, this new handler was "not at all meticulous about his personal appearance," she noted. His gray suits, brown shoes, and colorless personality helped him blend into any crowd. He was only in his mid-thirties, but his receding hairline and pronounced limp made him look much older. Elizabeth noted his Jewish nose and East Side accent.[67] His English was so good that she thought he might be a native-born American. To be sure, she laid a verbal trap for him.

"You know," she told him one day as they settled themselves on a bench in Central Park, "the Russians used to call me *umnitsa*."

He laughed appreciatively—she was, after all, quite a "clever girl." Then he suddenly caught himself. She had discovered that he spoke Russian. "All right," he admitted. "You caught me on that one; but I'm not a Russian—I'm a Lithuanian and proud of it."[68]

"Jack" was actually Joseph Katz, one of the most active NKGB agents in the United States. He handled many important American contacts, including Earl Browder and Harry Gold.[69] Over the next year, Elizabeth would meet him dozens of times and become rather fond of him. "[O]f all the agents I had met since Yasha's death, he was the most decent," she remembered later.[70] Apparently these feelings were not reciprocated. After Elizabeth defected to the FBI in the fall of 1945, Katz accepted his last orders from the Soviets in the United States. He agreed to kill her.[71]

But this potentially lethal end to the relationship was not at all clear when they met. Initially, Elizabeth was not much impressed by this man who had all the callowness of youth and the physical problems of old age.

Furthermore, "Jack" seemed just as determined as "Bill" to circumscribe Elizabeth's autonomy. At their second meeting, he demanded control of Mary Price. She "became somewhat incensed about this" and demanded to see his superior. At their next meeting, Katz told her that Moscow had granted her wish.[72]

In early November 1944, Elizabeth traveled down to Washington to meet "Al" at a Georgetown pharmacy. She pinned her standard red flower on her hat and picked up her copy of *Life*. She stood in front of the drugstore and waited.

Just as she began to worry that the meeting had been canceled, she heard the required code words. "I bring greetings from Moscow," said the man.

Like Elizabeth, Anatoly Gorsky (who used the name Gromov in the United States) was in his mid-thirties. He brushed his blond hair straight back on his head, and his expressionless eyes peered out from spectacles. He was short, fat, toothy, and "funny look-ing," Elizabeth remembered later.[73] "Dubiously I stared at him," she said, "noting his appearance of well-fed flabbiness, his well-tailored and expensive-looking clothes. Could this be the man I was to meet?"[74]

Elizabeth may have been dubious, but he certainly was the right man. Gorsky was not only the chief of NKGB operations in America but also the first secretary at the Soviet embassy. A "grimly effi-cient, humorless, orthodox Stalinist," according to Christopher An-drew and Vasili Mitrokhin, he had made a name for himself in London, where he had controlled the "Cambridge Five," the British spies who counted Kim Philby and Donald Maclean among their number.[75] Gorsky had followed Maclean to Washington when the British diplomat had been posted to the embassy there.[76] Once in Washington, Gorsky supervised agents, cultivated presidential advisers, and recommended assassinations. There was something about him, Elizabeth said later, that made "shivers run up and down your spine."[77] She had demanded to see someone at the top, and she had gotten her wish.

Thus began Elizabeth's relationship with her last—and most powerful—NKGB controller. In an elaborate pas de deux, the two champion manipulators tried to placate, deceive, and outwit each other. A survivor of the Stalinist purges, Gorsky plainly thought that he could handle this difficult American woman. Like his pre-decessors, though, he had no idea of the strength and shrewdness of his adversary.

Gorsky seemed to view Elizabeth as a child, and, like all bad parents, he attempted to solve this discipline problem with threats and bribes. The bribe came first. At their second meeting, in New York in November, he told her it was a memorable day. The top Communists in the motherland had awarded her the Order of the Red Star. If she ever went to Moscow, she would only have to show her star to be "wined and dined and treated like a princess."[78]

The honor was not a good choice. Although she appeared to respond with "cordial gratitude," Elizabeth was actually seething beneath the surface. She knew better than to go to Moscow, and some silly Russian decoration meant nothing to her.[79]

Gorsky had better luck with threats. At their third meeting, a week before Christmas 1944, he summarily informed Elizabeth that he was taking over *all* of her sources. "I'm afraid our friend Golos was not too cautious a man, and there is the risk that you, because of your connection with him, may endanger the apparatus," he explained. Meanwhile, she could decide if she wanted to continue with the underground in another location with new contacts. That was that; no more debate, no more angst. The decision had been made without her.[80]

The loss of her sources was upsetting enough, but then something else happened that night to anger Elizabeth even more. The two participants told dramatically different tales of what happened next. In her version, Gorsky sexually harassed her. He stared at her like "a trader about to decide whether to buy a horse" and said, suggestively, "I like you personally; I think we could work very well together." She was overwhelmed with "nausea."[81]

In Gorsky's version, though, his lonely, oversexed agent made a pass at *him*. She purred suggestively that he reminded her of her dead lover and talked of how she would like to start a family. In a panic, Gorsky wired to Moscow that his bosses should reconsider the matchmaking possibilities for his amorous agent. He wanted someone else to absorb her considerable sexual energy.[82]

It is impossible to know for certain who was telling the truth. But Gorsky did not have a reputation for sexual adventures, while Elizabeth did. Moreover, he told his version of the event at the time, whereas she told her side much later. In any event, whether he insulted her by propositioning her or by rejecting *her* proposition, the net result was that she felt insulted. That insult only strengthened Elizabeth's conviction to leave the Soviet service.

Over the course of the next month, Gorsky forced Elizabeth to turn over all of her contacts to him. She was exhausted, "mentally, and physically, from the strain of leaving them." They were, after all, her friends.[83]

At the same time, Gorsky insisted that she begin extricating herself from her two day jobs at World Tourists and U.S. Service and Shipping. Elizabeth had merely been filling in after Golos's death at World Tourists, but she loved her job at the shipping company she had helped create.[84]

She had run the companies well, but her brazen attempt to manage known espionage fronts while conducting espionage herself was insupportable to the new NKGB. The Soviets picked out her successor at U.S. Service and Shipping—an American Communist named Rae Elson—and directed Elizabeth to start training her.[85]

To further complicate her life, the Russians insisted that she had to leave her old apartment. She had been lax and unprofessional to allow her contacts to learn her phone number, Gorsky told her. The FBI could well be waiting for her when she came home. She knew he had a point. One day, she had been panicked by a clean-cut young man who knocked on her door and claimed to have the wrong address. He seemed to be "memorizing" her face.[86] But it was still hard to leave the bedroom she had shared with Yasha. As she packed up her belongings, she knew that she was leaving behind her memories of a happier life.[87]

When she moved into the Hotel St. George in Brooklyn Heights that spring, Elizabeth was a lonely, bitter, and paranoid woman desperate for companionship and security. Then, suddenly, in what seemed to be a tremendous stroke of luck at the time, she succeeded in finding a companion. As a result, though, she found that she was anything but secure.

On the last day of April 1945, she met a man at her hotel bar whose appearance brought back sweet memories from the past. Middle-aged, stocky, with thinning red hair and blue eyes, Peter F. Heller must have reminded her of Jacob Golos.[88] He was waiting for a room; she was waiting for someone just like him. They had sex that very day.[89]

At first Elizabeth was thrilled with the relationship. He was an attorney, he told her, and a lieutenant in New York's National Guard. He seemed a perfect catch—perhaps even marriage material.[90] She told John Reynolds that she planned to leave the company and get married.[91] For some reason, Reynolds seemed to dislike the man intensely, but Elizabeth was too addled by love to care.[92]

Then, however, Heller abruptly stopped calling her. Frantic to find him, Elizabeth discovered a Peter Heller listed in the phone book, but the person who answered seemed suspicious and demanded to know how she had obtained the number.[93] Finally, Heller resurfaced, but with a tale that was hardly reassuring.

He had been in a Navy hospital for a while, he told her. He had received "excellent care" because of his profession. He was, after all, a "big shot Government spy."[94]

The FBI later determined that Peter Heller was, in fact, a "crackpot" and a "bag of wind." He was not a "spy" but rather a former investigator for the New York State Parole Commission.[95] Currently, he was a part owner of a textile-trimming business bequeathed to him by his mother-in-law.[96] Elizabeth's new boyfriend was a married man who tried to pick up women by hinting at his undercover exploits as a superspy.

In this case, he picked up the wrong woman. It does not impress a top Communist spy to hear that her boyfriend is a big-shot spy catcher. Elizabeth understandably began to fear that this smooth-talking lothario had been sent by her enemies to seduce her. Here she had met the perfect guy, and it turned out he was, in all probability, bait for a "honey trap" aimed at her.

But which side was he on? "I was undecided in my own mind as to whether Heller was actually an agent of some U.S. Governmental organization or whether he was in some way connected with the Russians," she later explained.[97] One night, she could no longer stand the strain. She "threw a fit of hysterics very beautifully," telling him that she was truly a Russian spy and "frightened to death" of her bosses. Her announcement stunned Heller and convinced him that she was delusional.[98]

She reported the relationship to Joseph Katz—in part, no doubt, to gauge by his reaction whether Heller had been sent by the Soviets. Katz, in turn, told Anatoly Gorsky, who demanded a meeting with Elizabeth, the first since their angry encounter before Christmas.

Gorsky told Elizabeth in no uncertain terms to end the relationship. Heller was probably an FBI agent, he said. She should handle the breakup "diplomatically so as not to arouse his suspicions."[99] The whole affair only magnified the problems she already represented for the Soviets and their agents. The only solution, he said, was for her to move to the Soviet Union as soon as possible.

Elizabeth's highly developed survival skills served her well in this case. She demanded explanations and details. Wartime restrictions forbade her legal emigration to Moscow, and she adamantly refused to go "illegally"—that is, without papers.[100] Americans who went to the Soviet Union without proper documentation had a tendency to disappear without a trace. The whole idea "frightened me considerably," she later testified.[101]

Gorsky cabled Moscow about his growing frustrations with this difficult agent. Over the years, she had endangered dozens of valuable sources by her ignorance of the basic rules of tradecraft. This dalliance with a potential counterspy was the last straw. Elizabeth, he said, "is a serious and dangerous burden for us here."[102]

While Gorsky figured out how best to untangle Elizabeth's latest mess, he ordered her to go on vacation for a month or two.[103] He hoped that she would come back rested and ready for a new assignment in a foreign land. His Moscow supervisors agreed with his moves and suggested that he might try to find her a Party-approved husband so that she would have "no time to think too much [and] no time to practice romance, etc."[104]

Unfortunately for Gorsky and his bosses, though, Elizabeth had a lot of time to think during her long vacation in the seaside village of Old Lyme, Connecticut. One can imagine the balance sheet she drew up in her head. On the one hand, the NKGB had taken away her job, her friends, her apartment, and now her latest boyfriend. They were making noises about sending her to Moscow, and she knew what might happen to her there.

On the other hand, Heller's sudden appearance in her life seemed to suggest that the FBI might be closing in. Perhaps agents

A SERIOUS AND DANGEROUS BURDEN

were getting ready to arrest her at any moment. One way to avoid this, of course, would be to preempt an arrest by becoming an informer. But she knew what that would mean for her friends.

As she agonized over her decision, she began suffering from screaming nightmares. "Always it was the same one," she remembered later, "and always, no matter how thoroughly I waked myself out of it, I went back to it again." In the dream, she saw a firing squad aiming at a blindfolded prisoner. The prisoner might be Mary Price or another friend, but at the same time—in the inarguable logic of dreams—it was Elizabeth herself. "As I stood there, rooted to the spot with horror," Elizabeth continued, "the victim would suddenly wheel around and point his finger at me."

"Traitor!" he would yell. "It is you who have killed me."[105]

The alternative to becoming an informer, though, was equally terrifying. She knew now that the NKGB might deal with her as it had dealt with Juliet Poyntz. One day, she might vanish from her New York residential hotel, with a candle still flickering in her empty room.

At the end of her enforced vacation, she grew frantic waiting for something to happen. Rather than wait any more, she decided to act.

A young Elizabeth looks
pensively at the photographer
in this family photograph.
Courtesy Roger Turrill.

Jacob Golos initially
struck Elizabeth as
short and ordinary
looking, but she quickly
fell under the spell of
his "startlingly blue"
eyes. Russian Foreign
Intelligence Service.

When Elizabeth "dropped her mask," as the *New York World-Telegram* put it, many reporters were disappointed by her appearance. Library of Congress.

(opposite)
Initially, Elizabeth enjoyed the notoriety of being the "red spy queen." This 1948 portrait appeared in the *World-Telegram*. Library of Congress.

Former assistant treasury secretary Harry Dexter White was one of the most prominent men that Elizabeth accused of espionage. Library of Congress.

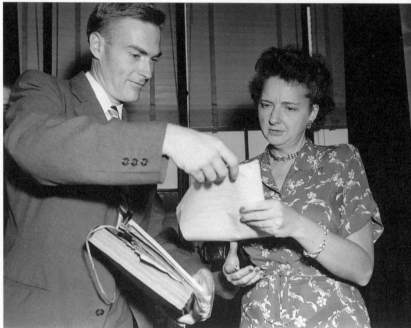

William Remington, shown here handing Elizabeth a document, hired private detectives to dig into her "sordid past." AP/Wide World.

Duncan Lee, right, denied Elizabeth's charges that he passed her secret information from the Office of Strategic Services. AP/Wide World.

Nathan Gregory Silvermaster supervised a ring of spies for Elizabeth. Acme.

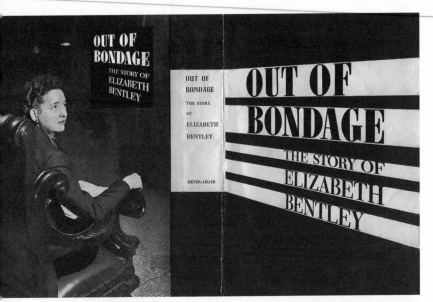

In her 1951 memoir, Elizabeth recounted her life as she wished it had been.
Courtesy Devin-Adair Publishers.

(opposite top)
Friend and fellow ex-Communist Louis Budenz helped arrange
Elizabeth's conversion to Catholicism. AP/Wide World.

(opposite bottom)
Elizabeth poses with her cat for a *World-Telegram* photographer shortly
after her religious conversion in 1948. "It's the first time in 13 years I've
felt like a human being," she said. Library of Congress.

Elizabeth admitted to lover and fellow ex-Communist Harvey Matusow
that she had invented some of her charges. AP/Wide World.

[5]
Get Rid of Her

t was pure, unadulterated fear that drove Elizabeth Bentley to the threshold of the FBI offices in New Haven in August 1945. She was disillusioned, of course; she was angry
and alienated from Communism in general and from the
Soviets in particular. But she had been disillusioned for two
years; this alone was not enough to drive her into the arms
of J. Edgar Hoover.

In her autobiography, she claimed that she had a religious
epiphany in Old Lyme: a vision of God speaking to her in the
steepled church of her forefathers.[1] But there is no hint of a conversion experience in the FBI statements she gave at the time. Instead,
there is just fear—fear of the Soviets and fear of the Feds.

On the day she chose to go to the FBI, the *New Haven Register*
featured a banner headline announcing the formal arrangements
for the Japanese surrender.[2] She never mentioned the atomic
bombings earlier that month in the many accounts of her defection, but they must have played a role in her decision. Elizabeth
and her sources had believed that the U.S.-Soviet wartime alliance
partially justified their espionage. Now that the war had ended,
she could no longer sustain any illusions about the U.S. government's tolerance of her actions. She knew what would happen if
she got caught.

She chose the FBI office in New Haven for a couple of reasons.
She was already vacationing in Connecticut, and the NKGB was not
as likely to notice her there. Just to be sure, though, she covered
her tracks well. She took the elevator in the unassuming business

building to a floor three stories above the FBI office, then stole down the fire stairs.

She took a deep breath and opened the door. Her knees shook as she approached the receptionist. Finally she found the courage to speak. "I'd like to see the agent in charge," she said.

As she waited on a nearby bench, she suppressed the urge to bolt.[3] She knew that she was taking a huge risk by coming here, yet she also knew that staying away could be even more dangerous.

The moment had come: the receptionist indicated it was her turn. Elizabeth swallowed her fear and walked into the small office.

Special Agent Edward Coady lit a cigarette and offered one to Elizabeth. As they settled back in their seats, he waited impassively to discover her purpose. Elizabeth drew nervously on her cigarette, then launched into her story.

She had come to file a complaint about a Lieutenant Peter Heller of the New York National Guard, she explained. A balding, fortyish man, he was passing himself off as a "big shot government spy." She had decided to talk to the FBI about him when he asked her if she wanted to spy, too.

As it happened, Elizabeth told the agent, she was the vice president of a shipping firm that sent packages to Russia. Heller had suggested that she might use her position to help the U.S. government.

Finally she came to the point. She feared this man might be impersonating a government agent. What could Coady tell her about him?[4]

Coady was thoroughly puzzled by this woman. He could tell that this Heller and his murky status with the government were not the real reasons for her visit. But he could not discern her true purpose.[5] He had never heard of Elizabeth Bentley. The bureau was not following her; apart from a few months in 1941, it had never followed her.[6] Neither, of course, had he heard of Heller. More important, though, he had no idea that the most significant

American agent of Soviet espionage ever to defect had just walked into his office.

Coady talked to Elizabeth for two hours before telling her that he could not confirm or deny the identity of any government agent.[7] He informed his supervisor of the encounter, who dutifully summarized the details in a memo to the FBI office in New York. The memo suggested that Bentley might be developed as an informant within the U.S. Service and Shipping Corporation, if in fact this company was involved in spying. The memo was headed: "RE: LIEUTENANT PETER HELLER; IMPERSONATION; ESPIONAGE."[8] At that point, the FBI was not sure whether it was dealing with a routine impersonation case or something more significant.

In New York, the field office assigned the "impersonation" case to Special Agent Frank Aldrich. He quickly discovered that Heller was a braggart and blowhard.[9] The impersonation case should be continued, he decided, but he did not see much importance in it. Consumed with preparations for his impending retirement, he put the New Haven memo aside for a few weeks.

The FBI later decided that Elizabeth's New Haven visit was a "'feeling out' process" in which "she wanted to indicate she had information but wanted it to be elicited from her."[10] If, in fact, she meant to pique the bureau's interest, she would have to try a little harder.

As Elizabeth concluded her vacation, the Soviet spy network in North America suffered its first major setback—without her help.

Throughout the summer of 1945, a young, disaffected clerk in the cipher department of the Soviet embassy in Ottawa began examining the secret files in his office. Igor Gouzenko looked for cables and memos that discussed Soviet espionage in Canada, then carefully folded their upper right-hand corners for later reference. On the hot, muggy night of September 5, he decided that it was time to execute his plan.[11]

After an early supper, he returned to his office. Drenched in perspiration, he closed the door to his office, opened his shirt, and stuffed 109 dog-eared documents inside. He worried that the suspicious bulge near his belly might give him away, but he hoped that a "sloppy shirt" would not seem unusual on such a hot night. He walked out of the building slowly, so as not to disturb the cables and alert the guards, and then boarded a streetcar.[12]

Gouzenko, like Whittaker Chambers, had access to documents that would prove his claims. Elizabeth would not enjoy that luxury. But at least she could rely on her street smarts, something that Gouzenko evidently lacked. His blundering attempts at defection stood in stark contrast to her careful, measured forays to the FBI offices.

Gouzenko simply planned to walk into a newspaper office or into the Canadian Justice Ministry and tell his story. The plan almost got him killed. Over the next twenty-four hours, he would try repeatedly and unsuccessfully to persuade Canadian journalists and law enforcement officers that he was not delusional. Finally, while he and his wife and child cowered in a neighbor's apartment, the police caught some NKGB agents breaking into his home. His bona fides now proven, the Royal Canadian Mounted Police began to debrief and protect him.[13]

The sweat-soaked documents spirited out of the Soviet embassy implicated several spies, including a British atomic scientist and Fred Rose, a member of Parliament who had worked with Jacob Golos.[14] The prime minister of Canada, Mackenzie King, considered Gouzenko's revelations so important that he personally flew to Washington to brief President Harry Truman.[15]

Had Elizabeth learned of Gouzenko's defection? If she had, of course, the knowledge would have given her even more reason to go to the FBI. But there is no evidence that she knew about it. Gorsky could have told her, but nothing in the NKGB documents or cables or in the FBI files indicates that he did.

Nor is there any evidence that the FBI suddenly became interested in Elizabeth because of the Gouzenko case. It is true that the bureau paid little attention to her before Gouzenko's defection, but only because she was deliberately unclear about the purpose of her visit to the New Haven office. The agents would not realize her importance until she spelled it out for them.

Gouzenko was the first person to alert U.S. officials that the Soviets had constructed a vast web of espionage in North America. He blew a hole in this web. Elizabeth, in turn, would tear it apart.

In the middle of September, Elizabeth returned to New York—and, directly contrary to Soviet orders, to her job at U.S. Service and Shipping.

Reynolds had begged her to come back to work because he was feuding with her successor, Rae Elson.[16] Elizabeth claimed in her autobiography that she agreed only because she feared that the Soviets would involve Reynolds in espionage and harm him and his family.[17] In her statement to the FBI, though, she indicated that boredom, money, and anger motivated her return.[18] A furious Gorsky telephoned Elizabeth and told her that he was coming up to New York to meet with her immediately.

Their September meeting was even more disastrous than their ill-fated Christmas rendezvous the year before. Earlier that day, Elizabeth had enjoyed a celebratory lunch with Reynolds, who had just been promoted to lieutenant colonel in the army. She had "several dry martinis" for the occasion.[19] As she staggered over to her appointment with Gorsky, she felt emboldened and uninhibited.

Al, she discovered, had planned her future for her. He ordered her to quit her job and disappear for a while. Then he would give her money to set up a small business—perhaps a hat shop or a travel agency—in a big city, he explained. After six months of establishing her cover, she would be given four or five agents to handle.

Elizabeth categorically refused. She was tired of the espionage game and especially tired of Soviet demands. Al then suggested an alternative: she could teach in a Russian school in Washington. She refused again and countered by insisting that Reynolds needed her at the shipping firm. But Al would not listen to her.

Elizabeth suddenly lost control. "I became so angered with him," she said, "that I told him in plain words what I thought of him and the rest of the Russians and, further, told him that I was an American and could not be kicked around."[20]

That was her version. According to Gorsky, she said considerably more. He reported to Moscow that she had come to their meeting drunk and told him that "she drank in order to tell in a drunken state that which she did not dare discuss sober." She denounced him and all other Russian agents as "gangsters" who "care only about Russia."

Worst of all, from Gorsky's perspective, were her threats. She implied that Golos, before his death, had been ready to defect to the FBI. Recently, Pete Heller had asked her to become an informant, she said, but she declined.[21] She seemed to leave hanging the possibility that she might change her mind.

It was obvious to Al that Elizabeth had the courage and the motivation to defy and destroy her spymasters. "Judging by her behavior," he said, "she hasn't betrayed us yet, but we can't rely on her. Unfortunately, she knows too much about us." Since she could "damage us here very seriously," he wrote, "only one remedy is left—the most drastic one—to get rid of her."[22]

Moscow's response was surprisingly restrained. Vsevolod Merkulov, Gorsky's supervisor, acknowledged that Elizabeth posed a "real danger," but he paternalistically suggested that all she needed was some money and a shoulder to cry on. Gorsky should "take all necessary precautions," he advised, but clearly the NKGB chieftain could not believe that this pathetic, lovelorn woman would really pose a threat to the most feared secret service in the world.[23]

Elizabeth realized that her drunken threats might have fatal consequences. As she explained later, she knew she was "living on borrowed time."[24] She was smart enough to know that no one should threaten the NKGB. Then, suddenly, she learned that she had reason to fear the FBI as well.

On October 11, the New York newspapers delivered some shocking news: "Daily Worker Editor Renounces Communism for Catholic Faith."[25] Louis Budenz, her old source, had abruptly abandoned the Party. His departure was so sudden that the *Daily Worker* "was caught with its ideological pants down and Editor Budenz's name still on the masthead," *Time* magazine chortled.[26] Budenz, who had been secretly meeting with the radio priest Fulton J. Sheen, announced that he had rejoined "the faith of my fathers" because Communism "aims to establish tyranny over the human spirit."[27] Two days later he announced that he would go on a nationwide lecture tour to expose the Communist menace.[28]

Budenz said nothing about espionage. But his clandestine contacts with Elizabeth would presumably provide juicy anecdotes for the proposed lecture tour. Moreover, though the newspapers did not mention it, Elizabeth must have surmised that the FBI was interviewing Budenz. All of Gorsky's concerns about her sloppy tradecraft had proved correct: here was a former source, now an enemy, who knew her real name and where she worked.[29]

As Elizabeth nervously weighed her options, the New York FBI office contacted her and requested an appointment to discuss the "impersonation" case.[30] On October 16, five days after her former source's well-publicized change of heart, she showed up at the field office in New York. The Soviets later saw this timing as more than coincidental. "Bentley's betrayal," Merkulov wrote in a memo to Stalin, "might have been caused by her fear of being unmasked by the renegade Budenz."[31]

This time, Elizabeth talked to a different agent in a much different setting. Instead of a small field office nestled in an ordinary business building, the New York FBI office was stationed in the imposing federal courthouse in Manhattan. She also had a different story to tell—though a story still far from the truth.

As she sat with Agent Aldrich, Elizabeth began to spin her story. The Pete Heller of her first FBI visit—the eccentric friend with bizarre espionage fantasies—was transformed into a much more menacing figure, a potentially dangerous agent of the worldwide Communist conspiracy. Before, she had claimed that Heller had urged her to tell the government about U.S. Service and Shipping.

Now, in a dramatic turnabout, she asserted that Heller had ominously warned her to *keep quiet* about her work at the shipping firm. In fact, she suspected that he might be a Soviet spy.[32]

Why did she tell this incredible tale? The bureau later concluded that she was still on a fishing expedition and not ready to commit herself.[33] Apparently, she thought that if she showed up at the FBI and mentioned the word "espionage," she could find out whether they were about to arrest her. If they were, she could suddenly come clean and take credit for defecting; if not, she could continue to weigh her options.

As the interview continued, Elizabeth dropped more intriguing nuggets of information for the startled agent. She had met many important Russian and American Communists through her job, she declared. She claimed that "she was closely tied in with people of whom she had suspicions and whom she believed to be Russian espionage agents." Suspicions? Believed? This was hardly a straightforward confession from a woman who had been a spy for eight years.

Almost as an aside, she mentioned the names of some of these possible spies. She dropped no bombshells that day; she betrayed no friends. She named Earl Browder and his brother William—no longer her friends and, at any rate, hardly concealed Communists. There was Jacob Golos (she had "rented a room" from him, she explained), who was of course dead. And then she casually dangled the name of Louis Budenz, the newly minted ex-Communist.

Lately, she admitted demurely, she had begun to feel "mixed [up] in some Russian intrigues and espionage." But the FBI must know all this, she said, because she was sure the bureau had been following her intermittently since 1941. Now, though, she might be ready to come forward with specific information.[34]

It occurred to Agent Aldrich that he might be dealing with a psychopath.[35] After all, he knew the bureau had *not* been following this woman. Moreover, she had no documentary proof, and she refused at that point to disclose specific names or incidents that were not already known to the bureau.

Aldrich's skepticism of Elizabeth's story and his own imminent retirement plans apparently prevented him from finding any urgency in her story. He wrote up a memo on her visit, but not until November 5—three weeks after her appointment. He did quickly phone Edward Buckley, another agent in the field office who was responsible for keeping tabs on Communist front businesses. Aldrich suggested that Buckley might want to follow up on Elizabeth's case. Assuming that she was not psychotic, Elizabeth Bentley might make a good informant.

In the memo on the interview, Aldrich laconically wrote that the "impersonation case on Lieutenant Peter Heller should be held in abeyance" until the bureau talked to Elizabeth again. It was beginning to look less and less like impersonation and more and more like espionage.[36]

Among the many facts Elizabeth had kept from Agent Aldrich at the October 16 meeting was her appointment the very next day with the top NKGB agent in the United States. On October 17, Elizabeth had another meeting with Gorsky.

She arrived sober and contrite. Over dinner at the Cornish Arms Hotel, she apologized to Al for her previous behavior.[37] He, in turn, was "very pleasant and sympathetic," apparently on Merkulov's instructions, and willing to overlook her drunken accusations. He even conceded that she could return to U.S. Service and Shipping.[38]

Elizabeth told Al that she was concerned about Budenz's defection. Overall, though, given her propensity for hysteria, Gorsky was surprised at how calm she seemed at the prospect of Budenz's informing on her.[39] He did not know that she had already made contingency plans in the event the FBI came calling.

Gorsky ended the meeting by handing her a plain white envelope containing $2,000 in $20 bills. The money came with no "strings attached," he said, and could be used to ease her "financial difficulties." They parted amicably.[40]

So amicably, in fact, that Elizabeth came to regret her decision to go to the FBI. For three weeks, Agent Buckley repeatedly called her at the number she had given Aldrich. For three weeks, Elizabeth refused to take the FBI's phone calls. She was "sick," she later claimed.

Obviously, she was reconsidering her defection. She had made up with the NKGB, and it seemed that the FBI was not about to arrest her after all. She had walked to the doorway of defection—and then decided not to go through it.

As it turned out, she hesitated only briefly. It was, ironically enough, a fight over money—a fight worthy of the most conniving, greedy capitalists—that finally convinced Elizabeth to answer the phone and betray her comrades.

About one week after her pleasant chat with Al, Elizabeth met with Lem Harris, a native-born American Communist with a Harvard degree, an "independent income," and a blue-blooded pedigree more impressive than Elizabeth's.[41] Son of a founder of a stock brokerage firm on Wall Street, Harris had given up his life of luxury to work on farms in the United States and the Soviet Union. Convinced that Communism provided the solution to the depression, he became the CPUSA agricultural expert and one of its chief fundraisers.[42] He also helped to handle finances for the Party. Like Elizabeth, he was used to giving orders rather than taking them.

Harris told Elizabeth that he wanted to examine the books of U.S. Service and Shipping. When she refused, he grew belligerent and demanded that she give him $15,000 immediately—the amount that the Party had originally invested in the firm. He had heard that the Russians were planning to take over the company, Harris said, and he wanted the CPUSA's money back.[43]

Furious, Elizabeth told him that it was the Soviets' responsibility to reimburse the Party, not hers. But Harris refused to take no for an answer. If she did not return the money, he said, he would "blow her to hell."[44]

Shaking with anger and fear, Elizabeth decided to seek help from the one man who understood the interlocking finances of

GET RID OF HER

Soviet intelligence and the CPUSA. Earl Browder had been booted out of the Party leadership in June for "right-wing deviationism," but years ago he had arranged the financing for her company.

In a secret meeting on October 26, Browder assured her that the Party would never sue her for the money. It was an illegal contribution, after all. However, he added ominously that the new leaders of the Party were not known for being reasonable or smart. "You can't tell what they will do down there," he said, "they are a lot of fools." In other words, Harris might well carry out his threat to kill her. After confirming Elizabeth's worst fears, Earl then refused to help her. What could he do in his present position? he asked.[45]

It was quite clear now to Elizabeth that her life was in danger. On November 6, when Special Agent Buckley called again, Elizabeth decided to answer the phone.

She told him quite honestly that she was upset and uncertain about whether she should talk to him. Buckley insisted, however, that if "she had any information regarding un-American activities" it was her duty to tell him.[46] Finally, she agreed to make her third trip to an FBI office the next day.

This time, the bureau realized the importance of her visit. Buckley told her to meet him at the subway station at Foley Square at 4:30 P.M. They told each other what they would be wearing, and Buckley instructed Elizabeth to carry a magazine. When she arrived, he slipped her into the federal building through "various exchanges of elevators." He and another agent, Don Jardine, began to question her.[47] She freely admitted that fear, not her "good old-fashioned New England conscience," as she later claimed, had driven her to them.[48]

This time she decided to tell all she knew. On that first day, Elizabeth talked for eight hours and gave a thirty-one-page statement. She would continue to speak with the New York office almost daily for the rest of the month. It all poured out of her: the Silvermasters, Mary Price, Duncan Lee, George Silverman, Helen Tenney, Maurice Halperin, Jack, Bill, and Al—every name she could remember. In the end, she would sign a 107-page statement naming more than eighty alleged Soviet spies in the United States.

Now, at last, the FBI felt the urgency of the situation. In the early morning hours of November 8, the New York office sent a frantic teletype:

> FROM NEW YORK TO DIRECTOR AND SAC URGENT. RE ELIZA-
> BETH TERRILL BENTLEY . . . ON NOVEMBER SEVENTH, NINE-
> TEEN FORTY-FIVE THE ABOVE MENTIONED SUBJ. VOLUNTARILY
> CAME TO THE NY FIELD DIVISION WHERE HSE [sic] FURNISHED
> INFORMATION RELATIVE TO A RUSSIAN ESPIONAGE RING WITH
> WHICH SHE WAS AFFILIATED AND WHICH IS PRESENTLY OPERAT-
> ING IN THIS COUNTRY.[49]

Based on Elizabeth's names and descriptions, Jardine and Buckley were convinced that she was telling the truth. "There wasn't any question in my mind that we hit gold on this one," Jardine says.[50] As the first telegram arrived at 1:55 A.M. in Washington, the New York office phoned headquarters to insist that top officials look at it first thing in the morning. The night-shift clerk hurriedly pulled all the available files and index cards on the names mentioned in the telegram.[51]

And there were many cards and files, for several of Elizabeth's sources had long been suspected of Communist sympathies by the U.S. government. Charles Kramer, Lauchlin Currie, and Harry Dexter White, for example, had been named by Whittaker Chambers. "We had files here, there and everywhere," Jardine says, "and she kind of sewed it all together."[52]

Over the next few weeks, Elizabeth completed her statement. Besides naming sources she knew personally, she also gave tantalizing hints about individuals whom she could not fully name. For example, Kramer had told her about an agent in the State Department who worked for Soviet military intelligence. The only thing she had learned about this mysterious agent was his last name, "Hiss." She thought his first name was Eugene.[53]

There was no Eugene Hiss in the State Department. But *Alger*

Hiss was already under a cloud of suspicion, thanks to Chambers. In the margins of Elizabeth's comments about Eugene Hiss, someone at the FBI made a handwritten notation: "Alger Hiss."[54]

Elizabeth also told what she could remember about an espionage ring of engineers in New York City. She described that evening in 1942 when Yasha had stopped the car on the Lower East Side and had met with a tall, thin man with horn-rimmed glasses. "[Golos] did not elaborate on the activities of this person and his associates," she said, "nor did he ever identify any of them except that this one man to whom he gave my telephone number was referred to as 'JULIUS.'" She added that she doubted that was his real name.[55]

There were moments of drama during the interrogation. On November 16, as Elizabeth met all day with special agents Thomas Spencer and Joseph Kelly, she told them how Al had tried to bribe her with the envelope stuffed with $20 bills.

The next day, as Elizabeth entered the hotel room where the agents were waiting, she opened her purse, took out an envelope, and casually tossed it on the bed, saying, "Here's some Moscow gold." For years, anti-Communists had been fulminating that the American Communists were bankrolled by money from Russia. Here was proof. The startled agents took the stash and put it in a safety deposit box.[56]

Elizabeth's initial statements to FBI agents would later serve as a benchmark for evaluating her veracity. During that first month, she stuck mostly to the truth—or at least what her sources had told her was the truth. She was not afraid to venture her opinions, but for the most part she clearly labeled them as opinions.

For example, she said that she had never met Harry Dexter White. She did mention that she regarded him as a "valuable adjunct" to the spy network because of his friendship with the treasury secretary. But she did not hint at the vast conspiracies she would later attribute to him once the newsreel cameras were turned on.[57]

She made it clear that Lauchlin Currie—as far as she could remember—did not give documents to her sources. Instead, he would pass information to George Silverman orally. One such briefing contained the gossip that the United States was "on the verge of breaking the Soviet code," she said. But she did not attach any special significance to that information. Far from indicating that Currie was one of her two most important sources, she allotted him only one-quarter of a page and two passing references in a 107-page statement.[58]

Elizabeth also mentioned that William Remington had told her about a new process for making rubber, but she added that "the information was quite vague and probably of no value even to a chemist."[59] She used similarly restrained language when she explained that Lud Ullmann had given her the "approximate schedule date of D-Day."[60] This revelation did not greatly excite the FBI agents who interrogated her. They knew that American military planners at the highest levels had briefed their Soviet allies about D-Day. She said nothing to imply that she had stolen precise information about the invasion.

All of those claims would come later.

Within days of Elizabeth's first statement, the FBI launched a massive effort to verify her charges. Tom Donegan, the FBI's counterespionage chief, led the effort. From the beginning, J. Edgar Hoover declared that there would be "no limit" to the number of agents assigned to her case.[61] By December 1945, seventy-two special agents were working on the biggest espionage case in the FBI's history.[62] Elizabeth had their attention now.

These numbers were necessary because the bureau wanted to follow, spy on, open the mail of, and listen to the phone calls of the men and women Elizabeth had named in her statement. Within two weeks, agents were following Maurice Halperin, Robert Miller, Victor Perlo, Greg Silvermaster, Helen Tenney, Lud Ullmann, Harry Dexter White, George Silverman, Charles Kramer, Duncan Lee, and several other lesser figures in the network.[63] The bureau also made plans to break into the Silvermasters' house.[64] Soon, reams of reports would deluge FBI headquarters detailing who had attended a party with Harry Dexter White and who had been invited for Christmas dinner at the Silvermasters.

The FBI minutely recorded all of the details of the lives of Elizabeth's former friends, sources, alleged sources, and alleged sources' sources. In addition, Hoover poured resources into an investigation of Elizabeth's vague mention of a man named Hiss. On November 28, as she prepared to sign her final statement, Hoover asked Attorney General Tom Clark for permission to tap Alger Hiss's phone. Clark responded with a scribbled note: "Edgar: Is this man now employed at the State Dept. If so, what do we have on him?" The FBI director responded that two defectors had now named Hiss. Clark approved the taps.[65]

The bureau also opened the mail going to Hiss and his wife, Priscilla, and began surveying Alger's every move. For the next two years, every person visiting the Hiss residence—even the preschool carpool driver for the Hisses' four-year-old son—was watched and noted by the FBI.[66]

The best way to catch these suspected criminals was, of course, to observe them committing a crime. To accomplish this, the bureau needed to "double" Elizabeth—to have her pretend to continue to work for the Soviets.

Of course, they needed her cooperation for this, but the FBI never doubted that Elizabeth would agree. She had, as one agent noted, "no choice in this matter." Wartime espionage was a capital offense. If she wanted the agents' protection—and if she wanted to avoid prison or even the death penalty—she would have to do what they asked.[67]

Elizabeth realized the delicacy of her position. At the beginning, when she was not sure whether she would avoid prison, she flattered the agents and emphasized her "patriotic" motives for helping them.[68] She cooperated with their plan to double her, although she confessed that she did not "relish" the assignment.

She also insisted that she did not want to profit from her crimes. When agents raised the subject of "compensating" her for potential "monetary losses" she might suffer while working as a double agent, she brushed aside their offer.[69] Her attitude on this issue would shift dramatically in the years to come.

Elizabeth began her new career as a double agent just a few weeks after her defection. She was scheduled to meet Gorsky on November 21, and the FBI planned to be there. Everyone involved was nervous. The bureau did not want Gorsky—or any other subject under surveillance, for that matter—to detect the tails. "We don't want to lose the surveillance, but we don't want them to become suspicious, either," wrote one top FBI official to another.[70] Nor did they want Elizabeth to "go overboard" during her debut as an actress. She assured them that she would be discreet and tactful.[71]

On the day of the meeting, the FBI followed Gorsky from the Washington airport to his rendezvous with Elizabeth at Bickford's Restaurant in Manhattan.[72] This time, as she observed with distaste Al's wolfish appetite and his "vulgar and offensive" language, there were G-men watching from the shadows.[73]

As usual, Gorsky was primarily interested in Peter Heller. Primed by the FBI, Elizabeth assured Al that she had completely dropped him after discovering he had a wife and three children. If she met him again, she said, she would "stick a knife in him."[74]

Elizabeth then dropped some "casual hints" about resuming her life as a spy. This was a crucial moment: the FBI was hoping that Gorsky would welcome her back into active espionage immediately. But Al did not take the bait. Elizabeth had said she wanted "a normal, peaceful, settled life," he explained, and now she had it.[75]

At least that's what she told the FBI. The agents could not overhear her conversation, so they could not verify how hard she had tried to win a job that she admitted she did not want.[76]

Their leisurely discussion was basically "innocuous," Elizabeth said, but something about it disturbed her. She could not quite put her finger on it, but Al seemed "cagey."[77] As he left the meeting, Gorsky "made vigorous and extensive efforts to lose anyone surveilling him." After talking it over with the agents, though, Elizabeth decided that his behavior was "routine procedure on his part rather than any present belief that he was being surveilled."[78]

She was wrong. Gorsky's suspicions had indeed been aroused. In his opinion, she had asked a lot of strange questions. Then, as he left the restaurant, he was alarmed to see three men following him in a car.[79]

The next day, his worst fears were confirmed. Back in Washington, he received a cable from Moscow. The Soviets had reliable information that their "clever girl" had outwitted them.

The early news of Elizabeth's defection was one of the NKGB's biggest intelligence coups ever. If she had succeeded in burrowing back into the Soviet underground in America, the FBI could have collected damning evidence against dozens of spies. But the Soviets countered the FBI's would-be mole with their own mole — a spy so highly placed that he was privy to the nation's top secrets.

This Soviet mole was Kim Philby, a Cambridge-educated star in the British secret service who had risen to be chief of Soviet counterintelligence by 1945. In other words, he was in charge of catching Soviet spies. He also happened to be one himself. Because the British, Canadians, and Americans shared intelligence information, Philby had learned immediately of the Gouzenko defection. He quickly informed Moscow.

J. Edgar Hoover tried his best to keep Elizabeth's defection secret. The FBI assigned her a male code name — "Gregory" — to help protect her identity and decreed that news of her case could not go to "*any* sources outside the bureau."[80] However, Hoover did not obey his own prohibition. On November 9, the day after Elizabeth's first statement, he met with Sir William Stephenson, the British station chief in the United States, and told him of her defection.[81]

Stephenson must have passed the information to Philby, for on November 20, less than two weeks after Elizabeth began her confession in earnest, Philby informed the NKGB of her betrayal. In a stunning reversal of fortune, the Soviets now had the chance to limit the colossal damage that Elizabeth could inflict on their spy networks.[82]

Realizing the stakes, the NKGB responded swiftly. In a November 23 cable, the Soviets instructed all station chiefs in the United States to "cease immediately their connection with all persons known to Bentley in our work [and] to warn the agents about Bentley's betrayal." The cable specifically told Gorsky to cease meeting with Charles Kramer, Victor Perlo, Helen Tenney, Maurice Halperin, and Lauchlin Currie, among others. Gorsky must also stop seeing top British agent Donald Maclean. In another cable, the NKGB told Akhmerov to inform Greg Silvermaster of the defection and to warn him to stop meeting with his sources.[83]

With the FBI watching, Akhmerov could not carry out this order himself. Instead, he sent a messenger, a Brooklyn man named Alexander Koral. On December 1, as the FBI looked on, Koral met the Silvermasters on a street corner, proceeded to their house, and delivered a brief message. There would be "no more visits," he said.[84]

Because of the successful delivery of that message, the FBI's massive undercover effort over the next eighteen months would be in vain. Thanks to Philby, Elizabeth would become the least successful double agent in FBI history.

Another American agent who received a warning of Elizabeth's confession was the tall, thin engineer who had made the mysterious nighttime phone calls to her apartment. "Julius," of course, was his real name: Julius Rosenberg had been supervising a spy ring of American Communist engineers since 1941.[85] He had also helped the Soviets establish contact with his brother-in-law, David Greenglass, a sergeant in the machine shop at the super-secret atomic bomb project in New Mexico.[86] On December 15, NKGB officer Alexander Feklisov visited the Rosenbergs' apartment and told Julius to burn all his notes and prepare to deny everything to the FBI.[87]

As a final precaution, Moscow ordered Akhmerov and Gorsky to return to the Soviet Union immediately. Overnight, the Soviets stopped all NKGB espionage in America.[88]

The Soviets also considered silencing Elizabeth permanently. On November 27, Gorsky discussed in a memo to Moscow the best way to kill her. Joseph Katz could do it, he said, but he was having trouble choosing the best method to use. After all, Elizabeth was "a very strong, tall and healthy woman," and Katz "was not feeling well lately." Perhaps the best method would be poisoning her food, he concluded.

Once again, however, the NKGB leadership restrained Gorsky and indicated that they had their own plans for Elizabeth. They did not disclose what those plans were.[89]

As the Soviets sought frantically to limit the damage from this catastrophic defection, Elizabeth continued to meet with FBI agents. She remained "completely cooperative" with the bureau up until the last day.[90]

On November 30, the agents gave her a statement to sign. The typed, single-spaced pages were neatly arranged in a half-inch stack. The names in the statement were all capitalized, and they jumped out at the reader. MARY PRICE. HELEN TENNEY. DUNCAN LEE. JACOB GOLOS.

Suddenly, she had another change of heart. She refused to sign. She might be sending some friends to prison, she explained. "She characterized the Americans' activities as being motivated by an ideology," one FBI agent wrote, "and that they felt that the information they obtained was to help an ally."[91]

The agents persisted, of course. It was too late to back out now. After they reminded her that the war was over and the Soviets were no longer U.S. allies, she agreed to sign.

Her new protectors were still suspicious of her, however. As she continued her sessions with the bureau, agents made plans to break into her apartment. They still were not entirely sure if "Gregory" was telling the truth.[92]

For the next year, Elizabeth was engaged in a dangerous, adult version of Let's Pretend. While she pretended that she was not an informer, the Soviets and her sources pretended that they did not know she was one. The Soviets, obviously, had the advantage.

On the surface, Elizabeth conducted her business exactly as she had for the past few years. She continued as the vice president of U.S. Service and Shipping, a job that paid a substantial salary of $9,600 a year.[93] This money bought her long vacations in Puerto Rico, trips to Turkish baths, and three-martini meals in fancy restaurants.[94]

Meanwhile, Elizabeth did her best to reenter the underground. Her attempts were stymied at every turn. Gorsky did not show up at scheduled meetings in January and March; he had left the country on December 7, but Elizabeth and the FBI did not know this.[95] Elizabeth surmised that he was laying low because of the fallout from the Gouzenko case in Canada. She remained convinced that her own defection was a secret. "I don't think they became aware of me as being a traitor at all," she testified later.[96]

She maintained this conviction even after she had an unsuccessful reunion with the Silvermasters. Acting on FBI advice, she called up her former friends in March and said that she wanted to meet them. Although they invited her to their house, they gave her a "very chilly" reception and said nothing of substance.[97] Elizabeth did not attempt to call on them again.

With one notable exception, the few people who would talk to Elizabeth were insignificant sources—too insignificant for the Soviets to bother warning.[98] But there was one major source who had *not* been warned. According to NKGB cables, Gorsky was supposed to inform Helen Tenney of Elizabeth's betrayal. Helen's new controller did set up a meeting with her in December, but for unknown reasons the controller never showed up or contacted her again. Helen thus had the unfortunate distinction of being the only one of Elizabeth's important sources who would talk to her during her years as a double agent.

Under FBI instructions, Elizabeth arranged a meeting with Helen at a Washington restaurant on March 13, 1946. She was immediately struck by Helen's thin, haggard appearance and nervous manner. After glancing around, Helen explained. "I didn't know whether or not I should come," she said. "J. Edgar's boys are chasing me."[99]

Elizabeth was taken aback. Of course FBI agents were chasing her; Elizabeth herself had set them on her trail. Two agents, in fact, were sitting at a table nearby. Was Helen playing some sort of clever game?

But her former source seemed completely sincere as she explained how the FBI had come to New York and asked questions of her family chauffeur. "I'm so glad you've come," she told Elizabeth. "After I lost my contact a few months back, I've been sitting and worrying, thinking that something must be wrong."[100]

Helen expressed concern that she might be putting *Elizabeth* in danger. Elizabeth reassured her friend "and told her she felt her fears were groundless."[101] The FBI's star informant later confessed that she hated herself that night. "She was coming to me in the expectation of finding a friend, and instead I was her enemy," she wrote.[102]

A few months later, when Helen's life took a tragic turn, Elizabeth was faced with an even more difficult choice. Helen began to lose her tenuous grasp on sanity when the State Department revoked her passport. The official cause was a technicality, but Helen feared that she faced imminent arrest. When she began telling her friends and family that she was a Russian spy, they urged her to seek help for her "hallucinations."[103]

In late August 1946, after what the FBI called "an exceptionally severe night of drinking," Helen took an overdose of phenobarbital. She remained unconscious for five days. When she woke up, she became hysterical whenever she heard anyone use the words "Russia" or "Russian."[104]

FBI officials could not believe their good fortune. They had always hoped that one of Elizabeth's sources would relent and corroborate her story, and now here was a source in the midst of a mental breakdown. When agents learned that Tenney wanted to meet Elizabeth at Longchamps restaurant in New York, the leaders of the FBI could hardly contain their enthusiasm. On January 16, 1947, Hoover himself telegraphed to New York his insistence that "Gregory" set up a meeting.[105] As Assistant Director Mickey Ladd explained in a memo, "[I]t is highly probable that Tenney may, in this state of mind, reveal some startling information to Gregory which is not known to the Bureau."[106]

Elizabeth, however, refused to go. In a marked deviation from her normal "100 percent cooperative" attitude, she protested that such a meeting in a public restaurant might prompt Tenney to "make a scene" or try to kill herself again. Either way, Tenney might "precipitate a police investigation which could definitely jeopardize Gregory's position."[107]

It was a peculiar argument. Elizabeth did not argue that the meeting might cause Helen to kill herself, but only that it might prompt her to kill herself in public—and thereby jeopardize Elizabeth's position. Perhaps she designed the argument to appeal to the coldly rational minds at the bureau. If she did, though, her strategy failed. As Ladd wrote, with notable understatement, "It is highly improbable that Tenney will commit suicide on the occasion of this meeting at Longchamps or at any time that she is in the company of Gregory, since it is known that she has confided with Gregory in the past and appears to have utmost confidence in Gregory."[108]

Of course, the meeting might push Tenney to suicide at some later time. But, Ladd reasoned, she might kill herself anyway, and it would be nice for the FBI to know what she had to say first. "In the event that she does commit an act of self-destruction in the near future," he wrote, "the question would always be in the Bureau's mind as to what Tenney had to disclose to Gregory."[109] Ladd and Hoover also hoped that Elizabeth would convince Tenney to see a psychiatrist. The agents could then induce the doctor to tell them everything she said.[110]

Elizabeth hesitated, then finally acquiesced. Three weeks after the bureau first urged her to set up a meeting, she arranged one. On February 7, 1947, the two former spies met at a Chinese restaurant on West 48th Street.

Helen was nervous and talkative. During the course of a two-hour meal, she told Elizabeth about her recent break-up with her boyfriend, her excessive drinking, and her overdose.

She had little to say about espionage, however.[111] Elizabeth told the agents that they had no hope of getting good information from her. Helen was still a committed Communist, she said, and a most unlikely informant.[112]

Elizabeth had drawn the line. However much she wanted to please her new friends at the bureau, she was not going to help them exploit or manipulate her troubled friend. As the pressure increased on Elizabeth in the months and years to come, though, such acts of nobility would become increasingly rare.

As Elizabeth struggled with her role in Helen's breakdown, she also faced a crisis at her day job. By the fall of 1946, U.S. Service and Shipping was almost broke. The Soviet tourist agency, Intourist, decided not to renew the company's exclusive contract with it. At the same time, the Department of Justice began pressuring the business to register as a foreign agent. In response, Reynolds decided to shut the company down.

Bentley and Reynolds's friendship dissolved along with the company. As the closing date neared, they began to quarrel over her severance package. Reynolds finally agreed to pay her almost a year's salary in severance and bonuses when the company folded in March.[113]

In January 1947, Elizabeth called Reynolds at his home, where he was recovering from viral pneumonia, and said that she needed the money right away. Reynolds angrily refused, saying that he would not pay her until the company shut its doors. It then occurred to him that Elizabeth might disobey his orders. He called his bank and prohibited her from cashing company checks. As he suspected, that very afternoon Elizabeth arrived at the bank and tried to deposit a company check into her own bank account.[114]

Reynolds quickly fired Bentley, took control of all of the finances, and hired a lawyer to tell her she would get just two months' salary in severance.[115] In his view, she was guilty of rank insubordination and appalling greed. She, though, saw the confrontation differently. She had built the company from scratch, and now this rich dilettante, this sham of a company president, was not going to let her get her money when she needed it. Never one for following orders, she just decided to take the money herself.

Distraught, Elizabeth could think of nothing but the money. She was so angry, she said, she just "felt like tearing up the office and locking the door and never coming back again."

But the confrontation did help her discover a winning strategy that she would find helpful in the future. She insisted that the FBI agents had to help her—or else. If they did not, she said, "she did not see how she could be of any value in the current investigation."[116]

The bureau agreed to help her arrange to sue for the money and even referred her to a lawyer. Tom Donegan, the agent in charge of Elizabeth's case, had resigned from the bureau and started his own law practice. At the FBI's recommendation, she hired Donegan and sued Reynolds for the money. Later, when Donegan became a prosecutor and Elizabeth was transformed from his client into his chief witness, this arrangement would become an embarrassment to the FBI.[117]

Eventually Elizabeth won the amount that Reynolds had originally promised her in severance, but the loss of her job would spell the end of her financial security. She tried to get a position comparable to the one she had held at U.S. Service and Shipping. She discovered, though, that most U.S. employers did not share the Soviets' commitment to employing women. As she explained later, employment agencies thought she was "crazy" to want an executive position. Finally, she found a job as an office manager at Ameritex Industrial Company, but she lasted there only one month. Steadily descending the ladder of business prestige, she took a job in May as a secretary at an American subsidiary of a British molasses company "because she had no money left," an FBI report noted.[118] She hated it, not surprisingly, but she was desperate.[119]

The loss of her high-paying job was an important turning point for Elizabeth. When she had a rewarding career and a hefty paycheck, she never thought of marketing her notorious life story. But when the money disappeared, so did her restraint. As she pounded away on her typewriter at her dead-end job, her thoughts began to turn to her old friend Louis Budenz. He had succeeded in launching a successful career as an ex-Communist professor, lecturer, and author. Perhaps she could do the same.

[6]
The Blonde Spy Queen

A s Elizabeth fumed over the slow pace of the FBI's investigation, bureau officials struggled to figure out their next move. All of the major players in the White House and the Justice Department helped plan that move, for they realized that this espionage case could have profound political implications.

The FBI's investigation of the "Gregory" case took place amid bitter partisan battles. Republicans had gained the upper hand in November 1946, when they took control of Congress for the first time in sixteen years. In the campaign, the GOP had highlighted President Harry Truman's ineptitude in handling the postwar convulsions afflicting the nation, from labor strife to inflation. But some canny Republicans also began to blast the president for employing suspected Communists. The election, said one congressman, was a choice "basically between communism and republicanism."[1]

Hoping to seize the initiative on the loyalty issue, Truman decided to set up his first program to test the loyalty of government employees.[2] Ultimately, the president established loyalty boards to investigate suspect workers. By cracking down on what Whittaker Chambers would call "the concealed enemy"—those who owed secret allegiance to the Communist Party—the president planned to steal the Republicans' thunder and avert a second Red Scare.

But Truman also faced concealed enemies in his administration. J. Edgar Hoover was working secretly to forge an alliance with the Republicans in Congress. In this war between the president and his FBI director, Elizabeth would provide Hoover with his most formidable weapon.

Unlike his predecessor, Harry Truman had been unwilling to flatter and placate Hoover; indeed, in private moments, Truman sometimes referred to the FBI as a potential "Gestapo."[3] For his part, Hoover despised the president. According to one of the director's top aides, "Hoover's hatred of Truman knew no bounds."[4] The FBI director never forgave Truman's decision to give jurisdiction over foreign intelligence to the newly created Central Intelligence Agency rather than the bureau. Furthermore, Hoover doubted Truman's commitment to fighting domestic Communism. As Kenneth O'Reilly has noted, FBI officials "viewed the administration itself as 'subversive' and sought to document Truman's alleged 'softness' on communism."[5]

In Hoover's view, Elizabeth's accusations proved the subversive tendencies of the Truman administration. The FBI bombarded the White House with reports of treasonous conduct by government employees, and yet Truman officials did not seem to care. The reason for this indifference was apparently the FBI's tendency in the past to cry wolf.[6] The bureau had deluged Truman officials with every rumor of the alleged Communist connections of various New Dealers, and some of the charges had been completely without foundation. As a result, Elizabeth's story did not stand out in this avalanche of accusations. Truman's failure to act, however, convinced Hoover of the president's incompetence—or worse.

Hoover was also suspicious and contemptuous of his immediate boss, Attorney General Tom Clark, whom he regarded as a political hack with questionable morals.[7] The FBI chief was already angry over the Justice Department's failure to prosecute the journalists and government employees who had been charged with leaking top-secret information to *Amerasia* magazine in 1945.[8] He did not trust Clark or the president to deal honestly with Bentley's allegations. Indeed, bureau officials feared that Clark and other Truman administration officials would turn the Bentley case into a "political football" in a Machiavellian attempt to embarrass Hoover and the FBI.[9]

In this conspiratorial atmosphere, worthy of Florence under the Borgias, the head of the Justice Department and the chief of the FBI had to agree on how to handle Elizabeth's accusations. Thanks to Kim Philby, this was not an easy decision. By early 1947, after more than a year of tailing, tapping, and scrutinizing every move of her agents, the bureau had not found any evidence of espionage.

As a result, any potential prosecutions would "hang by the thread" of Elizabeth's testimony alone.[10] "[T]he case is nothing more than the word of Gregory against that of the several conspirators," one of Hoover's top lawyers, E. P. Morgan, informed bureau officials.[11] The government could not prove that any information had been stolen, let alone that the alleged thieves willfully intended to aid a foreign power. The FBI's public relations chief, Lou Nichols, expressed the legal problems succinctly. "Obviously this whole group is wrong and as far as I am concerned they could be shot," Nichols confided, "but that is not legal proof."[12]

Knowing the weakness of these potential charges, Hoover feared most of all that Clark would attempt to prosecute the cases because *he knew they would fail.* As bureau official F. L. Jones put it, Truman's supporters "will then be in a position in 1948 to say that such charges of Communist infiltration made by the Republicans were investigated by the bureau and shown to be without foundation."[13]

To avoid this calamity, Hoover's preferred course of action in the Bentley case was to quietly dismiss her few sources who still worked for the government.[14] The great red hunter wanted to catch Communist spies, but he was "very, very reluctant" to prosecute them without stronger evidence, one of his chief deputies told Clark.[15] As Gary May has noted, this is "one of the unappreciated ironies of the postwar Red Scare."[16]

After recommending the quiet separation of Elizabeth's sources from the U.S. government, Hoover then went to work against the president he abhorred. In the spring of 1947, he secretly began to spoon-feed information to his favorites on the House Un-American Activities Committee. Hoover leaked his top-secret files to the committee members, suggested witnesses, and even gave them lists of questions to ask.[17] As one FBI official explained, the bureau wanted to use anti-Communists in Congress "in order to properly and factually bring before the American public what Communist activity has been going on in the government for many years."[18] Since he could not prosecute the spies, Hoover would encourage congressmen to publicize their alleged crimes, ruin their future careers, and embarrass the Democrats who had hired them in the first place.

Eventually, Hoover gave selected congressmen one particular file that he thought they needed to protect the national security and battle the current president. The file was marked "Elizabeth Bentley, Internal Security, Espionage."[19] Elizabeth's charges would form the foundation of the post–World War II Red Scare.

Once it became apparent that the government could not successfully prosecute Elizabeth's sources, both Hoover and the attorney general scrambled to protect themselves from congressional charges that they had bungled the case. Desperate to assure their critics that they had done all that they could, they poured resources into efforts that seemed certain to fail.

Hoover's strategy was to make one last, massive investigative effort. On April 15, 1947, the FBI descended on the homes and businesses of twelve of Elizabeth's most important former contacts. The agents held out the forlorn hope that these simultaneous interrogations would flush out the "weakest sister" and persuade him or her to "crack."[20] The FBI phrased this search for an informer in terms of weakness, not strength. There was no discussion of attempting to find someone *brave* enough to defy the NKGB. Instead, they looked for an informant who was "weak" and, by extension, unmanly or feminine.[21] As bureau officials had feared, though, none of the major figures admitted anything.[22]

But over the next few weeks, FBI field offices interviewed some of the other, minor figures, and one of these interrogations did turn out to be surprisingly helpful in a later case. When agents interviewed the hapless Abe Brothman, he admitted knowing Elizabeth and her successor, Harry Gold. The name of this mysterious chemist was new to the bureau. Although the FBI's investigation of him did not turn up any evidence of espionage at the time, the bureau added Harry Gold's file to its collection of potential Soviet spies.[23] Later, during the investigation of the theft of atomic secrets, this file would come in very handy.

Like Hoover, Tom Clark wanted to protect himself from charges that he had bungled the investigation. On the advice of his prosecutors, Clark finally decided to present the "Gregory" case to a grand jury. He knew that the jury would never return an indictment. But if the Un-American Activities Committee ever raised questions, "it would be possible to answer by saying that the Grand Jury had considered the evidence and had not deemed it sufficient to justify criminal action," as one internal memo put it. Clark decided to empanel the jury in New York, rather than Washington, on the assumption that his prosecutors could better control jurors outside the capital.[24] Tom Donegan, now in his new career as special assistant to the attorney general, presented the case, assisted by Assistant Attorney General Vincent Quinn.

Up to this point, the main actors in the proposed prosecution of the Bentley case had been two men: Hoover and Clark. But as the Justice Department prepared for the grand jury investigation, the woman who had prompted the case began to demonstrate that they could not take her cooperation entirely for granted.

In theory, the Justice Department controlled Elizabeth: the prosecutors could, after all, indict her for espionage. Or could they? In January, as the department first began to discuss the possibility of a grand jury inquiry, Assistant Attorney General James McInerney traveled to New York to *ask* Elizabeth if she would accept an indictment. She quickly let him know that she "would not consent" to such a course.[25] Since she was the only cooperative witness, they realized that they could not credibly threaten her with prison.

Elizabeth realized this as well. Beginning in January, after McInerney's visit, she began to test the limits of her relationship with the U.S. government. She first asked the FBI to arrange a vacation for her in Puerto Rico. Somewhat reluctantly, agents agreed. When she returned from her trip, she asked, for the first time, what was going to happen to the $2,000 she had received from Al. It was evidence, they tersely informed her.[26]

At the same time, she began to complain to the FBI about her health, her finances, and the government's treatment of her.[27] To relieve her anxiety and depression, she drank heavily in bars near her hotel.[28]

Once it finally began, the grand jury investigation only magnified her concerns. She complained that the inquiry would cause her to miss work and prevent her from searching for a better, more satisfying position. She also began to worry that her testimony would endanger her safety. As Donegan and Quinn tried to explain to Elizabeth her responsibilities in the investigation, she became "somewhat querulous and a trifle obstreperous," Special Agent Joe Kelly reported.[29]

After she began testifying, Elizabeth's personal life briefly improved. She met a businessman named Joseph Florentine, who lived near her hotel, and fell in love with him. They began an affair.[30] Florentine was her first boyfriend since Pete Heller and only her second since Golos's death.

But just as her depression started to lift, her worst fears about the grand jury investigation were confirmed. News of the inquiry began seeping into the press. In October, two conservative newspapers, the *Washington Times Herald* and the *New York Sun,* disclosed that a New York grand jury was investigating espionage charges against "high government officials." Some liberals wondered whether the leaks were designed to pressure the grand jury into returning indictments.[31]

Then, on November 21, *Washington Post* columnist Marquis Childs disclosed that the grand jury investigation had been prompted by a "woman of education" who had "approached the FBI with sensational reports of a spy ring in which she said she had played a part." The column also gave a generally accurate description of Elizabeth's spy network, including the use of a "basement room in a Washington residence in which she said the documents were microfilmed."[32] Hoover sent the column to Attorney General Clark, noting that it marked the "first time that the identity of the informant has been so nearly disclosed, especially the fact that the informant is a woman."[33]

As a result of the leaks, Elizabeth got "the jitters," a New York agent reported to Washington.[34] If it was in the newspaper, who else might know? She soon began receiving anonymous phone calls. The phone would ring, but no one would be on the line when she answered. She told the FBI that Party members often used this technique to harass defectors.[35]

Up to this point, she had not believed that the Communists— American or Soviet—had known about her defection.[36] The news leak, though, convinced her that she was now targeted for harassment—and perhaps worse.[37]

She had reason to worry. As she testified in New York, NKGB agents in Paris began to discuss plans for her assassination. The station chief there asked Elizabeth's old friend "Jack," otherwise known as Joseph Katz, if he was still willing to kill her. He was. But the hardened agents in Moscow balked at giving final approval. They decided to delay any assassination plans indefinitely.[38]

As she agonized over the meaning of those anonymous telephone calls, Elizabeth also fretted about her financial security. She made no secret of her "intense dislike" for her secretarial job.[39] She wanted a more responsible position with a higher salary.

She first suggested that the U.S. government might need her considerable skills in intelligence. She called the New York FBI office repeatedly, asking for the agents' help in getting a job with the Central Intelligence Group, the predecessor of the Central Intelligence Agency. The nervous agents told her that since the grand jury was still meeting, "it would seem more propitious for her to delay any such action."[40]

Obstructed on this front, she began to talk about writing "a book covering her experiences in Russian espionage and Communist Underground work." Again, the bureau told her no—at least as long as the grand jury was meeting.[41]

But she could not stop thinking about the possibilities of profiting from her life story. In December 1947, she asked the bureau "whether there were any objections to her contacting Louis Budenz to secure his advice concerning her idea of writing a book." Yes, there were objections, the agents told her; she must never approach Budenz without first getting bureau permission.[42]

Showing her usual respect for authority, Elizabeth sent a special delivery letter to Budenz the next day. She suggested that the two old friends might want to get together and discuss Helen Johns, the code name she had used with Budenz.[43] Her old pal immediately turned the letter over to the FBI.[44]

Her friends at the FBI were understandably worried. "[T]here appears to be little doubt but that she will probably become difficult to handle after the grand jury proceedings terminate," wrote Hoover aide Edward Tamm. They should come up with a strategy to keep her from "capitalizing" on her relationship with the bureau, he suggested.[45]

They would need that strategy sooner than they expected. Blocked from consulting with Budenz, Elizabeth began considering other ways to market her life story.

Meanwhile, the prosecutors struggled to conclude their secret grand jury investigation, unaware that their chief witness was plotting to expose the case. The frustrating inquiry seemed destined to end without indictments. Although the jurors believed Elizabeth and were "aroused and incensed" by her accusations, no other witness had corroborated her testimony.[46]

Like the jurors, Hoover was also aroused and incensed. He angrily reminded other bureau officials that he had never wanted to prosecute the case anyway. He feared a "most vigorous condemnation of the Department [of Justice] and particularly of the FBI" when the case concluded without indictments.[47]

Quinn suggested a way to avoid this potential public relations nightmare. The grand jury could continue to meet, and the Justice Department could present another related case for its consideration.[48] This case would include conspiracy charges against the

Communist Party for violating the Smith Act, the law that prohibited membership in organizations advocating the overthrow of the U.S. government. If the government could win Smith Act indictments, then "the no bill in the Gregory case would become much less significant and the resultant publicity would not be unfavorable," explained New York assistant special agent-in-charge Alan Belmont.[49]

Once again, though, Hoover was wary of damaging his bureau's reputation. He told Quinn that he was "just as adverse [sic] to presenting the Communist Party brief" as he had been to presenting the espionage case. He snidely suggested that the Justice Department hire some *"real"* lawyers to make sure that they had a case before they repeated the same mistake.[50]

To prepare the ground for the Smith Act indictments, the prosecutors called Elizabeth back to the stand on March 30, 1948. Quinn and Donegan peppered her with questions about the Communist Party's "plan to overthrow the government of the U.S.A. by force and violence."[51] Such evidence was crucial to winning Smith Act indictments, but Elizabeth refused to give it to them. She disputed their contention that violent revolution was a "principle or doctrine" of the Party.[52] At one point, she tentatively suggested that the Party might use revolution "as a last resort"; but she also insisted that American Communists never discussed violent revolution. "They would have lost an awful lot of membership had they ever said that," she said.[53]

She even contended that most American Communists never read Marx or Lenin and did not understand Communist doctrine. Communist literature was "dry as dust," and most members did not bother to slog through the dense prose, she said.[54] Her insistence on this point seemed to irritate Quinn, who interrupted her to ask if "people more intelligent than you" read such literature. Donegan smoothly posed another question before Elizabeth could respond.[55] The prosecutors did finally get her to concede that the Communist Party never officially "disowned" Leninist theory.[56]

Elizabeth also tried to explain—with some sympathy—the motivations of her sources. Many of them just wanted to help the

THE BLONDE SPY QUEEN

Soviets beat the fascists sooner, she said, and regretted that the U.S. government was not offering all the help that it could.[57] She also downplayed the significance of the material she had received. At one point, she objected when Donegan referred to the "complete" B-29 bomber program she had supposedly received from Ullmann. "I don't think he ever had that much," she said.[58]

If Elizabeth's testimony on March 30 was disappointing to the prosecutors, the session was even more troubling to her. She could not understand why Donegan asked her so many questions about Party doctrine. Upset and confused by the new direction of the questioning, she decided that it was time to implement her plan to strike out on her own.[59]

Elizabeth later claimed that she waited until after her "spring appearance" at the grand jury before she contacted the press.[60] This was not entirely true. Her final two appearances before the espionage grand jury were on March 30 and April 6, 1948. On April 1, five days before she was scheduled to appear for the last time, she called the offices of the *New York World-Telegram*.

This was one of the most fateful choices of her life. She had decided to spy; she had decided to defect; and now she decided to tell the world about it. None of these decisions worked out well for her, but in many ways the last one was the most disastrous.

In choosing her confidants in the media, Elizabeth showed her customary shrewdness. Nelson Frank and Frederick Woltman of the *World-Telegram* were, like Elizabeth, ex-Communists who now crusaded against their old comrades. Their newspaper, published by Roy Howard, had a reputation for trying its best "to tie the supposed Communist menace to the Democratic Party coattails," reporter Fred Cook later wrote.[61]

When Elizabeth made her fateful phone call to Woltman, she did not identify herself. She merely said that she had gone to Vassar with his former wife and had some information for him on the grand jury. He set up a meeting and invited Frank to sit in on it.

Frank, one of the paper's anti-Communist experts, already had experience in marketing tales of Communist espionage. In February, the FBI had received a tip that he had approached a movie producer and offered to sell information about the espionage grand jury.[62] When the bureau hauled him in for an interview, Frank sputtered that it was all a misunderstanding and insisted that he had no intention of leaking secret information.[63] Then Elizabeth walked into his life and dropped a potential gold mine in his lap.

At the meeting, the three ex-Communists chatted amiably for three hours. In the course of the interview, Elizabeth told the men about her relationship with Golos, her spying, her sources, and even her grand jury testimony.[64]

The two veteran reporters were bemused by the visit. Woltman, at least, was not sure she was telling the truth, though Frank apparently had no such qualms.[65] In any event, they told her that they could not write a story about her until the grand jury had finished its work. They also told her they planned to tell the FBI about her visit.[66]

The reaction there was immediate. *"This certainly is outrageous acting upon part of informant,"* Hoover scrawled at the bottom of one memo.[67] Under orders from headquarters, the New York agents tried frantically to reach their "obstreperous" informant. Finally Joe Kelly found her on the morning of April 5.

She was somewhat contrite. Explaining that "she had become nervous and distraught," she said that she had merely wanted to discuss her case with "someone who would understand the situation." She insisted that she had "absolutely made no proposition toward developing her story on a commercial basis." And she promised not to make any unauthorized contacts again. Kelly believed her.[68]

That was a mistake. Two weeks later, Elizabeth told the New York FBI office that she had, in fact, sought out Nelson Frank again. On April 16, she had dinner with him, followed by a "discussion of several hours' duration." She told him almost everything about her life as a spy. Far from being apologetic, she explained that these talks were therapeutic: they had "a most salutary effect on her health and peace of mind." She planned to see him again.[69]

Indeed, on April 25, she had dinner with him and his family at their home in the Bronx, where she charmed four-year-old William Frank by making him a beanbag.[70]

The two opportunistic ex-Communists soon agreed on a plan to publicize and market Elizabeth's experiences. They drew up a "home-made contract" designating Frank as her official ghost-writer.[71] On May 7, he notified the bureau that he was writing her autobiography—and preparing a multipart series for his paper.[72]

Frank did promise to hold back on publishing Elizabeth's story while the grand jury was meeting—or until another reporter threatened to scoop him. Because the Justice Department decided to seek indictments of Communist leaders, the inquiry continued for another two months.[73]

Then, on July 20, the grand jury indicted twelve CPUSA leaders for violating the Smith Act. At 5:55 P.M., FBI agents burst into Party headquarters and arrested five officials.[74] The next morning, Frank was startled to see a vague article in the *New York Sun* on the mysterious woman informant who had prompted the whole inquiry.[75] He no longer saw any reason to sit on his scoop.

That afternoon, New Yorkers rushing along the busy streets of the nation's largest city were stopped by a bold headline on the *World-Telegram's* front page: "Red Ring Bared by Blond Queen." The copyrighted story, by Frank and his assistant, Norton Mockridge, was packed with phrases from a pulp magazine. The *World-Telegram's* editors had rejected Frank's first draft and ordered him to give it "more life."[76] He had more than complied.

The article explained that an unnamed "svelte and striking blonde" had started the government probe that ended with the Communist leaders' arrest the day before. The "beautiful young blonde" had assuaged her "gnawing pangs of conscience" by informing on the spies she had controlled for the Soviet Union. Bowing to the FBI's concerns about jeopardizing the investigation, though, the articles mentioned only one name: that of Anatoli Gromov (Gorsky), who had left the country three years earlier.

The article gave no hint of the fear that had driven Elizabeth to the FBI's doorstep. Instead, it portrayed her as a naïf who ran to the U.S. government the moment that she realized her "once small service" for the Communist Party "had mushroomed into a gigantic, treasonable assignment." (As the FBI laconically noted, this patriotic explanation "is not consistent with information furnished" by Bentley.)[77]

Frank and Mockridge hyped the value of the information she had stolen, claiming that "the first plans of the B-29," "complete data on [the explosive] RDX," and "almost daily" figures on airplane production had been secreted in her knitting bag. Most important, the Russians had been "delighted" by Elizabeth's intelligence that American officials "were about to break the Russian secret code." The Russians had "presumably" changed their code immediately.[78]

Frank had every reason to "enliven" his stories. He wanted to please his bosses, who, in turn, wanted to sell newspapers and to imply that the Democrats had coddled Communists and endangered national security. He also wanted to package Elizabeth, his future meal ticket, in the most marketable manner. Hence the "svelte" young blonde who stole invaluable information.

But in making the story more sexy, Frank distorted and exaggerated Elizabeth's adventures. Although she *had* gotten a lot of information from Silverman and Ullmann on airplane production, she had never claimed before that the figures changed "almost daily." Although she had passed along Currie's warning about the code, she had no idea whether the Russians were "delighted" or not. She had never mentioned RDX in any of her statements to the FBI. Finally, Ullmann had given her some information on the B-29, but just months earlier in front of the grand jury she had insisted that she did not think "he ever had that much."

She did not, in fact, know how much he had. She could not remember, and in any case much of her stolen information had been on microfilm. She had simply stuffed the reels into her knitting bag and delivered them, unread, to her superiors.

The *World-Telegram* story was not the last word on the signifi-

THE BLONDE SPY QUEEN

cance of her espionage career. The quality of the information she stole would continue to grow with the passage of time.

Elizabeth had deliberately sought out public exposure, but she had not reckoned on becoming the "blonde spy queen." She protested to the *World-Telegram* about the way the reporters had caricatured her, then tried to drown her anger and anxiety in alcohol. The FBI was also angry with Frank for emphasizing how surprised agents had been by Elizabeth's sudden defection. He was "making us look like saps," Hoover complained. Frank apologized profusely and assured the New York agents that he and his paper wanted to "lean over backwards" to portray the bureau in a favorable light.[79]

For the first four days, the *World-Telegram* was the only paper that knew Elizabeth's real name—or what she looked like. One lurid story followed the next: "Super-Hush Veiled Red Spy Cells," "Citizens Tricked into Spy Ring by U.S. Reds," and so on.[80] In each story, Frank and his assistant made sure to mention the beauty of the mysterious spy queen.

Frank closely guarded the identity and integrity of his source. He knew that Elizabeth would eventually have to reveal herself to the rest of the press, but he wanted to control her and her image as long as he could. He quickly set about negotiating her first public appearance with a respected Senate committee, Senator Homer Ferguson's Committee on Expenditures in the Executive Departments.[81] By stage-managing her public appearance with a responsible group, Frank hoped to avoid the notorious House Un-American Activities Committee. Worried about HUAC's "unfavorable" reputation, Frank wanted to protect his source's credibility by distancing her from the more primitive congressional red-baiters.[82]

He did not reckon on the determination of HUAC investigators, though. Robert Stripling, a renowned committee staff member, was just as conservative but much shrewder than most of the congressmen he served.[83] When he saw the *World-Telegram* article, he wanted the "spy queen" for his committee.

Stripling claimed that sheer ingenuity led him to Elizabeth.

After recognizing Jacob Golos from the vague description in the *World-Telegram* stories, he looked up Golos's obituary and discovered that he had died in Elizabeth Bentley's apartment. He simply put two and two together, he said.[84] There was one problem with that story: the *New York Times* did not publish an obituary of Jacob Golos.[85] In reality, the committee must have gotten the tip from its good friends at the FBI. The bureau's public relations chief, Lou Nichols, was a productive source for HUAC chairman J. Parnell Thomas.[86]

The HUAC staff issued a subpoena for Bentley—with her correct name and address—on July 21, the same day that the *World-Telegram* began running its series on the supposedly anonymous spy queen.[87] Two days later, Stripling called Elizabeth and notified her that the committee knew her identity and would soon deliver a subpoena. Panicked, she called Nelson Frank for advice. He made it plain that he did not want her to appear before HUAC and ordered her to try to elude the committee's investigators. He then rushed over to her hotel, where at 10:30 in the evening he encountered the HUAC agents.

Frank was "very angry," according to Stripling. Proclaiming himself to be Elizabeth's "counsel" and "intermediary," he was "very nasty" with the HUAC agents, and accused them—with good reason—of finding Elizabeth through an FBI leak.[88]

Frank could not order Elizabeth to defy a subpoena, though, and she reluctantly agreed to appear the next Saturday, July 31. In the meantime, HUAC lost no time in building up public anticipation for her appearance. On July 26, the committee began leaking her name to the press.[89] Two days later, Elizabeth awoke to find her name on the front pages in Washington and New York.[90]

Nelson Frank did what he could to salvage his plans. "Red Spy Queen Drops Mask" read the headline over his lead story. He proceeded to give Elizabeth's name, address, and "age," which she lied about. (She sliced four years off her true age of forty.) He also published the first picture of her. It was as flattering as possible, with a soft focus and gentle lighting that created almost a halo effect. In the story, Elizabeth explained that she was not looking forward to the "publicity I shall now receive." But, just as she had cooperated with the FBI and grand jury, she was now prepared to help "any other American agencies which feel I can be of service."[91]

She was going to have two immediate opportunities to serve, as it turned out. To ensure that her public debut was before a more respected committee, Frank scheduled her Ferguson Committee testimony for July 30, the day before her HUAC appearance. For two days in a row, she would face the packed galleries and newsreel cameras that accompanied a contentious congressional hearing.

As Elizabeth began her first public testimony on July 30, the international and domestic political tensions of the early Cold War were in the process of escalating daily. The front pages of newspapers around the country displayed photos of hungry Germans clambering over the ruins of buildings to wave at American planes ferrying food to West Berlin. Sullen Russian officials explained they had blockaded the city because of "technical difficulties."[92] In the United States, candidates jockeyed for political advantage as the election of 1948 approached. Henry Wallace, the former vice president, won the nomination of the Progressive Party for the presidency. President Truman, meanwhile, inadvertently set the stage for the spy hearings by calling Congress into special session to come up with a plan to stop inflation. Forced to be in the capital during the worst part of the summer, Republican congressmen struck back by investigating the Communist infiltration of Democratic administrations.

The audience for Elizabeth's first congressional testimony, Senator Ferguson's Committee on Executive Expenditures, claimed jurisdiction over one small part of her story: how was the executive branch responding to charges that some of its current employees were subversive? The investigation was somewhat limited, though, because only two of Elizabeth's alleged sources still worked for the government in 1948, and one of them—Sol Adler in Treasury—she had never met. Primed by Elizabeth's secret FBI file, obtained from bureau public relations head Lou Nichols, the senators were forced to focus all of their outrage on William Remington, who was now in the Commerce Department.

The senators were relatively restrained in their questioning. They asked Elizabeth to mention only two names in public: Remington and Mary Price, the latter in an apparent effort to embarrass the Progressive Party, for which she now worked. Other than the senators' attack on the Wallace campaign, they stayed fairly focused.

In her first public testimony, "with a bunch of lights shining in my face and a great deal of hullabaloo," Elizabeth was similarly restrained.[93] In many ways, she was still rather sympathetic to her former sources. She called them "poor devils" and a "bunch of misguided idealists" who had been led astray by the "cheap little men" who ran the Party.[94] She made it clear that she was not sure if Remington knew his information was going to the Soviet Union. Even one of Remington's attorneys found her testimony to be "scrupulously honest."[95]

At the same time, however, she also began the long and gradual process of "improving" her story. For example, she had told the FBI that Remington had once discussed a new method of manufacturing rubber, but she had added that the information "was quite vague and probably of no value even to a chemist."[96] Before the committee, though, the formula was transformed from worthless gossip into "quite a complicated thing."[97]

Elizabeth did not seem to fully realize the magnitude of her sources' crimes until the next day, when she met with the House Un-American Activities Committee. There, goaded by some of the least principled members of Congress, she suddenly remembered details and horrors that had eluded her for the past three years.

The new Republican chairman of HUAC, J. Parnell Thomas of New Jersey, was typical of the anti-Semitic, anti–New Deal congressmen who dominated the committee. As Walter Goodman has written, "Here his disposition could find expression, his animosities find scope, his politics find fellowship."[98] In a few years,

Thomas would join some of his committee's targets in prison when he was convicted of taking kickbacks.

The chairman and his cohorts on the committee were eager to find evidence for their belief that the New Deal was, as Thomas himself said, "hand in glove with the Communist Party."[99] Richard Nixon, a freshman member from southern California, had defeated his opponent by falsely implying that he was supported by Communists and subversives. A powerful minority member, Mississippi's John Rankin, specialized in attacking the civil rights movement as Communist-inspired. As far as Rankin was concerned, the "un-American" in his committee's title referred to blacks, Asian-Americans, liberals, and Jews.[100]

The Bentley hearings provided Rankin with another forum for his diatribes. He emphasized the Jewish origins of her sources and fulminated that "this so-called 'civil rights'" was just "communistic bunk."[101] Other members joined Rankin in painting a picture of the American Communist as sneaky, Jewish, domineering, bloodthirsty, and dumb.

One might think that Elizabeth would be uncomfortable here. She had, after all, called Golos "the perfect Communist" because of his selfless devotion to humanity.[102] In response to the committee's vicious stereotypes, Elizabeth could have taken the opportunity—as she had in speaking to the FBI and the grand jury—to emphasize the benign motives of her sources, to put their actions in context, and to deny that they planned to use violence in the United States.

Yet she did not. Instead, she agreed with most of what the committee members had to say. She obligingly concurred that American Communists were plotting to overthrow the U.S. government, that there was "very little" difference between fascism and communism, that Russian farmers were "slaves," and that American Communists were "suckers."[103] She obsequiously maintained that subversive teachers had prevented her from learning American values in college—indeed, that Columbia had offered no courses on the American government.[104]

She refused to endorse the congressmen's rants only when Rankin asked her to agree that a "racial minority"—a reference to Jews—had seized control in Russia. "I am not clear about the racial minority," she demurred.[105]

In general, though, she could not have been more eager to assist the members of the committee. At one point, she even interrupted the chairman to say that she had forgotten to name someone.[106] If anything, she seemed positively enthusiastic about the prospect of informing on her friends. Of course, not all of her alleged sources were friends; some of them, such as William Taylor, she had never met. But that was not obvious from her testimony. For example, she referred to Taylor by his first name—"William was in the Treasury"—without clarifying that she had not dealt with him directly.[107]

Elizabeth also "improved" one key aspect of her story in her HUAC testimony. In 1945, she had mentioned to the FBI that Ullmann had given her the approximate date of D-Day, the allied invasion of Normandy.[108] The FBI had not bothered to follow up on this alleged transfer of superfluous information to an American ally.[109]

In 1948, with the Cold War under way, this story suddenly assumed ominous proportions, as if she had given military information to the Nazis. Although Elizabeth had not mentioned this nugget to Frank—or at least Frank had not written about it—she now made it a critical charge of her congressional testimony. "We knew about D-Day long before D-Day happened," she said, nervously puffing on her cigarette, "and we were right."[110]

Elizabeth's testimony did not need any embellishments. Her true story was scary enough. In her eagerness to please the congressmen and generate headlines, though, she was not satisfied with the truth. Just as she had improved her genealogy and reinvented her career in Italy, so she "remembered" new examples of the malevolence and cunning of her former friends.

Elizabeth's "improvements" in her story in 1948 were her own inventions, an apparent result of her desire to please her new anti-Communist friends and satisfy the hungry media. She was

THE BLONDE SPY QUEEN

not controlled by any outside interests, even the FBI. The bureau was on edge whenever she testified, anxiously awaiting any new "memories" that the congressmen's questioning might suddenly release from the deepest recesses of her mind. In her HUAC testimony, Elizabeth alarmed bureau officials by claiming that the FBI had watched her receive the $2,000 in "Moscow gold" from Al, which she and the bureau knew was not true. Assistant Director Mickey Ladd and New York special agents nervously discussed her testimony and concluded that it was "not entirely accurate."[111] The FBI did not, however, publicize her inaccuracies.

The only sour note at the hearing came when Rankin's desire for Anglo-Saxon racial solidarity temporarily trumped his antipathy for Communism. The Mississippian had startled Elizabeth near the start of the hearing by demanding to know why she had waited so long to tell the authorities what Greg Silvermaster had said about Lauchlin Currie and the secret code. As the proceedings wound to a close, he could no longer contain his outrage. How could she have taken the word of "a man named Silverman" and "a man named Silvermaster" over that of a "Scotchman"? He accused Bentley of "smearing Currie by remote control."[112]

The other committee members, though, commended Elizabeth for her courage, and even Rankin grudgingly tried to think of something nice to say near the end of the hearing. "I think you are rather late in seeing the light," he said, "but better late than never."[113]

Throughout her congressional testimony, Elizabeth worked to win the support of her interrogators. To accomplish this, she supported their prejudices and exaggerated her own importance. She also emphasized her own naïveté. She maintained that as an idealistic liberal she had been propagandized by subversive teachers and seduced by an older ideologue. The implication was clear: she should not be held responsible for her actions.

But as much as she tried to promote herself as a naive schoolgirl, Elizabeth could not control her image in the media. During her two days of public testimony, the reporters of America variously described, analyzed, lauded, and ridiculed her story. The reporters, who were almost all men, were fascinated by Elizabeth's status as a "lady spy." She seemed to be a freak: a woman in a man's profession, a woman who had betrayed her country. Bentley's image as a "red spy queen" highlights the gender tensions of the postwar period. The reporters' struggle to understand her deviance reveals cultural anxiety about changes in women's roles in the 1940s.[114]

To explain her to their readers, journalists fell back on popular stereotypes of female spies and Communists. Depending on which newspaper they read, Americans learned that Elizabeth was either a sex-starved, man-eating temptress or a sexually repressed, man-hating spinster.

Although Bentley's supporters made her out to be a Mata Hari, she had little in common with the Dutch stripper who had been executed by the French for allegedly passing state secrets to the Germans during World War I. After all, she neither slept with her sources nor seduced her government contacts. Moreover, as her critics noted, she did not look like a promising candidate for such a role.

But right-wing newspapers seemed determined to make her play that part. Even after she was "unmasked," Nelson Frank continued to assert that Elizabeth was glamorous and attractive—and, against all evidence, blonde. The *New York Journal-American,* a rabidly anti-Communist Hearst paper, also described her as a "shapely blonde" and a "blonde and blue-eyed New Yorker" who testified in a "form-fitting black dress" and who had "lured" secrets out of weak-kneed New Dealers.[115]

Liberals looked at the same woman at the witness table and saw an altogether different person. In general, they painted Elizabeth's charges, as Earl Latham has said, as the "imaginings of a neurotic spinster."[116] She had obviously imagined herself to be a femme fatale; perhaps she had imagined her life as a spy as well. A. J. Liebling, the *New Yorker*'s press critic, ridiculed her story and called her the "Nutmeg Mata Hari."[117] Joseph Alsop said she joined the party out of "genteel poverty, loneliness and frustration"—in effect, portraying her as a plain-faced spinster who became a Communist in a pathetic attempt to meet men.[118]

Murray Kempton later dedicated several pages of his book on thirties radicals to wondering why desperate "old maids" like Bentley were so likely to join the Communist Party. He cited the supposedly scientific findings of a researcher who claimed that "four out of five male Communists were described by their analysts as persons of real talent, while only two of five women subjects could be said to possess any talent at all." The female Communists were hostile, defiant women who were better "haters" than men. According to Kempton, Elizabeth was a silly woman who listened at keyholes like an "old biddy" and slapped police thugs with her pocketbook: a prime example of "a rather definite pattern" followed by "Comrade Woman."[119]

The war between the stereotypes—"Red Spy Queen" versus "Comrade Woman"—exposed the fears of the men who relied on them. The first few years after World War II were a time of great change in gender relations in the United States. During the war, as 13 million men joined the military, the government and the media had urged women to take defense jobs. More than 6 million women had responded, increasing the size of the female labor force by 57 percent.

As Elaine Tyler May says, women's war work "demonstrated that women could do 'men's work' and survive without men."[120] This was frightening to many men for economic and cultural reasons. Economically, of course, men feared that women would refuse to give up their jobs at the end of the war. But many men also had cultural concerns: they worried that American women were becoming too independent.[121]

Popular culture reflected this fear of strong women. Increasingly in the 1940s, the media portrayed assertive women as scary and unnatural. As Susan Hartmann notes, in contrast to the competent, decisive career women of the late thirties and early forties, women characters in mid-forties movies increasingly tended to be treacherous or helpless.[122] The archetype of the treacherous woman was the film noir villainess.[123] These "spider women" were dangerous precisely because they flouted traditional sexual morals and gender roles. Of course, the image of the evil woman did not arise suddenly in the postwar period; tales of wicked, seductive women like Eve and Salome appear in ancient literature and the Bible. But fears of the femme fatale are most common—and frantic—at times when a society is experiencing changes in the balance of power between men and women.[124]

The forties femme fatale image explains why some reporters were so determined to change Elizabeth's hair color. They wanted her to match a familiar figure: the "Bad Blonde," in Nora Sayre's phrase, who by 1948 was a stock character in film noir, detective fiction, and the early anti-Communist films.[125]

Assertive women were doubly threatening in the early years of the Cold War because female assertiveness was seen as a Communist characteristic. As Susan Douglas writes, if the United States was going to triumph over the Communist menace, "then *our* women had to be very different from *their* women."[126] "Their" women took masculine jobs and regarded their personal appearance as relatively unimportant; "our" women stayed at home and were extraordinarily feminine. Our women were chaste; their women scoffed at traditional sexual morals. Our women deferred to their husbands; their women bullied them. As Morris Ernst, the intensely anti-Communist co-counsel of the American Civil Liberties Union, noted in his *Report on the American Communist*, "[T]he tendency seems to be that in Communist marriages the wife is the more dominant partner."[127] Elizabeth was dangerous because she was not only a female criminal but also a Communist female criminal.

Elizabeth was the first "red spy queen," but other accused "lady spies" would receive similar treatment from the media. The cultural construction of the "spy queen" in these cases reveals similar tensions about masculinity and changing gender roles in the early years of the Cold War.

Just a few months later, for example, Priscilla Hiss would be vilified by reporters, prosecutors, and even alleged friends. Like the women in film noir, like some conservatives' fevered notions of Elizabeth, she was portrayed as the evil temptress who had led her husband down the road to treason and betrayal—or possibly even framed him to make it *appear* that he had gone down that road. In the eyes of Alger's friends, the brainy, Bryn Mawr graduate was "domineering," "hard," and, yes, "a femme fatale."[128] But Alger's opponents also saw Priscilla as the source of his problems. Richard Nixon, whose disgust for Priscilla seemed to grow over time, expressed anger in his own account of the Hiss-Chambers affair that he had not questioned Priscilla more intensely because she was "if anything, a more fanatical Communist than Hiss."[129] In 1986, Nixon wrote in the *New York Times* that this was a common pattern for Communist couples: "the wife is often more extremist than the husband."[130]

Ethel Rosenberg's case also demonstrates the anxiety about women's changing roles in the early Cold War. As a woman, Julius's wife was supposed to be more emotional, more committed to her family and children, and less interested in politics. Thus her stoic appearance made her seem even more evil than the alleged atomic spy who had married her. "There is a saying that in the animal kingdom, the female is the deadlier of the species. It could be applied to Julius and Ethel Rosenberg," intoned the *World-Telegram and Sun*.[131] The *Journal-American* told its readers that Julius's "deceptively lumpish" wife had been "even more immersed in communism and its requirements for regimentation" than her husband.[132] Before turning down her application for clemency, President Eisenhower wrote his son that the "strong and recalcitrant" Ethel had "obviously been the leader in everything they did in the spy ring."[133]

Elizabeth, a strong and recalcitrant woman herself, could have set him straight. Far from dominating her husband, Ethel was simply an accessory to his crimes.[134] The espionage stories in the newspapers, with their shrewish wives and svelte young seductresses, revealed more about the nation's Cold War cultural anxieties than about spies and spying.

Red queen or neurotic spinster, Elizabeth needed some proof for her allegations before many Americans were prepared to believe her. She rattled off dozens of names to congressional investigators, but she did not have a shred of evidence to prove her charges. Nor did she have a former confederate willing to back her up.

Then, on July 30, as Elizabeth testified to the Ferguson committee, the *New York Sun* announced an exclusive. An editor "on the staff of a national news magazine" could furnish "the vital link in the story of espionage and Red infiltration of the Federal Government."[135]

In the offices of *Time*, where Whittaker Chambers had enjoyed a comfortable job since 1939, the former spy read the *Sun* story and "turned sort of green around the gills," according to a friend.[136] He knew his story was going to come out now—though not in the forum he had intended. On August 2, he received a subpoena to appear before HUAC the next day. He was about to push Elizabeth off the front pages.

Chambers joined the committee members in the largest auditorium on Capitol Hill, the Ways and Means hearing room. There, he announced to the packed gallery that he, like Elizabeth, had joined the Communist underground in Washington. In fact, he had supervised a group of Communist government staffers who had apparently gone on in later years to spy for her. Both Bentley and Chambers had known Victor Perlo and Charles Kramer as Communists; Chambers also corroborated Bentley's charge that Harry Dexter White was a Communist sympathizer. His most shocking claim, though, was that Alger Hiss had been a secret Communist.[137]

Chambers did not charge his former friends with espionage at this time. Nevertheless, he told a powerful tale that confirmed many of Elizabeth's allegations. With his accusations against Hiss, he began the public examination of the Cold War espionage case that would remake the nation's politics. He had been called to testify because of Elizabeth Bentley.

Elizabeth had started a chain reaction that would transform American politics and culture. In August 1948, her career as a professional ex-Communist was just beginning.

[7]
False Witness

t was one of the most dramatic days in the history of the House Committee on Un-American Activities. Harry Dexter White, a balding, well-spoken architect of the postwar economic order, calmly and emphatically denied the charges made by Elizabeth Bentley and Whittaker Chambers that he had secretly aided the Soviet Union.

"The principles in which I believe, and by which I live, make it impossible for me to ever do a disloyal act or anything against the interests of our country," he told the spellbound hearing room. And what were his principles? The "American creed," he explained. "I believe in freedom of religion, freedom of speech, freedom of thought, freedom of the press, freedom of criticism and freedom of movement."[1]

Before the hearing, White, now a financial consultant in the private sector, had sent Chairman J. Parnell Thomas a note asking for rest periods of five or ten minutes for each hour of testimony. He was recovering from a severe heart attack, he explained. Now, as he testified, he impressed audience members with his dignity and patience.

Elizabeth's charge that he had helped to secure jobs for her sources was "unqualifiedly false," he asserted.[2] He did admit, though, that he knew some of those sources and had even enjoyed games of Ping-Pong, softball, and volleyball with them on occasion.

Thomas responded with snide humor. "For a person who had a severe heart condition, you certainly can play a lot of sports," he said.[3] Furious, White explained carefully that he had played sports *before* he developed a heart condition. The audience responded with thunderous applause. It was one of the low points of the HUAC chairman's sordid career. Three days later, White was dead of a heart attack. Progressive presidential candidate Henry Wallace summed up the feelings of many Americans when he called White "a victim of the Un-American Thomas Committee."[4]

White was the most prominent of the witnesses called in response to Elizabeth's testimony, but he was not alone in denying her allegations. Over the next month, a long list of her alleged sources paraded before the Thomas committee. Some—including Victor Perlo, Charles Kramer, George Silverman, Lud Ullmann, and the linchpin of the network, Greg Silvermaster—took the Fifth Amendment and refused to answer most of the committee's questions. But a few took different paths. Former presidential adviser Lauchlin Currie joined White in a resounding rejection of her story. "I emphatically deny," he testified, "that I ever knew, believed, or suspected that any statement of mine was repeated to any person acting under cover for the Soviet Government or any foreign government."[5]

Duncan Lee and William Remington also refused to take cover in the Fifth Amendment. Both Ivy League graduates admitted knowing Elizabeth and even chatting with her about their work. But they denied having any inkling that she was a Communist agent.

Lee told a story of a naive young man meeting an "attractive, well informed" woman who had been eager to make friends with him and his wife. Over time, however, Duncan and Ishbel Lee discovered that the woman they knew as "Helen Grant" was not what she seemed. "We came to the conclusion," he told the committee, "that she was a very lonely and neurotic woman, that she was a frustrated woman, that her liking and apparent ardent liking for us was unnaturally intense." When they tried to end the relationship with her, she cried and "did carry on" for half an hour.[6] Never at any time, he said, did he tell state secrets to her. Lee emphasized Elizabeth's emotional instability and implied that she might be seeking revenge for an unrequited friendship. Soon Alger Hiss would mount a similar defense against Whittaker Chambers.

It was William Remington, though, who would prove to be Elizabeth's biggest nemesis over the next several years. Ironically, Remington had not been a very significant source. But he had the distinction of being the only source personally known to Elizabeth who was still in the federal government when she went public with her allegations.

Like Duncan Lee, Remington admitted meeting Elizabeth, but he denied helping her to spy—at least knowingly. He claimed that Elizabeth had presented herself as a reporter for a liberal periodical. They had discussed the war on about ten occasions, he said. But he never gave her classified information or even realized her true purposes in talking with him.[7] The Ferguson committee did not find Remington's explanation persuasive, and neither did the regional loyalty board. The board soon recommended his dismissal from the government.[8]

The attacks by her former friends prompted no visible reaction from Elizabeth. When she bumped into Remington before a hearing, she greeted him pleasantly and showed no traces of guilt or anxiety.[9] Nelson Frank reported to the FBI that she "is being treated very well" and "and is enjoying herself."[10] To her friend Joe Kelly at the FBI, though, she confessed that she was "under severe strain."[11]

Elizabeth began to realize the awful consequences of making her story public. Rumors swirled around Washington that she was a "psychopathic case." Attorney General Tom Clark, distressed by her charges against prominent Democrats, tried to plant stories that she was a lunatic and a liar.[12] Meanwhile, Remington's lawyers retained a prominent private investigator to dig up dirt about her past.[13]

She also feared assassination. During her stay in Washington, her vulnerability to the NKGB was underscored by the presence of two guards.[14] She did in fact receive several threats. One note, scrawled in pencil and mailed from Massachusetts, warned her that her "spy story" would be the "last story you will ever write."[15]

The most bizarre incident occurred three thousand miles away on the Golden Gate Bridge. On August 4, a highway patrolman found a pile of women's clothing and a suicide note addressed to "E.T.B." near the center of the span. The note explained that the writer had "suffered," and she "didn't want my little baby to suffer what I've been through so I'm taking it with me." The letter concluded with a postscript explaining the lack of a signature: "Nobody would care about my name, except maybe Elizabeth."[16]

In Washington, Elizabeth was "considerably upset" by the alleged suicide, even though she did not know anyone in San Francisco. She worried that it might have been Rae Elson or Helen Tenney, but neither one had children.[17] Police noted several aspects of the incident that made them suspicious, including their failure to find any bodies.[18]

If the "suicide" was a hoax, then the mastermind of the plot must have known Elizabeth well. She was unstable, conflicted, and justifiably concerned about her physical safety. The drama at the bridge could have been designed to turn public opinion against an informer—and to upset an already disturbed woman.

The high political stakes of Elizabeth's testimony became more apparent with each passing day. On August 5, President Truman agreed with a reporter that the spy hearings were a "red herring" used by Republicans to distract attention from their failure to stop inflation.[19] His opponents responded angrily. Republican nominee Thomas Dewey's campaign manager attacked Truman for covering up Communist espionage, while HUAC charged the White House with refusing to help "protect the national security."[20] Senator Ferguson even raised the specter of impeachment.[21]

Meanwhile, newspapers and magazines reflected the growing fear of Communists abroad and at home. In New York, a state supreme court justice ruled that children could be taken away from parents who sympathized with Communism.[22] As the Berlin crisis continued, American readers increasingly saw the words "Cold War" in the headlines—though often still in quotation marks.[23]

Elizabeth's testimony provided the Republicans with a potent campaign issue for the upcoming election. She was charging, after all, that two Democratic administrations had first harbored Communists and then refused to believe the evidence that they were spies. Many Republicans did try to exploit this issue, with party vice presidential nominee Earl Warren attacking the administration for "coddling" Communists.[24] But the president proved remarkably successful in defending himself against these charges. His loyalty program and the Justice Department's Smith Act indictments proved that he was serious about suppressing domestic Communism, while his tough, anti-Soviet foreign policy gave the Republicans little chance to attack him on that front. Above all, the third-party candidacy of Henry Wallace provided Truman with an opportunity to show his revulsion for Communists at home.

The Progressive Party's nominee was a thoughtful, idealistic former vice president who believed that he should be sitting in the Oval Office himself.[25] If not for Franklin Roosevelt's decision to replace his liberal vice president with Harry Truman in 1944, Wallace would have been running for reelection in 1948. Wallace also resented what he saw as the president's overly bellicose foreign policy and insufficient commitment to racial integration.[26] He was determined to run in 1948 to advance progressive issues and force Truman to the left.

Wallace was naive, however, in believing that he could surround himself with Communists and still maintain liberal support. John Abt and Mary Price, among other secret and overt Party members, played significant roles in his campaign. This toleration for domestic Communists during a Red Scare helped doom the Wallace campaign.

Because Wallace provided a convenient target, Truman was able to survive the spy hearings and win reelection. As Alonzo Hamby has noted, "It was hard to use the Communist issue against Truman as long as Henry Wallace was running to his left."[27] By exposing the Communist elements of the Wallace campaign, the hearings gave the president an opportunity to demonstrate that the Communists *were* supporting a candidate in the 1948 election—and that candidate was not Harry Truman.

Although Elizabeth had given the Republicans an election issue, she herself did not play a role in the campaign. Red spies—even reformed ones—were hardly welcome allies on the hustings. In fact, Elizabeth disappeared from public view for several weeks before the election.

She made her last public statement for months on September 12, when she appeared on NBC's radio show *Meet the Press*. One of the reporters on the show asked her if she would repeat her charges outside the privileged halls of Congress. In later years, Elizabeth would become more circumspect about accusing individuals of crimes when she was not protected by congressional privilege. But in 1948, she was still relatively inexperienced in legal affairs and media relations. When the reporter asked her directly if she would name Remington as a Communist, she obliged. "Certainly," she said, "I testified before the committee that William Remington was a communist."[28]

To preserve his credibility, Remington had to respond. The young economist decided to counterattack on two fronts. First, he appealed his unfavorable ruling from the regional loyalty board to a higher body, the Loyalty Review Board. Then he sued his accuser for libel.

Over the next few months, Remington's lawyers played an elaborate cat-and-mouse game with Elizabeth as they sought to question her and she tried to avoid them. She did not want to accept service of Remington's libel suit, and she did not want to make it easy for other people to sue her.[29] After her appearance on *Meet the Press,* she abruptly dropped out of sight. Neither Remington nor the Loyalty Review Board, which wanted her testimony on Remington, could find her.

Remington's attorneys, Richard G. Green of New York and Joe Rauh of Washington, quickly realized that "a little process dodging on her part would be extremely useful in our fight before the

Loyalty Review Board," as Rauh craftily put it. In other words, her refusal to accept service of the papers in the libel suit made her look like a liar. Both attorneys filed depositions explaining their assiduous efforts to find her. Then they called the newspapers.[30]

Elizabeth's supporters hit back with some publicity of their own. An anonymous "friend of Miss Bentley" contacted New York newspapers in early November to explain her disappearance. It had nothing to do with the libel suit, the friend insisted. Physically and emotionally exhausted from her testimony, she had spent the last few months in religious seclusion. Then, on November 5, with her sponsors Louis Budenz and his wife, Margaret, looking on, Monsignor Fulton Sheen baptized her at a Washington church.[31] The woman who had sought community and acceptance in fascism and then Communism had found a new "ism" to give her life meaning. Elizabeth was taking refuge in Catholicism.

Elizabeth's conversion marked her final break with her past and her entrance into the world of religious anti-Communism. The Catholic Church had opposed atheistic Communism since the mid-nineteenth century. This opposition escalated after World War II when Communists in Eastern Europe imprisoned and tortured church leaders.[32] Besides their intense religious revulsion for Communism, American Catholics also had more practical reasons for leading the charge against domestic Communists. By vilifying "un-Americans," Catholics could prove their patriotism to Protestant Americans who had questioned it in the past. J. Edgar Hoover, for example, had not hired many Catholics before World War II. After the war, though, as he realized that their fierce anti-Communism made them valuable allies, he recruited an increasing number.[33]

Budenz, a prominent member of the anti-Communist Catholic lobby, encouraged Elizabeth to join the church. She valued his advice: he was, after all, one of the few friends she had left. Mary Price, Helen Tenney, John Reynolds and his wife—all of them despised her now. Budenz, the one link to her past who still accepted her, could be a role model and potential mentor. He could help ease her entrée into the high-paying world of professional lecturers on the Red Menace. He could also help ease her conscience by arranging her conversion to the religion that, he firmly believed, had saved his soul.[34]

Budenz himself had been brought back to the Catholic faith of his boyhood by the nation's "convert-maker" extraordinaire, Fulton Sheen. The monsignor, a phenomenally popular radio (and later television) personality, had established a reputation as the priest who converted American luminaries, including Congresswoman Clare Booth Luce, auto industry heir Henry Ford II, and journalist Heywood Broun.[35]

Sheen was also one of the nation's most prominent fighters of Communism. Several of his radio shows and books were devoted to the evils of Marxism. Unlike most religious anti-Communists, however, Sheen acknowledged the strengths and the appeal of Communism—and even the similarity of some of its doctrines to Christianity. "Communism is strong when it borrows some of the moral indignation that has been inherited from the Hebraic-Christian traditions; Communism is weak when it departs from that tradition," he explained in one sermon.[36] Sheen realized that good, caring Americans could be attracted to Communism. This nuanced view must have appealed to a woman who had loved a dedicated Communist and been one herself.

Elizabeth had strong emotional reasons for joining the long list of famous Americans who had been converted by the radio priest. Publicly, she explained that Catholicism filled a void in her life left by her abandonment of Communism, which had been, in many ways, her religion. In one interview, she described her conversion as "sort of like coming home . . . you'd be surprised how all sorts of things that have bothered you before just disappear, once you've got a faith in something."[37]

But Elizabeth had always been motivated more by opportunism than by ideology. And becoming a Catholic provided a great opportunity for an ex–red queen in 1948. The connection between the church and the anti-Communist lobby was obvious to her: after all, many of the FBI agents who handled her were Catholic. Louis Budenz was prospering as a Catholic professor, lecturer, and syndicated columnist ("Ex-Red"). Elizabeth had first decided to go public in an attempt to emulate his success. By converting, she could meet a host of conservative Catholics who could help launch her career and shape her image.

On November 15, the Loyalty Review Board chairman finally received a letter from his elusive, would-be witness. She would not be able to come to Remington's hearing, Elizabeth explained.[38] She had another engagement.

She did indeed. It was the dream of every American girl who ever felt unattractive and unpopular in high school: a triumphal return to the site of her adolescent humiliations. On November 21, the "sad and lonely girl" from East High School addressed 1,200 people at Rochester's Aquinas Institute.

Fulton Sheen she was not. She gave no convincing reasons for her interest in Communism, merely passing it off as the result of her "humanistic" education at Vassar. She described Communism as a "spirit of hate" and a "creed of hate," without explaining why she had adored a man she had described as the "perfect" representative of this hate-filled philosophy.[39]

The speech was no more honest than it was profound. In response to a reporter's question, she expressed surprise that Remington's lawyers were looking for her. "There has been no deliberate attempt at evasion," she protested. In New York, Remington's lawyer angrily refuted her story. "She has known for weeks that we are looking for her," he said.[40]

Now that Elizabeth had surfaced in public, Remington's lawyers decided to pounce. With the help of private detectives, Richard Green discovered that she was living at the Susan Devin Residence, a Catholic home for women in the Bronx. He arrived on December 15 to serve her with the libel papers. She was not there: she was delivering another lecture in New Orleans. But Green was sure she would be back.[41]

That night, at Loyola University in New Orleans, Elizabeth gave her now-standard speech on the dangers of Communism. Once again she expressed surprise that Remington's lawyers were looking for her and said they could see her "any time."[42]

She expressed similar bemusement when Green's private detectives finally tracked her down on December 29. Green triumphantly called the press and said he had caught up with her after a "twelve-week chase."[43]

But she was still not going to testify at the loyalty hearing. The next week she notified the Loyalty Review Board chairman that she would not appear at a new hearing for Remington. Then, confirming the loyalty examiners' growing conviction that she was unstable and unreliable, she began telling New York newspapers that she had never been asked to testify. In a brazen revision of the facts, she told *New York Post* reporter James Wechsler that she did not even know that Remington had appealed his case to the board because "they have never gotten in touch with me."[44]

The Loyalty Review Board members had had enough. "It seems to me that we have waited as long as we decently can trying to get this woman to appear," wrote one member, George Allen, to board chairman Seth Richardson. "She is obviously insufficiently converted and seems to be a constitutional liar."[45] The board gave Elizabeth a deadline of January 27 to respond.

Elizabeth's actions dismayed her boosters. Senator Ferguson angrily spelled out the implications for her lawyer. Her refusal to appear before the Loyalty Review Board would undoubtedly hurt her in the libel case and "reflect seriously upon credibility of all her testimony in other matters," he warned. The senator tried to call Elizabeth repeatedly, but she refused to take his calls.[46]

Lacking the testimony of his accuser, the Loyalty Review Board voted unanimously to clear Remington. It was the first serious blow to Elizabeth's credibility, but it would not be the last.

At the same time that Remington and Bentley were fighting in the courts and in the newspapers, Alger Hiss and Whittaker Chambers were engaged in a similar struggle. Chambers, however, had squirreled away documents to support his claims. When Hiss sued him for slander, Chambers decided to produce the documents—and to assert that the former State Department official had been a Soviet spy as well as a secret Communist. The "pumpkin papers," named after their temporary hiding place, prompted a grand jury to indict Hiss for perjury.

Each day the newspapers carried new signs that the Cold War had come home. The Hollywood blacklist prevented actors, writers, and directors with radical pasts from working again. In unions around the country, anti-Communists fought to expel Communists. And in New York City's Foley Square courthouse, twelve Communist Party leaders went on trial for violating the Smith Act. The government called several ex-Communists to testify, including informers Herbert Philbrick, Angela Calomiris, and Louis Budenz.[47] The prosecutors did not, however, call the red spy queen to the stand.

Elizabeth's testimony would not have helped the government's case. In contrast to Budenz, who contended that Communists used "Aesopian language" to conceal their violent intent, Elizabeth usually (though not consistently) testified that the Party did not openly avow violent revolution. On February 16 and 17, 1949, in secret testimony once again before the New York grand jury, which had reconvened to consider more indictments, she reiterated her belief that American Communists did not plan to overthrow the U.S. government. As the trial of Party leaders continued, she urged the government to register, rather than to outlaw, American Communists.[48]

Nor did she offer the prosecutors any hope for other cases. She again explained that she had not met most of her sources and had never seen them give documents to Silvermaster.[49] One juror asked if she had any documentary evidence for her charges. "Mercy, no!" she exclaimed. "You don't keep it." The juror begged to differ. "Mr. Chambers had some in a pumpkin," he said.[50]

Even without the distinction of appearing in the Smith Act trial, though, Elizabeth continued to build her career as a conservative ex–spy queen. She received numerous lecture invitations from Catholic and veterans groups happy to pay her $300 fee.[51]

She also testified frequently before Congress. At times she was "scrupulously honest," as she had been before the Ferguson committee. At other times she exaggerated the importance of her intelligence. One example of the latter occurred during her May 1949 testimony before the immigration and naturalization subcommittee of the Senate Judiciary Committee. The subcommittee, chaired by powerful conservative senator Pat McCarran, held hearings on a bill to tighten immigration laws to keep out radicals. But the senators went far afield in their questioning.

When the subcommittee's staff director, Richard Arens, asked her for examples of the intelligence she had stolen, she mentioned that she knew in advance about "projected raids on Tokyo." A few minutes later, Arens came back to the subject. "Did you have any information respecting the Doolittle raid on Tokyo?" he asked her. This famed raid, led in April 1942 by General Jimmy Doolittle, had boosted American morale at a low point in the war.

Elizabeth generated headlines with her definite reply. "Yes; we knew about *that raid,* I guess, a week or ten days ahead of time; yes." She explained that she had gotten the information from Lud Ullmann, who was a "specialist" on the B-29 program in the Pentagon.[52]

But Ullmann had not been in the Pentagon in April 1942 and did not have any access to intelligence on the Doolittle raid. Furthermore, Doolittle and his pilots had used twin-engined B-25s, not heavy, multi-engined B-29s.

When her critics later seized on this apparent invention, Elizabeth insisted that she had misunderstood the question. She had thought that Arens was talking about different Tokyo raids—about, in fact, some B-29 raids launched in late 1944. The FBI investigated her claims and concluded that she had been legitimately confused by the question.[53]

But Elizabeth had stopped seeing Ullmann two months before the B-29 raids. There was no way that she could have known about them "a week or ten days ahead." Moreover, she had said "that raid," not "those proposed raids." The noun was singular. Despite her later attempts to explain her errors away, it seems clear that she intentionally made the false claim that she had advance knowledge of the 1942 Doolittle raid on Tokyo.[54] She wanted to please her questioners, no doubt. She also needed to keep her name in the headlines if she wanted to advance in her new career.

Elizabeth made some assertions carelessly, without much concern for their accuracy, and did not suffer for them. Ironically, though, she suffered tremendously from her accusations against William Remington, who was indeed guilty of espionage and perjury. A truly penitent Catholic might have found some divine justice in it all.

Throughout 1949, the battle with Remington continued to depress and distract her. She knew that attorneys Richard Green and Joe Rauh were investigating her past, and she knew that they were getting help from some of her friends. One of her buddies in Florence, a fellow exchange student named Joseph Lombardo, had derogatory information about her that he was willing to share. After trying without success to get Elizabeth's academic records from Columbia, Lombardo told the FBI all he knew about her drinking, promiscuity, and Italian arrest record. The bureau told him not to mention it to anyone. Lombardo ignored that advice and talked to Remington's lawyers.[55]

Thanks to Lombardo's help, Green and Rauh soon had a treasure trove of information about Bentley's "sordid past": the alcoholism, the boyfriends, and the allegations of academic dishonesty. Their private detective agency worked diligently but unsuccessfully to find proof that she had been committed to a mental institution. Even without that proof, though, Rauh was gleeful about the information that they had found. He was sure that this intelligence would discredit the testimony of his client's sole accuser and convince her to settle the libel suit to avoid a public trial. Rauh was so confident that he even tried to sell Remington's story to Hollywood, with Bentley providing the "ever-present, brooding force of evil" throughout the proposed movie.[56]

First, though, Rauh needed to accomplish the difficult task of getting Elizabeth to answer questions under oath about her past. After months of protests and delays, she finally consented to give a deposition on September 7, 1949.[57]

She glided confidently into the law offices "as though she had never been ducking us," Rauh reported in amazement. Girded for battle, Rauh began pounding her with questions. Did anyone write her master's thesis for her? Did she know a Mario Casella? ("His name is familiar, but I can't place it," Bentley replied.) Had she been expelled from the university? Finally, her lawyer stopped the deposition after one hour, protesting that the questions had nothing to do with the libel suit. Although he was frustrated, Rauh could not help but be impressed by her performance. "She is a pretty smooth lady," he wrote to an acquaintance. "She can be pleasant and agreeable when she wants to and can lie without the slightest facial change. She is a worthy opponent in that sense, but I have the feeling that she is also deep down a very reckless liar who some day is going to destroy herself."[58]

The prediction came true sooner than Rauh expected. As she struggled to find a career and an income for the next phase of her life, Elizabeth asked Monsignor Sheen to help her obtain a position at a Catholic college. Sheen enlisted the aid of the National Catholic Welfare Conference, which wrote to Catholic schools around the country asking if they could find a place for her. In Chicago, at a small women's college named after the first cardinal west of the Alleghenies, a generous nun read the letter and decided to help. Sister Mary Josephine, the president of Mundelein College, agreed to hire Elizabeth to teach political science.[59]

Immediately after she finished her deposition, Elizabeth headed to Chicago to begin her new life. But the transition from Manhattan woman-about-town to religious instructor was not easy. She must have felt overwhelmed by her courses: the former C student with a background in languages suddenly found herself teaching international law, political science, comparative government, social theory, urban-rural sociology, and social psychology. This course schedule was inexplicably thrust upon an English and Italian major who said she had never read Marx. In return she received $3,500 a year—not a bad salary for the time but only about one-third the amount she had earned at the espionage fronts.[60]

Sister Mary Josephine was thrilled to give a new chance to this "former Communist courier who had travelled the rough, unhappy road to disillusionment." But some Catholics were not so pleased. The college had to withstand a "storm of criticism," the sister wrote to alumnae.[61] One admirer of the college, for example, wrote that news of Bentley's employment there "shocked and distressed" him.[62] Some alumnae questioned Elizabeth's "moral laxity."[63]

Sister Mary Josephine defended her decision to hire Elizabeth, but unfortunately the subject of her generosity did not live up to her expectations. The newly conservative and contrite Christian, the lecturer who held up her piety as an example for her students, led a less than exemplary life at Mundelein. She began "living openly and notoriously with a man not her husband." She was also charged with other, unspecified examples of "loose morals," presumably regarding her alcoholism. The college administration confronted Elizabeth with these charges, and she volunteered to resign.[64] Publicly, Mundelein announced that she had been released from her contract because she needed more time to testify.[65] Sister Mary Josephine remained on good terms with Elizabeth and continued to pray for her.[66] But it was obvious that she was not going to have much of a future in religious education.

As she negotiated a face-saving exit from the college, Elizabeth learned some more bad news from New York. The insurance company for NBC and General Foods, the sponsor of *Meet the Press*, decided to pay off William Remington rather than face an expensive libel trial. Over the vehement objections of Elizabeth's attorneys, they agreed to settle out of court for $9,000.[67]

Depressed and unemployed, Elizabeth moved back to New York.[68] She reeled from the double blow of losing her job and effectively losing the libel case. She was in a vulnerable and suggestible frame of mind.

FALSE WITNESS

Just as Elizabeth's credibility reached its nadir, the FBI was uncovering new evidence to support her original charges. These documents confirmed bureau officials' conviction that she was telling the truth—and helped to reenergize the postwar spy hunt.

At Arlington Hall in northern Virginia, U.S. Army codebreakers had been struggling since 1943 to read telegrams sent by NKGB agents in the United States to their supervisors in Moscow. The army routinely collected the cables but had not succeeded in breaking the Soviets' codes and ciphers.

But Arlington Hall analysts soon discovered that the Soviets had made a fatal error in enciphering their messages. Under the strain of total war, they had printed duplicate copies of their "one-time" pads. Late in 1946, Arlington Hall linguist Meredith Gardner decrypted a Soviet message for the first time. Soon he could read dozens more. The codebreakers later called their project "Venona."[69]

By the fall of 1948, the FBI was working with the cryptanalysts to verify Elizabeth's charges and to catch other Soviet spies. Then in September 1949 came a stunning revelation: Arlington Hall had decrypted a scientific report straight from the wartime atomic bomb project in Los Alamos. The FBI determined that the author was a British scientist named Klaus Fuchs.[70]

After British security officials confronted Fuchs, he admitted that he had transmitted top-secret intelligence about the atomic bomb to the Soviets over a period of years. His courier had been an American man he knew only as "Raymond."

The FBI immediately launched a hunt for Raymond. The agents had a description—a middle-aged white male, average height, round face—but little else to go on. Their best lead was Fuchs's suggestion that the courier knew something about chemistry or engineering.[71]

As FBI agents checked their files, they remembered an interesting tidbit from Elizabeth's original statement. Abe Brothman, "the Penguin," her first source, had been a chemical engineer. Furthermore, Brothman had given them the name of another chemical engineer, Harry Gold.[72]

Thus Brothman, himself an inconsequential source, had unwittingly given the FBI the key to solving the atomic espionage case. Brothman did not realize that Gold had been a trusted Soviet courier with many important contacts. The FBI now had the names of two suspect chemical engineers in its files.

When agents confronted Gold with charges of atomic spying, the retired courier confessed and told them about a soldier at Los Alamos who had aided him in espionage. With help from more Venona cables, the FBI identified this man as David Greenglass. When the bureau found Greenglass, he, too, quickly confessed and named his brother-in-law, Julius Rosenberg.[73]

Elizabeth had provided an important clue to solving what Hoover called the crime of the century. Soon, the government would require her testimony in the trial of the century.

In the winter of 1950, the nation's headlines told of Klaus Fuchs's confession, Alger Hiss's perjury conviction, and Senator Joseph McCarthy's charges that there were "205 card-carrying members of the Communist Party" in the State Department. But the woman who had prompted all of the charges and countercharges was unemployed, depressed, and broke.

One day in late January, Elizabeth used her connections in the anti-Communist Catholic community to make a significant phone call. It was to John Gilland Brunini, a prolific Catholic poet and the foreman of the new grand jury investigating her charges. She explained that she had met one of his friends in Chicago and wanted to pass along her greetings. He promptly invited her to lunch.[74]

If the New York Catholic anti-Communists had organized themselves into an official group, Brunini would have been the president. At different times in his long career, he directed the Park Association, the Catholic Poetry Association, and the Temple of Religion at the 1939 World's Fair. His critics privately called him "Cardinal Spellman's poet laureate," a title he would have embraced. He knew the most powerful players in the Manhattan Catholic community, including a wealthy, philanthropic dowager, Lady Armstrong of the Ladies of Charity. A sincere and devoted anti-Communist, he was also, one Catholic acquaintance said, a "politician and an opportunist" who was always on the lookout for a chance to make a buck. He could be, in short, a valuable mentor to a down-on-her-luck ex–spy queen.[75]

Elizabeth had a distressing—and disingenuous—story to tell. She had been forced to quit her job at Mundelein because of her constant service to the U.S. government, she claimed. Luckily, the kind Lady Armstrong was paying her hotel bills. If not for this true lady of charity, she would be out on the street.[76]

Moved by her plight, Brunini suggested a solution: she could write a book. This was not a new idea, of course. Back in 1948, she had drawn up a contract with Nelson Frank. But nothing had ever come of that plan. Now Brunini wanted to revive it.

When Elizabeth protested that "she needed income immediately and further knew nothing about writing," Brunini explained that she could get an advance with an outline and a sample chapter. As it happened, he was publishing a book that year with Devin A. Garrity, owner of the Devin-Adair publishing house. He would be happy to help her find a publisher and put together a proposal.[77] Thus Elizabeth set out to write a book with the foreman of the grand jury still investigating her allegations.

As her unofficial literary agent, editor, and mentor, Brunini had an interest in boosting Elizabeth's credibility and raising her public profile. He received some valuable intelligence that would help him in this quest in late April. At a dinner with reporters, he learned that the FBI had found evidence that Remington had committed perjury when he denied Party membership under oath. The bureau planned to present this evidence to a congressional committee and a Washington grand jury—not to Brunini's jury. Deeply angered, the foreman spent a "sleepless night" before resolving to urge his jurors to demand the right to question Remington.[78] If successful, this inquiry could reveal the flaws in Truman's loyalty program and, not incidentally, restore his coauthor's credibility. As Gary May has concluded, "Political extremism and personal gain led Brunini to choose action."[79]

Brunini was the guiding force behind the Remington perjury investigation: he researched the evidence and suggested witnesses. His major discovery was that the FBI had failed to question Ann Remington, who was now Bill's ex-wife. The foreman demanded that the prosecutors subpoena her.[80] Under intense pressure from Brunini and prosecutor Tom Donegan, Ann Remington finally broke down and admitted that her husband had paid Party dues to Bentley and passed her some information.[81]

Here, at last, was the "weak sister" who could corroborate Elizabeth's charges. Ann Remington was the first person from Elizabeth's espionage days who did not portray her as a fantasist and a psychopath.

Elizabeth relished the opportunity to exact revenge from the man who had falsely denied her charges and investigated her personal life. On May 18, she testified about Remington before Brunini's grand jury—and did her best to ensure his indictment. The most notable change in her testimony concerned Remington's knowledge of the ultimate destination of his information. Just two weeks earlier, in new testimony before HUAC, she had called Remington a "minor figure" in her espionage activities and explained that he "thought the information was going to the American Communist Party." When he had stopped spying, she had said, "it wasn't too great a loss to us."[82] Before the grand jury, though, she transformed Remington into an important, knowing NKGB agent. Because of his value, Elizabeth and the Soviets had "hated to let him go."[83]

On June 8, Brunini's grand jury indicted Remington for perjury. It was the first indictment based on Elizabeth's allegations.

Elizabeth readied herself for a new role. Already an experienced witness before congressional committees and government agencies, she would now testify in a criminal trial. Soon, in fact, her services would be needed in three major trials. After Remington's indictment in June, the FBI arrested Julius and Ethel Rosenberg later that summer. In addition, based on Gold's confession, the government charged Abe Brothman with obstructing justice.

The trials of Brothman, Remington, and the Rosenbergs would all begin in the next several months, with Elizabeth providing essential testimony.

As she waited for her court dates, Elizabeth squirreled herself away to write her autobiography. In Westport, Connecticut, she rented a room from a local family and focused on her manuscript. As usual, she needed constant lubrication to perform. "She smoked like a fiend and drank like a fiend," remembers George Pancoast, whose family rented to her. But she seldom went out and never entertained visitors as she worked hard to make her deadline.[84] When she did leave her room, she traveled to New York to meet with her collaborator.

The prosecutors did not learn of Brunini's work on Elizabeth's book until October, four months into her career as an author. Even then, Elizabeth warned Brunini not to tell the Justice Department about their collaboration, but he disregarded her advice—apparently because he was worried that Remington's private detectives might beat him to it.[85] Justice officials were not pleased by the news. Elizabeth's trademark style of manipulation and deception had infuriated the NKGB; now it was the U.S. prosecutors' turn.

In a conversation with Tom Donegan, Brunini explained that Bentley and her publisher wanted to pay him for his work, but he was not sure, given his position as foreman, whether he should accept. Outraged, Donegan told him that "under no circumstances should he do this."[86] Worried that the incident "might be used to good advantage by the defense," Donegan demanded to know if the foreman and the spy queen were sleeping together. Brunini insisted that they were not.[87]

Donegan had other worries as well. With three trials turning on her testimony, the prosecutors needed to ensure that Elizabeth came across as a credible witness. Yet soon after they discovered her secret literary dalliance with her grand jury foreman, they nervously noted more signs that she could prove vulnerable in court. Their chief witness, they concluded, might be descending into madness.[88]

Elizabeth began hearing clicks on her telephone; she started seeing mysterious figures in the shadows. One day she pointed out two "tails" to special agents Tom Spencer and Jack Danahy. The "tails" paid no attention to her, and the agents were convinced that she was neurotic. When she complained that she was followed to church and then to breakfast, an exasperated agent commented that she was only writing a book and not worth tailing.[89]

But the NKGB had considered killing her, and it had assassinated other defectors. Although no one was following her at this point, her fear was certainly reasonable—and her fear had saved her life a few years earlier. Considering the NKGB's record for silencing defectors, the FBI was remarkably unsympathetic to her concerns.

Her newfound friends in the Manhattan anti-Communist community passed along rumors that fed her fear. Elizabeth frequently dined out on her status as a celebrity ex-spy, enjoying dinners and cocktail parties with anti-Communist journalists and crusaders. She now counted among her friends Senator Joe McCarthy, Hearst journalists George Sokolsky and Howard Rushmore, HUAC staff director J. B. Matthews and his wife, Ruth, and attorney Robert Morris, who would soon become staff director for the Senate Internal Security Subcommittee. It was a warm, sociable community. In the years to come, Sokolsky would loan her money, Ruth Matthews would provide emotional support, and Morris would try to solve her numerous legal problems.

At one party, which was attended "by a number of prominent anti-Communists," right-wing journalist Victor Lasky told her that Remington had hired private detectives to shadow her. Morris gave her similar information. Actually, Remington's detectives were merely interviewing people who had known Elizabeth, rather than attempting to follow her. When Morris subsequently learned that Remington "did not have that kind of money," Elizabeth was even more worried. The "tails," she decided, must be Russian. She changed hotels and demanded police protection.[90] Ten days before the Brothman trial began, the New York FBI office reported that Elizabeth was "bordering on some mental pitfall which, of course, would be almost disastrous to the prosecution of the Brothman and Remington cases, as she is without doubt the principal witness in both."[91]

Finally, the prosecutors also worried that the exposure of Elizabeth's personal life could be "disastrous" to their cases. They knew, for example, that Remington's attorneys were investigating her "sordid past." Just what traps might they spring on her when she took the stand?

To ensure that they were not surprised in court, the prosecutors directed the New York FBI agents to "obtain in detail any derogatory information concerning her past life, particularly concerning any moral indiscreetness." On October 13, Special Agents Danahy and Spencer picked her up and drove her to an isolated section behind the Tavern on the Green in Central Park. For two hours, the G-men sat poker-faced in the car and listened as their star informant talked about the part of her past she had hoped to keep secret forever.

Elizabeth confessed to "some occasions where she had been indiscreet" but denied the suicide attempt in Florence. She maintained that she was "quite naïve in so far as sex was concerned" until she became a "real Communist," thus conveniently forgetting her numerous affairs as a fascist. Perhaps the most notable example of wishful thinking was her claim that she occasionally got drunk but "was not what could be called a drinker."[92]

It was her life as she wished it had been. The FBI agents and prosecutors understood this, but they also knew that her basic charges were accurate. "She may have tucked away some items about her personal life," Danahy says, "but she leveled with us on the espionage all the way."[93] They just hoped that those "items" would stay tucked away, undiscovered by defense attorneys.

The first test of the government's espionage prosecutions came in November 1950 when Abe Brothman went on trial.[94] Though Brothman was a minor agent, the Justice Department saw his case as a dress rehearsal for the more important trials to come.[95] In particular, they wanted to see how Elizabeth held up under pressure.

They need not have worried. Composed and demure in a purple wool suit, she entered the court by a side door and stared searchingly at the man she hoped to send to prison. After promising to tell the court the whole truth, she calmly recited her history of dealings with "the Penguin."[96]

Her story was now filled with an urgency that it had lacked in her FBI debriefing. In that earlier interview, she had said that Golos was "somewhat discouraged" with Brothman, and she could not recall any details about his blueprints. Now, with her anti-Communist supporters badly needing an espionage conviction, she remembered some damning facts. One blueprint was for a chemical kettle at the U.S. Army arsenal in Edgewood, Maryland, she said, and Golos had been "very much interested" in obtaining it.[97]

During her cross-examination, she patronized and corrected defense attorney William Kleinman, at one point objecting to his use of the term "Russian" agents. "They were Soviet agents," she observed primly. "I am distinguishing because Russian means a nationality, not a country." At another point, when Kleinman asked where a conversation had taken place, she explained, unhelpfully, "Wherever I happened to be with him at that moment." When she chided the defense attorney for having "forgotten" his facts, Kleinman erupted in anger to the judge. "Will your Honor tell the witness not to reprimand me?"[98]

The reporters at the trial were impressed by her grace under fire. When Kleinman sought to embarrass her by dwelling on her relationship with Golos, she "admitted her intimate relations with the spy with no hesitation or hint of embarrassment," the *New York Herald Tribune* noted with amazement. The *New York Times* reported that she was "completely composed."[99] The press viewed the jury's quick guilty verdict as a vindication for the FBI, the prosecutors, and Elizabeth herself.

Her next chance to defend her credibility and silence her critics came at William Remington's trial two months later. On the stand, she once again improved her story about Remington's "now-famous" synthetic rubber formula. Instead of a "worthless" jotting on a scrap of paper, the formula was now "super-secret" and "an extremely complicated thing." She now described Remington—formerly a "minor source"—as a key agent whose information had been judged "very excellent" by Golos.[100]

It was the cross-examination, though, that really tested her. Remington's lawyer, William Chanler, slashed into her, questioning her morals, her fascist past, her financial interest in a conviction, her literary arrangement with Brunini, and even her affair with Peter Heller. Elizabeth, though, stayed cool and composed. In a few cases, she simply denied Chanler's allegations—and lied in the process. For example, she denied that she had ever discussed Communism with Heller or that her fear of him had driven her to the FBI. This was not true, as Chanler could have proven if he had been given access to her first statement to the FBI. She also denied that Heller had picked her up in her hotel lobby by offering to buy her a drink. "I am not likely to do such things, so I don't imagine it happened that way," she said. For the most part, though, she avoided direct lies. Instead, she parried Chanler's thrusts by dismissing his arguments as "picayune" and irrelevant.[101]

Throughout Chanler's long interrogation, she remained "calm and unruffled," "self-possessed," and a "formidable witness," in the view of reporters covering the trial. She was obviously smart, one unfriendly columnist observed; she had that "quick and almost feline shrewdness that some women develop who have to make their way with their wits." With her prim, tolerant smiles, she was almost condescending to the famed trial lawyer charged with destroying her credibility.[102] The courtroom observers had no idea that this clever, carefully controlled woman also suffered from neuroses so severe that she had to drink herself into oblivion to ease the pain.

The jury returned a guilty verdict after just four and a half hours.[103] The man who had sued her, investigated her, and publicized her notorious past was going to jail. No wonder she had flashed that patronizing smile so often during the trial. Elizabeth might still be depressed and anxious, but she knew that she was now on the winning side.

She was far from finished with court appearances, though. Just a few weeks after Remington's conviction, the government needed her services at the atomic espionage trial of Julius Rosenberg, Ethel Rosenberg, and their friend Morton Sobell. The government had several witnesses against the Rosenbergs, including Harry Gold and Ethel's brother, David Greenglass. But Elizabeth played a significant role in the prosecution's plan for victory.

The prosecutors needed Elizabeth to testify that Julius Rosenberg was one of Golos's spies. On this point, she was not completely cooperative. In a strong assertion of independence, she told the FBI before the trial that she could not visually identify Julius. She had been too far away from him that night in 1942, she said.[104] But she was happy to testify to the late-night phone calls. On the stand, over furious objections from the defense, she told her story of the mysterious calls.

She also obligingly explained that all Communists were potential or actual spies for Moscow. "The Communist Party being part of the Communist International," she said, "only served the interests of Moscow, whether it be propaganda or espionage or sabotage."[105]

Defense attorney Manny Bloch subjected Elizabeth to a withering cross-examination. Contemptuous of her morals and incredulous of her testimony, Bloch spent some time establishing that she had enjoyed "relations" with Golos without the benefit of marriage. He demonstrated that she had profited from her tale, and he implied that she might have made up the story about the phone calls in order to increase her market value. Bloch did not attempt to maintain courtesy or civility. When she misunderstood one of his questions, he sneered, "Are you a college graduate?"[106]

But Elizabeth shrewdly refused to be drawn into traps. When he asked her to "characterize" her relationship with Golos, she snapped: "I don't feel I am called upon to characterize it. That is up to you."[107] She resolutely resisted his attempts to say how many lectures she had given, how many times she had testified, how many sources she had, and how much money she had earned.[108]

Elizabeth's testimony helped the government to win the case both at the trial level and later on appeal. In turning down the Rosenbergs' appeal, Judge Jerome Frank wrote that she "supplied the missing link connecting the Communist Party with the Soviet Union."[109]

On April 5, 1951, Ethel Rosenberg, an accessory to espionage who had refused to help the government prove its case against her husband, was condemned to die with him in the electric chair. Two weeks later, Elizabeth Bentley, a top Soviet spy who had stolen national secrets for seven years, held a press conference. Her life was about to be serialized in a women's magazine.

The editors at *McCall's* were initially leery of handling Elizabeth's story. When her publisher asked the magazine to serialize her autobiography, called *Out of Bondage,* one *McCall's* editor pronounced the book to be "one of the most fascinating documents" he had ever read and a "sure-fire success." But he worried that Elizabeth was "on the verge of being discredited." In January, he sought the advice of FBI publicist Lou Nichols. Would the magazine get burned if it ran her life story? Nichols scoffed at such a suggestion and pointed to Elizabeth's composure under cross-examination in the Remington trial. If her enemies were going to discredit her, he said, they would have already done so.[110]

Some critics did attack the magazine for running the series. Many Americans questioned whether a traitor—even a reformed one—should profit from her crimes. At the press conference announcing the serialization of her book, one reporter asked, "Miss Bentley, do you think this exposé of yours will help your country as much as your spying hurt it?" Once the articles began appearing, some readers angrily upbraided the magazine for glorifying treason and espionage.[111]

Elizabeth responded, quite sensibly, with a defense that was carefully crafted to absolve her from responsibility while enhancing her respectability. She decided to portray herself as a sort of Communist June Cleaver.

The headline of the June installment of her story said it all: "I Joined the Red Underground with the Man I Loved." Elizabeth described an ingenuous "college girl"—never mind that she was thirty when she met him—who fell under the spell of a handsome, powerful, older lover. He had her, as her book title said, in bondage. She worried about him; she idolized him; she obeyed him. At one point, when she momentarily balked at one of his orders, he rebuked her, and she felt "ashamed" of her "momentary rebellion." Their main regret, she said, was that they never had children.[112]

Both in its serialized form and in its expanded hardcover version, the most remarkable part of *Out of Bondage* was Elizabeth's portrayal of her relationship with Golos. After all, they had been Communists who did not believe in the "bourgeois" convention of marriage. Yet Elizabeth conveniently skimmed over this problem, at times with breathtaking audacity. "With wifely pride—*although, of course, we were never married*—I began to realize that Timmy was a far more important person in the Communist party than I had ever remotely dreamed," read the first sentence of her second installment.[113]

In effect, Elizabeth constructed a new image of herself: neither Mata Hari nor vengeful schoolmarm but rather a conventional housewife who had meekly obeyed her "husband." It was a frank appeal to the suburban *McCall's* readers. "I'm just like you," Elizabeth seemed to be saying, "except that my husband turned out to be a Russian spy." Her self-constructed image also helped to deflect blame: she had, after all, done only what Yasha had asked her to. How could she know it was wrong?

She did certainly follow the lead of her lovers in political matters. Moreover, she had frequently allowed men to take advantage of her—though, ironically, Yasha treated her better than any of her other lovers. But Elizabeth was not a demure girl with fluttering

eyelashes and a commanding husband. She had led a most un-
conventional life, from her rejection of marriage to her choice of
careers. She had successfully planned her defection to avoid assassination by the NKGB and imprisonment by the U.S. government.
She had recently demonstrated that she could outwit top lawyers
on the witness stand. Now, her distorted portrayal of her life was
one more example of her practicality and her resilience. She was
shrewd enough to change her life story in a way that suited the
times and her own needs.

Elizabeth also strove to paint herself as a defender of traditional sexual morality. This mistress of a NKGB agent was shocked
to discover that the Soviets sometimes used sex to gather information. As she explained to her gentle readers, Yasha stunned her
with the information that the Russians had evil plans for Mary
Price. "They want to set her up in an apartment, buy her fancy
clothes, and let her use her wiles on men who would be useful
to the cause." Luckily, Yasha, despite his Soviet training, shared
Elizabeth's basic American family values. "If anything happens to
me," he told Elizabeth shortly before the end, "take care of Mary.
Don't under any circumstances let her be turned over to them."[114]

It is certainly true that Elizabeth tried to get the Soviets to
drop Mary Price as a source. A Soviet telegram from 1944 con-
firms this. However, the Soviets thought that Elizabeth made the
request simply because she did not like Mary.[115] Price herself said
that Elizabeth had ample reason to despise her because she had
rejected her homosexual advances.[116]

Moreover, Elizabeth herself told different versions of this story
at different times. In 1945, she told the FBI that Mary had asked to
be let out of the underground and had, in effect, saved herself.[117]
In 1949, she told the grand jury that she, Elizabeth, had discovered the Soviets' evil plans for Mary and had resolved to save her
from their "clutches."[118] By 1951, it was the tenderhearted Yasha
who had recoiled in horror at Moscow's plans for Mary and directed Elizabeth to save her. In hopes of avoiding jail, impressing
her newfound conservative friends, and satisfying her own emo-

tional needs, Elizabeth seemed to be reinterpreting her life as a morality tale.

Elizabeth probably wanted to believe the story that she told in *Out of Bondage*. It was much more reassuring to edit out all of the unpleasantness—the drinking, the disastrous love affairs, Yasha's wife and child. It was also easier to attribute her mistakes to an outside force that had held her in "bondage" and from which she had now escaped.

She had also ceased to see a simple dichotomy between "truth" and "falsehood." Although she testified in public that *Out of Bondage* was "all absolutely true," at other times she said that she "dramatized" some incidents and even called it a work of "fiction."[119] She had formidable survival skills, and one of those skills was her ability to lie. She lied to others and to herself. She tried desperately to convince herself that ultimate truth lay in Marxism and then Catholicism, that she was not a drinker, and that Yasha had never been married. At some level, though, she must have doubted her own comforting stories. She used the alcohol to banish those doubts—and her inescapable guilt.

In the end, *Out of Bondage* exuded "a smell of phoniness" for many readers. Reviewers had a difficult time finding the right words to convey their disgust. "It is very hard to decide whether to treat *Out of Bondage* . . . as tragic, or as ludicrous, or as terrifying, or as pathetic," wrote Joseph Alsop.[120] All in all, the book read as if the author "had almost as grievous a tussle with Freshman English at Vassar as she had later with her New England conscience," one reviewer noted.[121]

But Elizabeth cannot be held solely responsible for the "schoolgirlish" tone of her book. Apparently, she had worked hard on a first draft, but all the evidence suggests that Brunini rewrote most of it.[122] Later, he insisted that he only proofread the manuscript, yet the testimony of Devin-Adair employees and FBI documents indicates otherwise. At one point, for example, Elizabeth told the FBI that Brunini was "not getting the copy out as fast as the publisher desired"; so she had sent him some roses to encourage him.[123]

Moreover, Brunini's unpublished writings are remarkably similar in style to *Out of Bondage.* He once wrote a manuscript, for example, called "Everyday Murder," which featured chapter titles like "A Tryst and a Corpse" and "Fingerprints in Rouge." The sweaty, stylized sentences in that manuscript ("his heart gave a sickening pound as he saw the corpse") are similar to the false drama in *Out of Bondage* ("I glared at him menacingly. . . . He seemed to shrivel in his chair").[124] Ironically, Elizabeth's portrayal of herself as a deferential female was accurate in one respect: she let a man write much of her book.

Thomas Sloane, Elizabeth's editor at Devin-Adair and one of Brunini's close friends, also had a hand in shaping the manuscript. Sloane lived in Westport near Elizabeth, and he rewrote so much of her book that she denounced him as a Communist.[125]

Two men, in short, helped plan, write, and edit a book by a woman aimed at female readers. Their assumptions about gender roles, combined with Elizabeth's strained attempt to portray herself as a victim, created that phony smell noted by so many reviewers.

One other male writer contributed in a small but substantive way to *Out of Bondage* and in the process encouraged Elizabeth to lie in her book. Richard L. Stokes happened to be ghostwriting another anti-Communist exposé in East Hampton, Long Island, just as Elizabeth was struggling with her rough draft on the other side of the Long Island Sound. Stokes was a recent convert to Catholicism who had quit the *St. Louis Post-Dispatch* in 1949 to "devote himself to Catholic journalism." In his weekly column for the diocesan press, Stokes alarmed even fellow conservatives with his rants against the "unholy entente between White House and Kremlin."[126]

As Elizabeth tried to meet her publishing deadline, Stokes was helping George Racey Jordan write an account of the treachery and espionage he had witnessed as a Lend-Lease administrator during World War II. Jordan claimed that the Soviets had used Lend-Lease shipments to ferry stolen documents, uranium ore, and the printing plates for German occupation currency.[127]

The occupation money scandal had been a hot topic in the American press a few years earlier. In 1945, the United States had given the templates for occupation currency to the Soviets, who had proceeded to print millions of dollars worth of new German marks and distribute them to their soldiers. Because the U.S. Army had foolishly decided to redeem the marks with hard currency, the Russians' lack of restraint at the printing presses ended up costing the American taxpayers a quarter of a billion dollars.[128]

A 1947 congressional investigation had blamed the army for the fiasco. Jordan and Stokes, however, wanted to revive the issue—and to connect it to the now infamous Treasury official who had played a role in the disaster, Harry Dexter White.

Stokes met Bentley that summer of 1950 as they worked on their manuscripts. When he asked her if she knew anything about the currency scandal, she "was generous enough to drop work on a book of her own" to help him research it, Stokes later wrote.[129] Actually, she was more than that: she was generous enough to fabricate information for him.

The currency issue represented a new low for Elizabeth. She had exaggerated many of her stories, including the importance of Remington's contributions and the supposed advance notice of the Doolittle raid and D-Day. But this was the first time she invented something out of whole cloth. It also marks the first time that someone—intentionally or not—planted a story with her.

After meeting Stokes, Elizabeth inserted into *Out of Bondage* a paragraph alleging that she had been "able through Harry Dexter White to arrange that the United States Treasury Department turn the actual printing plates over to the Russians!"[130] In other words, American officials had not simply made bad policy choices; instead, a Russian spy had secretly manipulated policymakers and swindled the taxpayers.

But she had never told this story to the FBI.[131] She had not mentioned it to congressional investigators, grand juries, or prosecutors. There is no documentary evidence from Venona or from the Soviet archives that she had anything to do with the decision to transfer the plates. Moreover, Bruce Craig has thoroughly examined this issue and determined that Harry White himself did not play a "decisive" role in shaping the policy, either.[132]

Perhaps she thought that her invention did not matter because White was dead. Perhaps she had ceased to distinguish between truth and falsity. In any event, Elizabeth Bentley was truly becoming a false witness.

[8]
Somewhat Hysterical

n the fall of 1951, Elizabeth tried to start a new life and put the anguish of the past few years behind her. In September, she bought a charming old house on several acres of land in the shoreline community of Madison, Connecticut. The resort town reminded her of the summers she had spent at the beach as a child. It was the first home she had ever owned.[1]

The *New Haven Register* ran a picture of the area's newest resident relaxing in her home.[2] Not even the most imaginative journalist could portray her as a Mata Hari now. Overweight, tired, and unhappy, she showed the strains of the last three years in her face. As she sank back in her chair and stared at the camera, she did not look like an advertisement for attaining inner peace through religious conversion.

Because she frequently left Madison to testify or to deliver "Communist menace" lectures, she needed a caretaker and handyman. She hired a local man named John Burghardt Wright. Soon local gossips were saying that he took care of more than just her house.

Like many of Elizabeth's previous boyfriends, Wright was older, self-important, and married to someone else. He had a short fuse and a taste for alcohol, which could be a dangerous combination. His criminal record included arrests for breaking and entering, breach of the peace, assault, aggravated assault, and assault to kill.[3] A doctor who examined him found the fifty-three-year-old to be "below average mentally, a braggart and an adolescent type."[4]

She had managed to find a boyfriend even more inappropriate than Peter Heller.

Wright made himself at home at Elizabeth's house in Madison. He began drinking her whiskey, charging liquor to her account at the local drugstore, and "acting as if he were one of the household rather than just an employee." She thought about firing him but then succumbed to the "black influenza" and could not get out of bed. When her priest tried to talk to Elizabeth about her unseemly relationship with her caretaker, she became so angry that she barely spoke to the father again.[5]

She suffered from financial as well as emotional problems. The sales of her book had been disappointing, and she had not yet found another teaching position. She still liked to party, with trips to the Caribbean, lots of liquor, and many "callers in the late evening and early morning hours." But she was having trouble paying the bills.[6]

As she tried to book lecture engagements, she smoldered with anger over her lack of financial success as an ex-Communist witness. Her mind began to turn to the $2,000 in "Moscow gold" that she had so casually tossed on the bed in front of the startled FBI agents back in 1945.

She had asked the FBI before about the money she had received from Gorsky. Tom Donegan, though, had made it clear that he would not even think about giving it back to her until after the Remington case was resolved.[7] And it was far from resolved: Remington had appealed his conviction, and in August 1951 the appellate court had ruled that the judge's charge to the jury had been too vague. The panel threw out the conviction but not the indictment.[8] A new trial loomed on the horizon.

Elizabeth, however, was not going to give up easily on the money. When bureau officials asked her to relinquish any claim to the cash, she informed them that her lawyer had a different opinion. The money belonged to her, she said, and she wanted it back.[9]

This posed a dilemma for FBI officials: they could hardly let

her keep the "fruits of the crime," yet at the same time they did not want to "antagonize Miss Bentley." Finally, Alan Belmont, now an assistant director of the bureau, devised a solution worthy of Solomon. The FBI would pay her $2,000 for "her assistance and services." In return, she would sign away her claim to the Moscow gold.[10] Through a feat of bureaucratic legerdemain, the bureau had transformed a payment for Soviet espionage into a payment for services rendered to the U.S. government.[11]

This was Elizabeth's first, tentative foray into blackmailing the FBI. Her success would embolden her to try it again.

As her anxiety and anger mounted, Elizabeth reached for her familiar crutches: too much liquor and the wrong sort of men. By the spring of 1952, she could no longer control her alcoholism. In March, she alarmed her conservative friends when she failed to show up at a Knights of Columbus lecture in Great Neck, New York. When her escort arrived at her hotel to drive her to the lecture, she complained that she had had too much "penicillin." The only cure, apparently, was to go down to the bar and have a few drinks. After an hour and a half, she was too "ill" to deliver the lecture. Elizabeth's religious friends and sponsors, Margaret Budenz and Lady Armstrong, called the FBI in great concern over her welfare.[12]

She recovered sufficiently to give a lecture in Toledo the next month, but disaster struck when she returned. As she had planned, John Wright met her at the New Haven railroad station on April 30, and the two of them went out for some drinks. By the time they stumbled back into Elizabeth's car, they had downed some ten highballs between them.

They quarreled over who should drive. Finally, Elizabeth took the wheel and began to drive erratically. Wright later told the FBI that she had taken a considerable number of barbiturates and prescription drugs in addition to the alcohol. Alarmed, he grabbed the wheel and pulled the keys from the ignition. She responded by slapping him with her gloves, and he "blew his cork and hit her with a right cross." He belted her with such force that she fell out

SOMEWHAT HYSTERICAL

of the car. She cowered and tried to run away from him, but he shoved her back in the car and drove her to Madison.[13]

The beating had been vicious. Several of her teeth were loosened, "two of her lower teeth had gone completely through the lower part of her face," and her face was swollen and scarred.[14]

During the week after the assault, John kept Elizabeth a virtual prisoner in her home. If she told anyone about the beating, he said, he would expose her drunken, "unladylike" behavior to the world. She clutched hot compresses and guzzled martinis to ease the pain. Finally, when her cuts became infected, she asked him to drive her to New York City to see a doctor. Once free of her "caretaker," she decided to call in the FBI.[15]

Both Elizabeth and the bureau had a compelling interest in intimidating Wright and covering up the whole affair. Elizabeth realized that this could "ruin her career as a lecturer."[16] The FBI realized that it could end up freeing William Remington—and endanger the Brothman and Rosenberg convictions. The bureau, however, did not want to get its hands dirty in the sordid affair. So it prevailed on the U.S. Attorney's office—and in particular, an ambitious young assistant U.S. attorney named Roy Cohn—to solve the problem.

Cohn's critics would later accuse him of a host of crimes, including suborning perjury, obstructing justice, bribing judges, and even committing murder.[17] He was never convicted, but to his enemies that only proved his skill at covering his tracks. Soon Cohn would become known across America as Joe McCarthy's henchman. He cut his anti-Communist teeth, though, on the espionage cases starring Elizabeth Bentley.

Elizabeth gave him one of his first opportunities to find creative—some might say unethical—solutions to vexing legal problems. Bentley's beating was "the most serious problem he had faced since coming into the United States Attorney's office," he told the FBI.[18] The government needed to find some way to keep its chief witness safe, emotionally stable, and out of the headlines.

Cohn first set up a meeting for the prosecutors, the FBI, and

Elizabeth's physician, Dr. Samuel Groopman. Elizabeth, however, refused to let them make major decisions concerning her life without consulting her. So she and Lady Armstrong showed up, unannounced and uninvited, to the meeting. It was a chaotic scene: Elizabeth, Cohn, and Dr. Groopman all tried to talk at once, and throughout the discussion Elizabeth sobbed, chain-smoked, and talked "almost irrationally." Cohn and Agent Tom Spencer regarded her with thinly concealed disgust. Cohn called her a "spoiled child," while Spencer wondered whether his formerly "cooperative" informant had become unhinged by the beating or by the drinking. Perhaps, he wondered, clutching at the ultimate male explanation for irrationality in females of a certain age, it was menopause.[19]

From Elizabeth's perspective, though, the U.S. government was failing to recognize her sacrifices on its behalf. After her years of service, she was unemployed and nearly penniless. Yet male ex-Communists were profiting nicely: Louis Budenz was "wealthy," and Whittaker Chambers was about to make a "small fortune out of his writings."[20] She could not understand why she was an object of ridicule while they were heroes.

The group at Dr. Groopman's office agreed on one thing: they needed to get rid of John Wright. Cohn quickly came up with an audacious plan. He decided to scare the abusive boyfriend out of Elizabeth's life. The infamous legal hatchet man was about to become a crusader against domestic violence.

Cohn told Elizabeth to entice Wright to New York under false pretenses. When he arrived, he was hit with the full force of the U.S. government. FBI agents whisked him to a meeting with two prosecutors and Special Agent John Danahy. U.S. Attorney Myles Lane told Wright "to get out of Bentley's life" or else he would haul him before a grand jury for tampering with a witness.[21] (He was, of course, technically tampering with a witness, though not for the usual reasons.) Lane gave him a subpoena "which was marked on a continuing basis" and warned him that any contact with Bentley would result in his immediate summons.[22] It was, as Wright later complained, a "scare meeting" designed to intimidate him.[23] Cohn

SOMEWHAT HYSTERICAL

had used bare-knuckle tactics, and they worked. Wright did not
bother her again.

On May 29, 1952, a star-studded gallery of anti-Communists
faced a friendly Senate panel investigating Communist espionage.
Elizabeth was among them. The government had solved her problem and put her back to work.

The occasion was the denouement of the Senate Internal Security Subcommittee's investigation of Owen Lattimore and the Institute of Pacific Relations. Senator Joe McCarthy had charged that
Lattimore, an obscure academic and onetime State Department
consultant, was the "top Russian spy" in the United States. Elizabeth had appeared before this body once before, when she had
disappointed the members by maintaining that she did not know
anything about Lattimore.[24]

But this time, perhaps unsettled by her recent personal troubles,
she made some extravagant claims. The subcommittee's counsel
during both her appearances was Robert Morris, a New York anti-
Communist and one of Elizabeth's good friends. Under his questioning, Elizabeth agreed that Soviet agents still infected the inner
councils of the U.S. government, despite the failure of the FBI to
find any. It was impossible to detect these agents because they dis-
guised themselves so completely. "For example," she said, "often
they were told to pose as right-wing Republicans or Fascists."[25]
Actually, not one of her sources had ever posed as a fascist or even
as a Republican, but the subcommittee did not press her for specific examples.

She also startled her listeners by claiming that she personally
knew of two undiscovered espionage rings. This allegation directly
supported McCarthy's claim that there were still traitors "shaping
policy" in the highest echelons of the government. Later, a befuddled FBI agent would scramble to figure out what she was talking about. It turned out that her account of the two "unexposed
rings" was, to put it mildly, exaggerated. One, she said, was Alger
Hiss's "ring" (which, arguably, had been exposed and consisted of
him alone); about the other, she could say nothing at all.[26]

Had her right-wing friends planted these stories with her? Was she being controlled? There is no evidence that the FBI was persuading her to give false testimony; on the contrary, the bureau continued to be alarmed by the new variations in her story. She did, of course, get some ideas from her activist friends. Brunini had encouraged her to augment Remington's role, for example, and Richard Stokes had told her about the occupation currency scandal. Robert Morris's presence on the Senate subcommittee staff might have prompted her to improve her testimony there.

But this was not a simple case of powerful male puppeteers pulling the strings of a docile marionette. Harvey Matusow, her lover and friend, explains that she was too strong-willed to allow anyone to control her. "I think she would have rebelled against that," he says.[27] Although Elizabeth incorporated some new stories into her memory to please her friends, she also refused opportunities to invent memories that would enhance her importance and help her sponsors. She refused to identify Julius Rosenberg. She refused to discuss Owen Lattimore. Once, her good friend J. B. Matthews, a prominent member of the ex-Communist network, asked her about an alleged proposal by Harry Dexter White to confiscate German companies. Far from tailoring her memory to fit Matthews's political purposes, she replied definitively that she "wasn't aware of any such thing."[28] Like the NKGB and the FBI before them, the anti-Communist activists found Elizabeth Bentley to be a most perplexing, inconsistent, and unruly ally.

Several weeks after Cohn rescued her from her abusive lover, Bentley demanded the prosecutor's help again. This time her problem was money—or rather the lack of it. She had already gone through the Moscow gold and her royalties. In fact, she could not afford to pay her income taxes, even though the ever helpful Cohn had introduced her to an accountant who managed to lower them substantially. She owed some $600 in medical and household bills, yet she had only $150 in cash. A thousand dollars would see her through the summer, she said. Cohn agreed to ask the bureau for help.[29]

SOMEWHAT HYSTERICAL

The agents in New York were not happy to be asked. They grumbled that she was notoriously "improvident," unstable, and generally a tough informant to handle. Perhaps, they suggested, she was going through menopause. But what could they do? "There is no question," wrote Agent Spencer, ". . . but that something will have to be done for this woman, at least until the Remington trial is disposed of."[30]

After complaining about her numerous weaknesses, the New York special agent in charge reluctantly conceded that "we do owe her some debt" because of her services to the government.[31] The bureau agreed to give her $50 a week for at least three months.[32] Seven years after her first foray into the FBI offices, Elizabeth had finally become a paid informer.

Shortly after she went on the U.S. government payroll, Elizabeth again required Cohn's services. On August 29, 1952, she was driving Lady Armstrong and two children to the railroad station in New Haven when she hit another car. She did not stop. The owner of the damaged car wrote down her license number and called the police. On Elizabeth's trip home from New Haven, she was stopped and arrested by the Connecticut State Police.[33]

Upset, nervous, and "very uncooperative," Elizabeth told the surprised troopers that she worked for the FBI and demanded the right to call the bureau.[34] When they finally allowed her to call the New Haven office, she told Agent Joe Casper that he must get her out of jail. The FBI, once again, turned the nasty problem over to Roy Cohn.[35]

Cohn swung into action. He called Police Commissioner Edward Hickey and urged him to let Elizabeth go and—even more important—to keep the whole case quiet. Hickey talked to the local prosecutor, who agreed to release Elizabeth without bond. She was later found guilty of failing to yield and fined $9.[36]

But her troubles were not over. Two weeks later, she lost control of her car, ran off the road, and damaged her 1939 LaSalle "beyond repair."[37] As she recovered from the accident at home, she grew desperate and lonely. She called the only people she could turn to, her "friends" at the New York FBI, and demanded that they drive her to see Dr. Groopman in New York. Disgusted and reluctant, they finally decided that they had no choice but to appease her.[38]

In their view, she was a most unpleasant passenger. "Throughout the trip from Madison to New York City," an unusually descriptive FBI memo noted, "she was rambling and incoherent in her speech, . . . engaged in backseat driving, weeping, sleeping, fingering a small crucifix, chainsmoking and was quarrelsome and demanding throughout the trip." Once they arrived, she insisted that the agents had to register her in her hotel and call her doctor. When they refused, she made a scene in the lobby.[39]

The agents were at the limits of their patience. Not only was she abusive, irrational, and ungrateful, but she was also becoming quite a bore, according to a memo to headquarters by the strained New York special agent in charge. "[S]he remains extremely talkative and inclined to dwell on her various problems to the exclusion of almost all other conversation," he wrote. She was a drunk, yes; but her problems went beyond alcohol. "[S]he is becoming increasingly emotionally unstable even when not under the influence of liquor." It *must* be menopause, he concluded.[40]

Nevertheless, J. Edgar Hoover and his men needed to protect her "credibility as a witness."[41] If the agents had not come to this conclusion on their own, Elizabeth was happy to connect the dots for them. She needed assistance and she needed money, she said, to obtain "the necessary peace of mind so that she would be a satisfactory witness in the forthcoming retrial of William Remington."[42] She told agents that if she did not get $1,000 immediately, "she would feel disinclined to cooperate in future interviews or to make further appearances as a witness."[43]

Bentley was not just asking for money; she was demanding it. Taking a cue from the heroic strikers of her Popular Front days, she staged a "sit-down strike" in Roy Cohn's office and refused to move until her demands were met. Most immediately, she required transportation; her car was wrecked, and she wanted the bureau to provide a chauffeur.[44]

Cohn called the New York FBI office and proceeded to beg. Could some agents check on her once a week and drive her around

Madison? Absolutely not, he was told. The FBI "would not and could not act as a nursemaid to Bentley." The bureau, moreover, was fed up with her constant demands. "It is the opinion of the Agents handling her," wrote Assistant Director Alan Belmont, "that she is probably cracking up emotionally."[45]

Maybe Cohn could find some Justice Department money to keep her happy, bureau officials suggested. Cohn did succeed in getting some funds "from a source whose identity he did not disclose" to help Elizabeth rent a car.[46]

But this was not enough. She wanted her $50 weekly payments continued, and she wanted a lump sum to settle her debts. With "great reluctance," New York bureau officials advised headquarters that they needed to pay her off "in order to assure that she will be a favorable government witness in the coming Remington retrial and other matters in which the Bureau may desire to utilize her services."[47] Headquarters grudgingly agreed, while admonishing the New York agents to learn to control their "increasingly neurotic" source.[48] "You should inform her," Hoover told his New York office, "that any further trouble may necessitate our terminating any further weekly payments to her."[49]

Once she realized that her blackmail had worked, Elizabeth's attitude changed dramatically. Special Agent Lester Gallaher told his superiors that her "mental and emotional condition" had improved "to a considerable extent" by the end of October. An agent who interviewed her in Madison the following month reported with relief that she was "most friendly and cooperative."[50]

Yet the money had begun flowing in too late. Between the time of her "sit-down strike" and the FBI decision to put her on the payroll, Elizabeth had done something that would seriously endanger the bureau's efforts to salvage her credibility. She had told someone that she was lying.

Elizabeth first met Harvey Matusow in the offices of her publisher on October 3, 1952. She made a habit of visiting the Devin-Adair offices that miserable fall, seeking payments of her dwindling royalties and encouragement during her "blue periods." One morning, she bumped into a charming young man peddling his own book. An ex-Communist like herself, he wanted to write a book called *The Reds Rock the Cradle*.[51] Like her, he had joined the Party out of idealism; also like her, he had abandoned it with a vengeance and become an FBI informer.

Matusow admired Elizabeth's spy queen "gimmick" and had come up with a gimmick of his own. He was, he said, the former leader of the Kremlin's youth movement in America. He had just finished a turn as an investigator for the Ohio Un-American Activities Commission and was about to embark on a lucrative campaign tour for Republican candidates. After some pleasant conversation, the spy queen and the Boy Stalinist made a date for that night. It was Matusow's twenty-sixth birthday.

That evening at the Rochambeau restaurant, the two star witnesses enjoyed a long dinner and several drinks. Throughout the meal, a few of Matusow's friends and acquaintances dropped by the table for short chats. Matusow dominated the conversation with long-winded denunciations of the Communist associations of various actors and activists, while Elizabeth nodded amiably in agreement. Her date had burst into national prominence thanks to his talent for exaggerating his own accomplishments, and that night was no exception. One woman who briefly joined the group found him to be "unstable mentally, an egomaniac, and an intense individual who demands everyone's attention."[52]

When Matusow and Elizabeth were alone, though, he gave her a chance to talk. She told him of the stress she was under. She could not find a job, she complained, because the FBI and Roy Cohn were constantly demanding her testimony, and she had already spent all her money from her book. As she told her story, she began to cry.

She angrily contrasted her position with that of her new friend. "[Y]ou are a man, you are young, you can go out and find a job," she said. "I can't. I have to continue doing this sort of thing." But how many times could she tell the same story? To keep her services in demand, she had to invent new revelations, she said. "I just have to continue to find information to testify about."[53]

SOMEWHAT HYSTERICAL

At least, that was Matusow's account of the evening. Many people later questioned it. He did not tell anyone about the conversation for more than two years. He and Elizabeth were the only ones present when she allegedly admitted to lying, and she vehemently denied that she had said any such thing.[54] Matusow, on the other hand, would later confess to being a "perpetual and habitual liar."[55]

But, in this particular case, there is much circumstantial evidence to support Matusow's version. The dinner took place right at the time when Elizabeth was most vulnerable. In early October 1952, she was frequently drunk, depressed, and bitter.[56] She had not yet received any assurance from the FBI that her $50 weekly payments would be continued or that her debts would be paid off. She must have felt comfortable with Matusow, whom she called "quite a character."[57] In contrast to the staid anti-Communists who normally took her to dinner, he liked to "do the town" and have fun.[58] And she had, after all, exaggerated her testimony in the Remington case and invented new allegations about the conveniently dead Harry Dexter White. Could she, in a moment of vulnerability and sympathy with her companion, have expressed some bitterness about the constant pressure for new revelations?

At one point in the dinner, according to Matusow, Elizabeth did something that was very consistent with her behavior that fall. She complained that she was not being adequately compensated for her services to the government. The FBI would need to find another witness, she said, because she was "sick of being used." If they wanted her testimony, she said, they would have to pay her for it.[59]

They did, of course, start paying her for it. Three months later, a mollified Elizabeth, secretly enjoying a weekly stipend from the U.S. government, testified at the second trial of William Remington.

Elizabeth's testimony could have been a disaster for the FBI and the prosecutors. Her depression, her self-pity, and her drinking had continued unabated. Every night of the week, she would go out with Matusow, who, though eighteen years her junior, was the new "quasi-man in her life," as he now describes it. They would go to a bar on the corner of Eleventh Street and Sixth Avenue, where Elizabeth would drink and Harvey would entertain her. At the end of the evening, he would take her home and pour her into bed. Every couple of weeks, they would sleep together, but usually she was too drunk. She talked of her pain at her "frivolous treatment" in the press. "She didn't understand the hostility," Matusow says. "She never got to the point where she could handle it." She also complained to him about her poor treatment by the FBI and her lack of true emotional support from her new anti-Communist friends. "She felt that she'd been used and abused," he says.[60] At one point, she confessed to her friend Ruth Matthews that sometimes she thought she "should step out in front of a car and settle everything."[61]

Once again, though, despite her emotional problems outside of court, Elizabeth performed well on the stand. As usual, she was somewhat snappish and impatient under cross-examination. When Remington's new attorney, Jack Minton, asked her who had helped her with her book, she replied with angry sarcasm: "I sat on a Manhattan telephone directory and wrote it myself." She corrected his word choice, the premise of some of his questions, and even the speed of his interrogation. "All right, never mind," the judge told her at one point. "Don't give him instructions."[62] But like his predecessors, Minton could not shake her self-confidence. She again succeeded in creating the illusion of a calm, controlled, and even patronizing witness, a Sunday school teacher somehow dropped into the middle of an espionage trial.

The FBI was pleased by her performance. The day after her testimony, the New York office told headquarters that she had "conducted herself in a creditable fashion" and recommended continuing her weekly payments for another three months. After the jury found Remington guilty, Hoover approved the recommendation.[63]

As the FBI prepared to continue Elizabeth's payments, though, she suddenly found another way to support herself. Increasingly concerned about Elizabeth's drinking, depression, and complaints

SOMEWHAT HYSTERICAL

about money, J. B. and Ruth Matthews worked assiduously to find her a job.[64] They finally succeeded in February 1953. At the urging of one of Elizabeth's Catholic sponsors in New York, the mother superior at the College of the Sacred Heart in Grand Coteau, Louisiana, offered her a job teaching political science.[65] Elizabeth was "ecstatic," Matusow says.[66] She accepted immediately.

The job at Sacred Heart symbolized a new chance. "She felt like her life could be put together again," Matusow remembers. She wanted to burrow down in her new role as teacher and protect herself, using the job as a "shell" against the outside world.[67]

Before she left for Louisiana, the FBI wanted to ask her more questions. Agents were hoping to gather enough evidence to prosecute Victor Perlo. Suddenly, though, Elizabeth had another attack of the "flu," this time requiring her hospitalization. The New York office asked for permission to pay her $100 "because of her hospital confinement and delayed departure and *since her cooperation is essential in any contemplated prosecutive action on Perlo.*"[68] Elizabeth, it appeared, was not entertaining any more questions unless she was paid for the answers.

Down in Grand Coteau, Elizabeth once again settled into the life of a schoolteacher. She lived on the grounds of the college, gave anti-Communist lectures in the surrounding areas, and earned a reputation as a fairly good teacher. But she soon discovered that she could not stay in a "shell" and shut out the rest of the world. The most controversial phase of her witnessing career was to come.

Richard Stokes had published more details about Harry Dexter White and the occupation currency "swindle" in a conservative magazine in late 1952. He gave considerably more information than Elizabeth had included in *Out of Bondage,* including the startling "fact" that her NKGB handler had *directed* her to obtain currency samples. Elizabeth had implied in her book that Ullmann had volunteered them to her. Moreover, Stokes claimed, when Moscow could not counterfeit the "samples" from Ullmann, the Russians had asked White to get the printing plates themselves.

"To the astonishment of Miss Bentley and Major Ullmann," he wrote, "White took this new commission in his stride." Finally, Stokes contended that the $2,000 Elizabeth had received from Gromov/Gorsky was actually a "bonus" for her part in wresting the plates from what the spymaster had called "American imbeciles."[69]

The occupation currency scandal quickly became a partisan issue. The battle lines in the fight over domestic Communism remained the same, but now the Republicans had the upper hand. The GOP had won back the White House and both houses of Congress in 1952, in part by branding the Democrats as soft on Communism. In the Senate, Joe McCarthy used his new chairmanship of the Government Operations Committee to continue his assaults on alleged Communists in the government. Alarmed by Elizabeth's new charges, a McCarthy subcommittee summoned her to Washington again.

She appeared on October 21, 1953, and proceeded to spin the most preposterous lies of her career. Before McCarthy, Senator Karl Mundt, and her old friend Roy Cohn, now the McCarthy committee's counsel, she confirmed every detail of Stokes's article. She said that she had received "instructions" from Akhmerov to "put pressure on Mr. White," who obliged by providing stolen currency samples. Later, the Soviets told her to demand the actual printing plates from White. She "took it for granted that the objective had been attained."[70]

The national media were astounded. So was the FBI. The bureau searched its files in vain for any references to occupation currency. When Special Agent Tom Spencer called her in Louisiana to ask why she had never mentioned this before, she responded that they must have forgotten.[71]

The reason she had not told the FBI earlier, Bruce Craig has concluded, is that the whole "scheme" was a complete fabrication.[72] During that summer in Westport in 1951, as she was struggling with her manuscript, she had met Stokes and learned about the currency disaster. Perhaps to please him, perhaps to make herself more important, she had "remembered" Harry White's role. She

SOMEWHAT HYSTERICAL

discussed the currency issue only briefly in *Out of Bondage*. But once Stokes wrote the details in a published article, she was forced to defend her story publicly.

The occupation currency policy in Germany was a disaster for the U.S. government. It was not, however, the result of espionage; it was the result of incompetence. By lying about her role in the scandal, Elizabeth obscured its true causes, prevented investigators from learning the truth, and exacerbated public paranoia about Soviet espionage.

Her deceptions stemmed from her decision to earn a living as a professional ex-spy. To keep her services in demand, she needed to continue to come up with fresh allegations. But when she invented new, demonstrably false charges, she gave ammunition to those who were hoping to destroy her credibility and cast doubt on her whole story. Her lies about White convinced some observers that she was lying about everything—and they were determined to prove it.

The currency hearings were just one part of Elizabeth's publicity blitz that fall. Dwight Eisenhower's attorney general, Herbert Brownell, raised her profile even higher in early November when he charged that the Truman administration had known about Elizabeth's charges against White and had still promoted him. Truman heatedly denied the allegations.[73]

In response, Hoover and Brownell went before a red-hunting congressional committee, Senator William Jenner's Internal Security Subcommittee, to refute the former president. In his testimony, Hoover—whom Jenner introduced as the "custodian of the nation's security"—for the first time publicly endorsed the veracity of his star informant. "All information furnished by Miss Bentley, which was susceptible to check, has proven to be correct," Hoover intoned.[74] The testimony thrilled Elizabeth and "made her feel like a different person," she told a bureau friend.[75]

As the partisan battle raged on, NBC's *Meet the Press* invited Elizabeth to discuss the Harry Dexter White furor. Under aggressive grilling by a panel of reporters, Elizabeth remained calm, self-confident, and noncommittal. Like a politician staying on message, she warned of the Soviet espionage threat without permitting the reporters to pin her down on specifics. She also praised Hoover and the FBI. Her supporters were pleased and proud. A bureau summary of her appearance lauded her conservative, intelligent responses to "loaded" questions and her "commendatory" remarks about the FBI. Hoover himself had listened to the program and remarked that she had done a "very good job."[76]

There was one moment in the show when Elizabeth briefly lost her composure. Robert Riggs of the Louisville *Courier-Journal* asked her why she had become an informer. "I dislike that term very much," Elizabeth snapped. The reporter explained rather lamely that he did not mean the word "in a derogatory sense." Elizabeth responded angrily on behalf of herself, Chambers, Budenz, Matusow, and all other ex-Communist witnesses who did not like to be called stool pigeons. "We were trying to help this government," she said. "We do not consider ourselves as tattletale people."[77]

During the interview, Elizabeth assured the panel that she had given all her information to the FBI.[78] One week later, though, she once again surprised her supporters with new charges. Capitalizing on the interest in White, she wrote a copyrighted series of articles in the *New York Daily Mirror*. She—or, more likely, her ghostwriters—used the staccato sentences and lurid modifiers of pulp fiction to describe how she was "cast in the Communist mold, blinded by its dogma, enslaved by its discipline." Luckily she had survived to tell the "terribly, incredibly dangerous" story of Soviet espionage in America.[79]

Most of the "specific acts of treachery" she described were recycled from her previous testimony and her book. But she also "dressed up" some of the incidents to give them more "reader appeal."[80] For example, she had earlier reported that the United States was "on the verge" of breaking the Soviet code, according to Lauchlin Currie. She had never before said that the Russians had any response to Currie's revelation. But now, in this version of the story, the delighted Russians had *directed* her to find out

SOMEWHAT HYSTERICAL

more details about the code.[81] In an internal memo to Hoover, the New York special agent in charge conceded that the code-breaking story was a "more colorful portrayal" of the incident than he had heard before and that Elizabeth "may be augmenting facts originally known to her" with information from her anti-Communist friends.[82]

She also charged that Silvermaster had instructions to seek help from White and Currie if he ran into any security problems. Elizabeth saw fit to reveal these Soviet instructions to the *Daily Mirror* readers but not to the FBI.[83] Finally, she played up White's role in the espionage ring, charging that he had urged Treasury Secretary Henry Morgenthau to exchange secret information with other government agencies. White then funneled all the secrets to the Soviets, she said. The New York agent again speculated that Elizabeth had picked up this information from other sources and decided to claim credit for it "because of the current interest in White."[84]

The FBI, although a bit befuddled by her new charges, was pleased by her "very favorable" references to the bureau.[85] This, in essence, was the source of the tension between Elizabeth and the FBI. On the one hand, the bureau was frustrated by her erratic behavior and confused by her exaggerations; on the other hand, Elizabeth served the bureau's political purposes. She warned of the Soviet threat, while praising the FBI's ability to handle that threat. Given her political value, Hoover was determined to protect her reputation and her credibility. She was not, however, going to make it easy for him.

When Hoover decided to give Elizabeth his imprimatur, it seemed to be a safe move. The one man who had challenged her credibility, William Remington, was discredited and behind bars. But a few months later, the FBI chief may have wished that he had been more equivocal. In February 1954, another man decided to follow Remington's lead and attempt to destroy her.

Elizabeth had briefly mentioned William Henry Taylor, a former Treasury Department economist, as a Silvermaster source in her

1945 statement to the FBI. She had named him publicly in her 1948 HUAC testimony, when she falsely implied that she knew him ("William was in the Treasury"). She charged that he passed information, including one of his own reports on wartime China, to Silvermaster. Like Remington and Brothman, Taylor was a small fish in Elizabeth's school of secret agents. But her charges against him carried symbolic importance. Now an employee at the International Monetary Fund, he was the last of her alleged sources to remain in public service.

The FBI and Congress had vigorously investigated the charges: at one point Taylor was simultaneously under subpoena to the House Un-American Activities Committee, the Senate Internal Security Subcommittee, Joe McCarthy's subcommittee, and federal grand juries in New York and Washington. The various inquiries turned up evidence that he had joined some leftist organizations and was friendly with several Bentley sources, including Silvermaster, White, and Ullmann.[86] But the case against him boiled down to Elizabeth's charges alone.

In September 1953, the International Organizations Employee Loyalty Board began investigating the case. Two months later, the *Washington Daily News* published a story on the inquiry.[87] Taylor decided to file suit against the Scripps-Howard newspaper—and to attack the credibility of his sole accuser.

Elizabeth's credibility, of course, was vulnerable to attack on many points. But the Taylor charges, ironically, were not among them. She had merely reported to the FBI what Silvermaster had told her—namely, that Taylor was his source. Scholars still do not know if Silvermaster told her the truth. Although Taylor's name has not surfaced in either the Soviet archives or the Venona cables, he could have been known by a cover name that has not yet been identified.[88] In any event, Elizabeth herself did not lie when she reported Silvermaster's information on Taylor.

But, to save his career and his reputation, Taylor had to demonstrate that Elizabeth was a liar. He hired Howard Dejean, a lawyer in Opelousas, Louisiana, to get a statement under oath from her. Dejean promptly subpoenaed her for a deposition.

SOMEWHAT HYSTERICAL

The subpoena reminded Elizabeth of the Remington case: the private detectives mucking about in her past, the embarrassing questions at the deposition, and the public exposure of her love life. She grew furious and irrational. The Communists, she said, were out to destroy her, and she was not going to let them.[89] The subpoena directed her to go to Dejean's law office on February 8. She did not show up.

When Dejean tried to start contempt proceedings against her, the entire force of the U.S. government swung into action, once again, to rescue its celebrated witness from her own self-destructive behavior. Elizabeth's open defiance of the legal system could have disastrous consequences for the FBI. Bentley was subject to a subpoena, wrote Assistant Director Alan Belmont, "the same as anyone else." Her continued intransigence "conceivably could affect her future value to the Government as a witness."[90]

Neither the FBI nor the Justice Department wanted her cited for contempt; and even the judge, "because of the prominence of Miss Bentley," did not want to cite her.[91] But he could not allow her "to flaunt the authority of his court."[92] The judge finally decided to persuade Dejean to delay contempt proceedings and serve her with another subpoena.

Dejean appeared to relish this challenge. On April 28, he burst into Elizabeth's classroom at Sacred Heart, dropped the subpoena on a table in the front of the room, and dashed out. Infuriated, Elizabeth told the New Orleans FBI that she had been "terrorized" by this "attack on my personal liberty." She wanted Dejean jailed for breaking and entering and for impersonating a U.S. marshal, even though, she admitted, "at no time did Dejean intimate that he was acting in the capacity of a United States Marshal." She demanded that the whole matter be brought to the personal attention of Hoover and the attorney general.[93] This was a delicate situation for the Justice Department. The prosecutors realized that she had no justification for ignoring the subpoena, yet they did not want "to alienate Elizabeth Bentley in any way."[94]

Their New York colleagues had warned the New Orleans agents that Elizabeth was a self-pitying "hypochondriac" who was frequently drunk and, even worse, "undergoing the menopause."[95] Now the Louisiana G-men had to agree that she was a handful. This lunatic woman, wrote a New Orleans agent, was "irrational and illogical and her talk impressed me as being that of a demented person."[96] Ominously, she seemed to be blackmailing the bureau into offering "some sort of protection or guidance to her." If they could not control her, an agent concluded, eventually she would commit the worst sin of all: "she will embarrass the Bureau."[97]

This could not be permitted. So, on May 17, the bureau convinced an angry, recalcitrant ex–spy queen to obey the subpoena and show up at Dejean's office in Opelousas.

Considering all of her efforts to avoid it, Elizabeth's deposition was something of an anticlimax. They could make her show up, but they could not make her answer any questions. She kept insisting that she needed time to consult her notes and documents. She conceded, though, that she would have to give a complete statement later.

Near the end of the interview, Taylor's lead attorney, former congressman Byron N. Scott, listed several documents that he wanted to question her about at a later date. In particular, he said, he would like to ask about *Out of Bondage*.

Elizabeth could stand it no longer. "I don't see why any reference is being made to my book," she blurted out. "That's fiction."

Dejean dashed over to a notary public and gleefully swore out an affidavit recounting the conversation.[98] Her critics could now pose a troubling question. If the book she had called "absolutely true" was actually "fiction," then why should they believe anything she said?

That summer she seemed free of the demons that had plagued her throughout the last few years. Lester Gallaher, another of her long-suffering contacts in the New York FBI office, wrote with relief that she seemed to be "in good spirits, friendly, and in a better state of mental health" than in the past. She was even able to make the daily commute to Manhattan, where she began work on her Ph.D. thesis at Columbia.[99] In the fall, she returned to Sacred Heart and the classroom, hoping for continued calm and quiet.

Elizabeth's emotional health was always fragile, though, and any stress could bring out her paranoia, her depression, and her tremendous thirst. Over the next academic year at Sacred Heart, the stresses multiplied along with the rum and whiskey bottles in her trash.[100]

The first blow came in November 1954. At Lewisburg Penitentiary in Pennsylvania, William Remington attracted the attention of a group of young thugs in the cell across the hall. They despised this young man of education and privilege who had inexplicably turned on his country and become a "damn Communist" and a "traitor." One morning, as Remington slept, they crept into his room and slugged him repeatedly with a brickbat. The handsome Ivy Leaguer died two days later. He was thirty-seven years old.[101]

Elizabeth had suffered from nightmares about betraying her friends. Now, she was indirectly responsible for one friend's death. There is no record, though, of her precise reaction. When reporters called, she refused to comment.[102]

She could not avoid commenting on her next public ordeal. The previous summer, the press had begun reporting that Harvey Matusow had changed sides—again. He claimed that he had lied under oath and now wanted to "undo some of the harm" wrought by his false testimony.[103] In January 1955, the ex-ex-Communist swore that he had testified falsely in two criminal trials. The next month, he decided to expose his old girlfriend as another false witness.

On February 21, Matusow, a favorite witness of the red-hunting right, returned to the august chambers of the U.S. Senate to tell the Internal Security Subcommittee that he had been a liar. And, Matusow added, he was not alone. Elizabeth had confessed to him that she did not tell the truth. He told the story of the emotional evening at the Rochambeau. "Miss Elizabeth Bentley, I believe, gave false testimony," he explained.[104]

Down in Grand Coteau, Elizabeth became hysterical. After telling New Orleans agents that she had no idea what Matusow was talking about, she called her old friend from New York, former special agent Joe Kelly. She was "considerably upset," Kelly reported, and apparently had been drinking.[105] She did not tell the straitlaced Kelly, who had been alarmed by her earlier accounts of her sexual activities, of the extent of Matusow's betrayal.[106] This was not just a case of a dinner companion revealing a confidence; this man had been her lover.

Viewing Matusow's charges against Bentley as a potential "planned attack on the Government's security program," agents began interviewing all possible eyewitnesses to the Bentley-Matusow dinner.[107] In the end, though, both Congress and the bureau's director decided to let the matter drop. While the FBI desperately wanted to refute Matusow's allegations, discretion seemed the better part of valor in this case. As the New York special agent in charge pointed out to Hoover, "[A]ny airing of that period of Bentley's life during October, 1952 would perhaps cause more serious embarrassment to the Bureau."[108]

Just as the Matusow allegations were fading from the front pages, William Taylor and his attorneys launched another assault on Elizabeth's credibility. On March 28, 1955, Taylor filed a 107-page brief with the International Organizations Employee Loyalty Board that challenged Elizabeth's veracity and the bureau's handling of her case. The chairman of the loyalty board told the FBI that Taylor's brief was "a diabolically clever attack on Bentley and the Government's loyalty program as a whole."[109]

Taylor pointed out several inconsistencies and embellishments in Elizabeth's story. Some of his charges were, as the FBI noted, "ridiculous and not worthy of comment."[110] For example, she had once mistakenly testified that she gave the Perlo group's dues to Golos, though he was dead by the time she took over the unit. She had also mangled some names and dates. Taylor merely highlighted her "ordinary, human, errors," Hayden Peake has concluded, "errors of no real consequence to the main thrust of her allegations."[111]

But though Taylor could not disprove the essence of her

SOMEWHAT HYSTERICAL

charges, he did point out some troubling contradictions in her tes‐
timony. She had deliberately obscured the history of her original
venture to the FBI, alleging that she had told her whole story to
the New Haven office in August 1945. The truth, as FBI memos
showed, was that she did not really confess until November. She
had lied about her October meeting with Gorsky, claiming that it
had been under FBI surveillance. Taylor also highlighted her ex‐
aggerated claims about D-Day, the Doolittle raid, and the occu‐
pation currency plates. Some of these embellishments may have
been accidental, but some were deliberate lies.

In an internal study, the FBI conceded that Elizabeth was guilty
of some "inconsistencies," but the bureau still strove to uphold
the truthfulness of its most celebrated informant.[112] When Taylor
raised seemingly immaterial points, the FBI ridiculed him. When
he raised more substantive ones, the FBI officials explained that
sometimes Elizabeth talked too fast and caused stenographers to
misquote her.[113] At any rate, the officials contended, it was only
natural for her to make some mistakes. "When considering the vol‐
ume of information furnished by Bentley, it is understandable why
she may have forgotten some items."[114] It was also understandable
why the bureau may have chosen to overlook some of her previous
lapses of judgment and memory.

As Elizabeth reeled from the Matusow and Taylor charges, she
received another blow from a completely unexpected source. Her
friend and protector, the U.S. government, accused her of cheating
on her taxes.

Elizabeth knew that the Internal Revenue Service had been in‐
vestigating her for some time. Back in 1952, the agency had noti‐
fied her that it did not accept her accountant's method of averag‐
ing her book royalties over a three-year period. She owed $3,700,
the government said. But Elizabeth had brushed off official de‐
mands for payment.[115] A woman who had manipulated the NKGB
and the FBI was not about to be intimidated by the IRS.

But she did not count on the efficiency and independence of
tax agents in the field. In June 1955, they confiscated her bank ac‐

count and notified the press. The mother superior at Sacred Heart then asked her to resign.[116]

Elizabeth's response to the newest crisis was typical. On the one hand, she was paranoid and delusional. She told the FBI that various people were out to get her, including Communists in the IRS. Yet she also cleverly combined appeals for sympathy with outright blackmail to get what she wanted.[117]

Ultimately, to resolve her tax case Elizabeth would call on the help of Roy Cohn; Deputy Attorney General William Rogers; bureau public relations chief Lou Nichols; Attorney General Herbert Brownell; the U.S. attorney in New Orleans; former Senate Internal Security Subcommittee counsel Robert Morris; Hearst columnist George Sokolsky; the IRS commissioner and his chief counsel; the chief counsel for the Treasury Department; two congressmen; J. Edgar Hoover; and countless FBI field agents. Her hold on all these powerful men was simple: they must help resolve her tax case quickly and quietly, or else she would "blow the lid off the administration."[118]

The pleas and threats worked. Officials in the Justice and Treasury Departments helped Elizabeth's lawyer to negotiate a compromise. Elizabeth agreed to pay the IRS $1,000, and the U.S. attorney agreed to beg the mother superior to take her back.[119] By September, she had returned to Sacred Heart.

The FBI helped her out by giving her $100, which Elizabeth accepted gratefully. She hoped, though, that the agents did not think "she was only cooperating with the Bureau for a financial return."[120] The agent who handled her asked for permission to give her another $50.[121] J. Edgar Hoover, exhausted by his ex–spy queen's repeated threats, responded that the bureau should not "interject itself into the midst of Bentley's difficulties by offering her additional funds at this time."[122]

Elizabeth's "difficulties" continued to increase in the new year. On January 4, 1956, the International Organizations Employee Loyalty Board ruled that there was no "reasonable doubt" of William Henry Taylor's loyalty. Byron Scott, Taylor's attorney, announced that the decision was "the strongest attack yet made on the credibility of Elizabeth Bentley."[123] The *Nation* was even harsher, proclaiming that the verdict "completely discredits the testimony given by Miss Bentley in this and other proceedings."[124]

This analysis was unfair. The chairman of the loyalty board explained that Elizabeth's veracity was not an issue because she had never met Taylor.[125] The board had simply decided that her secondhand reports were not sufficient cause to fire him.

But the decision certainly damaged Elizabeth's credibility as a witness. She told the FBI that Scott's statements were just "the opening barrage of an attack" on her integrity. Once again, she saw a Communist plot. There might very well be a connection, she said, "between Taylor and some officials of the United States Treasury Department" who were harassing her over her taxes.[126]

As she sank into depression and paranoia once again, Elizabeth learned some more bad news. She was about to lose her job. Sacred Heart, the nation's oldest Catholic women's college, planned to close its doors in June. Elizabeth called her friends in the New Orleans FBI office and confessed that she was "becoming very discouraged and despondent about her situation."[127]

It was even worse than she acknowledged. Sacred Heart was continuing its precollegiate school and academy, but Elizabeth had not been asked to stay on. There was too much "gossip" in the local area about her, including the maintenance men's tales of those rum and whiskey bottles in her garbage.[128]

Her powerful Catholic friends had helped her find two teaching positions, and she had been unable to keep either one. Though a competent teacher, she was unable or unwilling to abide by the strict moral code imposed on Catholic instructors. Deeply angered by her treatment at Sacred Heart, Elizabeth added one more "ex" to her résumé and abandoned the Catholic Church.[129]

As usual, she had a difficult time finding a school that would hire an informer. But just as she began to despair of making a living, she was given one more chance. In September 1956, she received word that the Cathedral School of St. Mary, a tony, Episcopal girls' school on Long Island, had offered her a job teaching sixth-grade home room and junior high English and French. It was not exactly the professorship she had hoped for, but it was a steady income. She accepted immediately and moved into a residence at the school.[130]

At St. Mary's, she "was one of the best-loved teachers at the school," according to a student. Some of the fifth-graders looked forward to being in her classroom the next year.[131] However, she could not escape her past. In January 1957, her picture appeared in the newspaper next to a review of the movie *The FBI Story*. The students suddenly realized the true identity of their middle-aged English teacher, and they began to gossip about her dangerous and glamorous past.

One of the girls in her class gushed to her parents: "Did you know Miss Bentley was a mistress . . . Did you know someone said they found a man murdered in her apartment when she was a Communist . . . Did you know that her Autobiography has some real 'moments' in it?"[132]

Her mother was not amused. She threatened to withdraw her two daughters from the school, complained to the bishop, and wrote to the national chairman of the Daughters of the American Revolution. The parents had not been allowed to vote on whether they wanted their daughters "subjected" to a person who might inspire delinquency in minors, she objected. "[S]he became a stool-pigeon to save her own neck—and I repeat—she has been a weak and twisted personality."[133]

The parent protest was successful. At a school dinner in June, the dean told Elizabeth that they would not invite her back to teach the next year. The school was not "entirely satisfied" with her as a teacher. Elizabeth was "not too happy about this," another teacher told the FBI, but "there was nothing she could do."[134]

The Cathedral School of St. Mary was Elizabeth's last chance at true respectability. Once again depressed and impoverished, she moved back to Connecticut. Eventually, the former spy, professor, and shipping company executive found a clerical job at a con-

SOMEWHAT HYSTERICAL

struction company. On nights and weekends she took courses for a teaching credential at Trinity College in Hartford.

One night after class, she had a "blackout" as she drove home. When she regained consciousness, she was back at the college. She had suffered from blackouts, the "black influenza," the "flu," a "virus," and "too much penicillin" many times in the past, but this was different. She was taken to a hospital and given psychiatric care. After a week, a doctor released her and allowed her to resume her job and her classes. The hospital bills were enormous, and she had to sell her house in Madison—the only house she had ever owned—to pay them. Her psychiatrist advised her to stop dwelling on her past and to start a new life for herself.[135]

Elizabeth decided to take his advice. After thirteen years of working as a bureau informant—of threatening, blackmailing, and, of course, helping J. Edgar Hoover and his men—she decided that she wanted out. For a time, the agents had been her friends, confessors, chauffeurs, therapists, and supervisors. But their constant visits also reminded her of the mistakes she had made, of the mistakes that continued to haunt her and prevent her from finding happiness.

She did not make the break easily or without regrets. On May 26, 1958, she chatted amiably with New Haven FBI agents and impressed them with her "friendly attitude" as they set up a meeting in two days to go over some cases with her.[136]

That night, though, she thought over the meeting and its implications. Was this going to be her life? Was she always going to meet with crewcut agents, stare at photographs, answer their questions, relive the past? The next morning, she showed up at the New Haven office and said that she did not want to meet with agents—not the next day, not ever. She said she "wanted to make a complete break with her past life, that she wanted to build a new life as a school teacher, that interviews with agents, INS and Government committees about her past always served to keep her in a highly nervous state." She was sick of this "delving into the past" and of the severe headaches that came with it.[137]

The FBI agents remonstrated with her: it was her patriotic duty, after all. But she was not convinced. The next day, she arrived at her appointment "in a highly nervous state" and told the agents that she was no longer available for interviews. Her "mental health" could not stand the repeated questions. She was done working for the FBI.[138]

After some consideration, Hoover decided to give his "highly nervous and tense" informant some space. The FBI kept tabs on Elizabeth but did not contact her for nearly a year. In April 1959, New Haven agents broke the long period of silence by calling on her at her rooming house in Hartford, where she had a temporary job teaching English and French at a nearby Catholic school.

She greeted the agents pleasantly, then became evasive. As she concluded the conversation, she grew "very nervous, emotional, and non-responsive," in the words of the FBI agent.[139] Perhaps her "highly emotional state" was due to menopause, one official conjectured.[140] (According to the FBI, Elizabeth Bentley had the longest menopause in recorded history.) In any event, the bureau agreed to leave her alone.

But Elizabeth discovered that she still needed the FBI's help. As she searched for a teaching job, she found that others would not join her in agreeing to forget her past. In August 1959, just a few months after she had refused to help the FBI, she wrote to her hero: the man himself, J. Edgar Hoover. "Lately it has come to my attention," she told the director, "that there are still some unenlightened people who still believe that I am not a loyal American." Could he please write her a letter of recommendation "which would for once and all allay doubts in the minds of school superintendents and principals and the general public as well?"[141]

Hoover wrote a letter quoting his Jenner committee testimony, stating that her information appeared to be accurate.[142] It was hardly a ringing endorsement of her loyalty, but it pleased Elizabeth. It also helped her to get her next—and final—job. In the fall of 1959, Elizabeth Bentley, Vassar graduate and college and prep school instructor, snagged a job at a penal institution for girls.

Long Lane School in Middletown was not really a jail. As Elizabeth explained to her new pen pal, Hoover, "[W]e have no bars, no wardens and we attempt to rehabilitate the young through kindly and understanding discipline." She hoped, in this small way, to "build up good citizens," defeat Communism, and "contribute to a better America."[143]

Hoover responded politely to Elizabeth. It was in his interest to do so. After all, as an FBI official noted for the file at the bottom of his letter, "It is believed we should express an interest in the continued progress of Miss Bentley inasmuch as her services may still be needed at some future date."[144]

Indeed, her services were needed. The next year, the director suggested that the New Haven agents might try contacting her again to ask her assistance in identifying more potential Communists and spies.[145] When the agents came by, Elizabeth was "friendly and cooperative" and "expressed praise for the Director." After agreeing to answer questions about cases of the "utmost importance," she told them that she had received her teaching certificate and a master's in education. She needed to find summer employment, though. Did the agents know if the FBI approved applicants at the General Dynamics plant in Groton?

The agents believed that her desire for a job at a defense contractor—and her apparent fear that the FBI could blackball her from such a job—might have contributed to her "cooperative attitude."[146] In the relationship between Elizabeth and the FBI, it was always hard to determine who was using whom.

Epilogue

n her last years, Elizabeth continued her periodic consultations with the FBI and her cordial correspondence with the director. She taught classes at the reform school, put out the school publication, and avoided the public spotlight.[1] At one point, the school administration told her that although she was a wonderful teacher, she would be "happier" elsewhere.[2] This time, however, Elizabeth was able to weather the storm and keep her job.

She desperately sought connection with the few friends she had left. She plaintively wrote to Ruth and J. B. Matthews that she had not heard from them in a "long time."[3] When George Sokolsky wrote her a perfunctory note, she gushed that she could not express "how much your kind and understanding letter meant to me." She wanted to see him very much, she said, and she would make a trip to New York as soon as she was free of the "virus" that had been troubling her.[4]

On November 18, 1963, at the age of fifty-five, she entered Grace New Haven Community Hospital. She underwent surgery on December 2 and died the next day. The official cause of death was abdominal cancer.[5] One of the frequent causes of this condition is chronic alcoholism.

She had notified the New Haven FBI office—the site of her first, tentative attempts at defection—of her illness. The agents noted her "warm regard and affection toward the Bureau to the end." Her funeral, held at the Holy Trinity Episcopal Church in Middletown, was as sad and lonely as her life. Although the service was announced in a local newspaper, the only people who came were those who could not deny their obligations to her. In the cavernous church sat a few relatives and some special agents of the FBI.[6]

Two years earlier, when Whittaker Chambers had died, the *National Review* had put out a special memorial issue. *Time* had devoted almost two full pages to recounting and celebrating the life of its most famous editor. When Elizabeth died, the *National Review* allotted a paragraph for her obituary, while *Time* gave her two sentences in its "Milestones" section. The magazine identified her as a "frumpy New Englander."[7]

All of the obituaries misunderstood her role as a spy. They called her a "mistress of master-spy Jacob Golos" and a "courier," rather than giving her the credit (or blame) she deserved for controlling dozens of agents. Most of the newspapers continued to poke fun at her by emphasizing her "dowdy" appearance and quoting some of her shallower assessments of Communism. Lacking access to secret documents, the reporters failed to communicate the monumental importance of her defection for Soviet espionage.[8]

The obituaries also underestimated her political importance. *Time* noted that she "helped convict" Remington and the Rosenbergs. Yet she had done far more than that: she had toppled the first in the row of dominoes that led to the convictions of Hiss and the Rosenbergs and to the deaths of Remington and Harry Dexter White. The *New York Times* observed that her accusations had helped "set the tone" of American political life in the 1950s.[9] But they had also helped define the partisan warfare of the early period of the Cold War and discredit the radical and liberal causes that she had supported for years.

Many obituaries painted a picture of a flighty female, an "overwrought neurotic woman" in search of a man to take care of her.[10] In part this was a reaction to the patently false image she had constructed of herself as a naive and conventional "housewife." On the other hand, she had no choice but to portray herself this way. She needed sympathy, and in the 1950s she figured that this was the best way to get it.

The real Elizabeth Bentley had been a strong woman who defied limits, laws, and traditions. Her cousin remembers her as "a women's libber before there was women's lib."[11] She smoked when the university forbade it; she drank when her father crusaded against drink. She ran a shipping company at a time when women had few opportunities in business. She enjoyed sex and had lots of it, even when her family and neighbors were scandalized by her behavior. She deceived and manipulated the NKGB, the most brutal and murderous secret police agency in the world, and lived to tell the tale.

She had also outwitted the FBI. In public, J. Edgar Hoover extolled her truthfulness; in their secret memos, though, agents called her "demented," "hysterical," "demanding," and "neurotic." Yet she understood that they needed her as much or more than she needed them. She used this knowledge to her advantage for years, until the constant reliving of her mistakes proved too traumatic.

Elizabeth always seemed to hope that she could escape the consequences of her decisions to betray her country and to betray her friends. To an extent, she succeeded. She calculated correctly that she could save herself from NKGB assassins by going to the FBI. She also arranged her defection so that she never had to spend a single day in jail. But she made a fatal error in assuming that she could profit from her crimes by ignoring the FBI's admonitions and taking her story to the newspapers.

Not only did she fail to make much money, but she also found herself ridiculed in the press. She realized, with mounting anger, that her gender prevented her from achieving the success of her fellow ex-Communists who happened to be men. Her bitterness, mixed with her guilt, exacerbated her substantial emotional problems and her addiction to alcohol.

She had many regrets. "I think if she had it all to do over again, she wouldn't do it," says Harvey Matusow.[12] Elizabeth had never been in "bondage" to anyone or anything; she made her own decisions. In the end, she paid the price for them.

Notes

PREFACE

1. Eleven prominent college textbooks of American history discuss defector Whittaker Chambers but do not mention Bentley. See Faragher et al., *Out of Many;* Henretta et al., *America's History;* Brinkley, *The Unfinished Nation;* Boyer et al., *Enduring Vision;* Nash and Jeffrey, eds., *The American People;* Divine et al., *America, Past and Present;* Garraty and Mc-Caughey, *The American Nation;* Blum et al., *The National Experience;* Thernstrom, *A History of the American People;* Norton et al., *A People and a Nation;* and Jordan and Litwack, *The United States.*
2. Goodman, *The Committee,* 245; Carr, *The House Committee on Un-American Activities,* 90.
3. Phone interview, Harvey Matusow, July 11, 2001.
4. "Memorandum of Conversation with Mrs. Hinckley," August 23, 1950, Rauh Papers, Library of Congress.
5. Phone interview, Jack Danahy, July 9, 2001.

CHAPTER ONE

1. Bentley's family tree can be partially traced at www.ancestry.com and www.familysearch.com. I am also indebted to Roger Sherman genealogists Al Streit and Robert Corey for helping me research this question.
2. Dan Anderson, "Elizabeth Bentley Stirs Home Town," *New York Sun,* August 4, 1948; Bentley/Turrill marriage certificate, courtesy of New Milford Town Clerk, in author's possession. The spellings are taken from the certificate. May Turrill's name is rendered as Mary in some documents, but her nephew says the family called her May. Phone interview, John Turrill, August 2, 2001.
3. Anderson, "Elizabeth Bentley Stirs Home Town."
4. Ibid.
5. Cecil B. Dickson, "Key Witness in Congress Red Spy Quiz Tells of Happy School Days in Rochester," *Rochester Democrat and Chronicle,* August 14, 1948.

6. Bentley's NKGB autobiography, 229. I am very grateful to Allen Weinstein for sending me Alexander Vassiliev's notes on this document, which is located in the closed KGB archives in Moscow.

7. "Spy Queen Bookish Girl, Says Aunt," *New York Journal-American,* July 29, 1948.

8. Bentley, *Out of Bondage,* 6.

9. "Miss Bentley Dimly Recalled as '25 Graduate of East High," *Rochester Democrat & Chronicle,* August 4, 1948.

10. "Key Witness in Congress."

11. "Miss Bentley Dimly Recalled."

12. "Key Witness in Congress"; Bentley's NKGB autobiography, 229.

13. Bentley, *Out of Bondage,* 69.

14. On changes for young women in the 1920s, see Fass, *The Damned and the Beautiful,* 260–326.

15. Richard Green to Joseph Rauh, October 28, 1948, Rauh Papers, Library of Congress.

16. Quoted in Peake, afterword to *Out of Bondage,* 223.

17. Report, November 16, 1945, Silvermaster file, FBI, 65-56402-25, 7.

18. "Spy Queen Bookish Girl, Says Aunt."

19. U.S. Senate Subcommittee on Immigration and Naturalization, *S. 1832,* May 13, 1949, 108.

20. Cohen, *When the Old Left Was Young,* 196–97.

21. Bentley testimony in grand jury records of "United States of America vs. Alger Hiss," February 16, 1949, 6442.

22. Quoted in Joanne Bentley, *Hallie Flanagan,* 118.

23. Ibid., 100–102, 114.

24. "Miss Bentley Dimly Recalled"; "Key Witness in Congress."

25. Bentley's NKGB autobiography, 230.

26. Silvermaster file, 65-56402-25, 5.

27. Solomon, *In the Company of Educated Women,* 133.

28. Bentley's NKGB autobiography, 231.

29. Cedar Hill Cemetery records, Hartford, Connecticut.

30. For Bentley's sexual activities in Florence, see "Memorandum of Conversation with Dr. Lombardo," October 4, 1950, Rauh Papers, and Peake, afterword, 280 n. 47.

31. For the records of the disbursements of her financial aid, see the records dated November 3, 1933, and February 13, March 22, May 14, and June 9, 1934, Archives, Università di Firenze.

32. Quoted in Gary May, *Un-American Activities,* 78.

33. Rauh to Green, October 26, 1949, Rauh Papers; "Memorandum of Con-

versation with Mrs. Hinckley," August 23, 1950, ibid.; Green to Rauh, October 28, 1948, ibid.

34. Hayden Peake and Jack Danahy have heard these rumors. Phone interview with Danahy, July 9, 2001; discussion with Peake, April 26, 2001. There is no reference to abortions in the FBI files, but Danahy says that such personal information would have been kept separate and confidential.

35. See, for example, memo re: Gregory, October 23, 1950, Silvermaster file, 65-14603-4318.

36. Phone interview with Harvey Matusow, July 11, 2001.

37. See, for example, Green to Rauh, October 28, 1948, and the discussion of her alcoholism in Chapter 8.

38. Elizabeth admitted her membership in the GUF in "United States vs. William Walter Remington" (1951), 1092. On Italian fascism's appeal for Americans, see Diggins, *Mussolini and Fascism,* passim.

39. Reale Università degli Studi di Firenze, *Annuario per l'Anno Accademico 1933–1934,* 55, 270, 320, Archives, Università di Firenze.

40. "Memorandum of Conversation with Dr. Lombardo."

41. Rebecca West, *The New Meaning of Treason,* 88.

42. Archivio centrale dello Stato, Roma: Ministero dell'Interno, Direzione generale pubblica sicurezza, Divisione affari generali e riservati, categoria A1, 1936, busta 15, Casella prof. Mario; Archivio centrale dello Stato, Roma: Ministero dell'Interno, Polizia politica, fascicoli personali, pacco 259, Mario Casella.

43. "Memorandum of Conversation with Dr. Lombardo." In her dealings with the FBI, Bentley denied most of the allegations made about her behavior in Florence, including the suicide attempt. However, William Remington's attorneys found sources to corroborate many of the charges.

44. Green to Rauh, October 28, 1948. Bentley's master's thesis, "Il Bel Gherardino," is available in the rare books department of the Columbia University Library.

45. Bentley, *Out of Bondage,* 3.

46. Hope Hale Davis, "Looking Back at My Years in the Party," *New Leader,* February 11, 1980, 13.

47. Bentley, *Out of Bondage,* 3.

48. Memo re: Mrs. Lini Moerkirk Stouman, December 5, 1945, Silvermaster file, 65-56402-118.

49. Bentley, *Out of Bondage,* 5.

50. Ibid., 7.

51. Ibid., 10–18.

52. Ibid., 18, 19–27.

53. Klehr, *The Heyday of American Communism,* 179–81.

54. For histories of the Communist Party of the U.S.A. that tend to emphasize Soviet control, see Klehr, *The Heyday of American Communism;* Haynes and Klehr, *The American Communist Movement;* and Klehr, Haynes, and Firsov, *The Secret World of American Communism.* For studies that stress the uniquely American aspects of the Party, see Isserman, *Which Side Were You On?;* Kelley, *Hammer and Hoe;* Ottanelli, *The Communist Party of the United States;* and Lieberman, *My Song Is My Weapon.*

55. Kazin, *Starting Out in the Thirties,* 85.

56. Silvermaster file, 65-14603-4318. See also "Memorandum of Conversation with Mrs. Hinckley."

57. On gender and sexuality in the CPUSA, see Rosalyn Baxandall, "The Question Seldom Asked: Women and the CPUSA," in Brown et al., *New Studies in the Politics and Culture of U.S. Communism;* Horowitz, *Betty Friedan and the Making of the Feminine Mystique,* 129–32; Gosse, "'To Organize in Every Neighborhood, in Every Home'"; Trimberger, "Women in the Old and New Left"; Dixler, "The Woman Question"; and Weigand, *Red Feminism,* 15–27.

58. Wechsler, *Age of Suspicion,* 59.

59. Quoted in Healey and Isserman, *Dorothy Healey Remembers,* 60.

60. Gornick, *The Romance of American Communism,* 42, 91, 56, 132.

61. "Will Dr. Butler Act?," *Nation,* November 7, 1934, 523. See also related articles on the controversy, all in the *Nation:* "Fascism at Columbia University," November 7, 1934, 530–31; "President Butler and Fascism," November 14, 1934, 550–52; "The Casa *Is* Fascist," January 30, 1935, 117–18, 129–30; "Fascist Victory at Columbia," April 3, 1935, 377–78, 388–89.

62. "Columbia Student, Refused Loan, Charges Discrimination by Officials of Casa Italiana," *Columbia Spectator,* October 17, 1935.

63. "Fascism at Columbia," *Columbia Spectator,* October 18, 1935.

64. "Police Action Averts Riot at Casa Italiana Protest; Blackjack Attempt Fails," *Columbia Spectator,* October 21, 1935.

65. "Youth in Soviet 'Enthusiastic,' Says Bingham," *Columbia Spectator,* November 6, 1935.

66. "Socialism and War," *Columbia Spectator,* November 7, 1935.

67. This narrative of Bentley's encounters with Poyntz is taken from the November 30, 1945, Bentley statement to the FBI, 65-56402-220, 3–4; Bentley, *Out of Bondage,* 45–84, passim; and Peake, afterword, 228. Bentley

spelled the name "Glazer," but Poyntz's friends Herbert Solow and Carlo Tresca wrote it "Glaser."

68. Tanenhaus, *Whittaker Chambers,* 131.

69. For descriptions of the underground, see ibid., 79–81; and Haynes and Klehr, *Venona,* 57–73.

70. Tanenhaus, *Whittaker Chambers,* 131.

71. See draft manuscript by Carlo Tresca, "The Communazi Lady Vanishes," in Poyntz file, box 10, Solow Papers, Hoover Institution. See also draft manuscript by Solow, "One Year of the Poyntz Mystery," and personal memo titled "Graubard Interview" in the same file.

72. Bentley, *Out of Bondage,* 48.

73. Ibid., 52–55.

74. See letter, Mark Graubard to Herbert Solow, November 8, 1939, Poyntz file, box 10, Solow Papers.

75. Bentley, *Out of Bondage,* 74.

76. Ibid., 75–76.

77. Gitlow, *The Whole of Their Lives,* 333–34.

78. Gallagher, *All the Right Enemies,* 174–75. See also Cave Brown and Mac-Donald, *On a Field of Red,* 345; Tanenhaus, *Whittaker Chambers,* 131; Tresca, "The Communazi Lady Vanishes"; and Solow, "One Year of the Poyntz Mystery."

79. Bentley's NKGB autobiography, 242–43; Bentley, *Out of Bondage,* 78–91; November 30 Bentley statement, 5–7; Peake, afterword, 229.

80. Compare *Out of Bondage,* 92, with Bentley's NKGB autobiography, 242–43.

81. Wechsler, *Age of Suspicion,* 81.

82. Bentley, *Out of Bondage,* 93.

83. November 30 Bentley statement, 9.

84. Bentley, *Out of Bondage,* 94–95.

CHAPTER TWO

1. Bureau of Investigation Reports, NARA, College Park, Md., RG 65, Box 2, File 61-39; Box 42, 61-1195; Box 68, 61-2469; FBI Reports in DOJ Case File 149-189, RG 60, NARA; Weinstein and Vassiliev, *The Haunted Wood,* 85; Bentley, *Out of Bondage,* 206–8; Cave Brown and MacDonald, *On a Field of Red,* 341; Haynes and Klehr, *Venona,* 94.

2. Bureau of Investigation Reports, RG 65; Haynes and Klehr, *Venona,* 94.

3. Letter, Kuzbas president to secretary of the Comintern, October 8, 1925, 515-1-507-111, RGASPI Archives, Library of Congress; letter, Golos to C. E.

Ruthenberg, April 20, 1926, 515-1-720-49, ibid.; Weinstein and Vassiliev, *The Haunted Wood,* 85–86; report, January 7, 1946, Silvermaster file, FBI, 65-56402-420, 4; Primakov, *Ocherki Istorii Rossiyskoy Vneshney Razvedki.*

4. Weinstein and Vassiliev, *The Haunted Wood,* 85.

5. Primakov, *Ocherki Istorii Rossiyskoy Vneshney Razvedki.*

6. Cave Brown and MacDonald, *On a Field of Red,* 341.

7. Memo, Coyne to Ladd, December 20, 1945, Silvermaster file, 65-56402-133, 4.

8. Weinstein and Vassiliev, *The Haunted Wood,* 86.

9. Ibid., 94; Primakov, *Ocherki Istorii Rossiyskoy Vneshney Razvedki.* For the sake of simplicity, I have used "NKGB" throughout this manuscript to refer to the Soviet intelligence service. However, the agency went through several name changes during Elizabeth's service. It was the NKVD from 1934 to 1941, then the NKGB for a brief time, then the NKVD again from 1941 to 1943, then the NKGB again from 1943 to 1946. After three more name changes, it became the KGB in 1954 and remained so named until the collapse of the Soviet Union in 1991. Benson and Warner, *Venona,* ix n. 6.

10. Budenz, *Men without Faces,* 39.

11. Weinstein and Vassiliev, *The Haunted Wood,* 224.

12. Cave Brown and MacDonald, *On a Field of Red,* 341.

13. Celia Golos found a job as a librarian near Moscow and received a state pension after Golos's death. Primakov, *Ocherki Istorii Rossiyskoy Vneshney Razvedki.*

14. Quoted in "Memorandum of Conversation with Golas' Relatives," October 10, 1950, Rauh Papers, Library of Congress.

15. Bentley, *Out of Bondage,* 94–96. Ironically, Golos was apparently influenced by Edward Bellamy's metaphor of an unsteady, overcrowded coach for *capitalist* society. See Bellamy's *Looking Backward,* 5–6.

16. Bentley, *Out of Bondage,* 94–98.

17. Ibid., 98.

18. Ibid., 99.

19. Report, January 7, 1946, Silvermaster file, 65-56402-420.

20. Bentley, *Out of Bondage,* 99–100.

21. Ibid., 102.

22. Ibid., 103–4.

23. November 30, 1945, Bentley statement to the FBI, 65-56402-220, 10.

24. Bentley, *Out of Bondage,* 104–5.

25. Bentley testimony in grand jury records of "United States of America vs. Alger Hiss," March 30, 1948, 2762.

26. See Haynes and Klehr, *The American Communist Movement,* 92–94; and Isserman, *Which Side Were You On?,* 32–38.

27. Bentley, *Out of Bondage,* 106–7.

28. Tanenhaus, *Whittaker Chambers,* 24–33, 40–56.

29. Ibid., 46.

30. Ibid., 56–60, 70–81.

31. Chambers, *Witness,* 335–36.

32. For the case against Hiss, see Weinstein, *Perjury;* Tanenhaus, *Whittaker Chambers;* Maria Schmidt, "The Hiss Dossier," *New Republic,* November 8, 1993, 17–20; Eric Breindel, "Hiss's Guilt," *New Republic,* April 15, 1996, 18–20; Eric Breindel and Herbert Romerstein, "Hiss: Still Guilty," *New Republic,* December 30, 1996, 12–14; Theodore Draper, "The Case of Cases," *New York Review of Books,* November 20, 1997, 13–18; and Weinstein and Vassiliev, *The Haunted Wood,* 4–10, 38–49. For defenses of Hiss, see Theoharis, *Beyond the Hiss Case;* Smith, *Alger Hiss;* Eric Alterman, "I Spy with One Little Eye," *Nation,* April 29, 1996, 20–24; and Lowenthal, "Venona and Alger Hiss." Other, more dated defenses of Hiss include Zeligs, *Friendship and Fratricide;* Levitt and Levitt, *A Tissue of Lies;* Jowitt, *The Strange Case of Alger Hiss;* Tony Hiss, *Laughing Last;* and Cook, *The Unfinished Story of Alger Hiss.* Alger Hiss has written his own defense in *Recollections of a Life* and *In the Court of Public Opinion.*

33. Tanenhaus, *Whittaker Chambers,* 123, 131; Weinstein and Vassiliev, *The Haunted Wood,* 10–11.

34. Weinstein and Vassiliev, *The Haunted Wood,* 89–90. Weinstein and Vassiliev received special access to NKGB documents as part of an arrangement between their publisher and Russian intelligence. The Russians have since closed the archives, so other researchers cannot check the documents cited in *The Haunted Wood.*

35. Ibid., 90.

36. Primakov, *Ocherki Istorii Rossiyskoy Vneshney Razvedki.*

37. Tanenhaus, *Whittaker Chambers,* 136, 144.

38. Ibid., 159–60.

39. Chambers, *Witness,* 463–66.

40. "Underground Espionage Agent," notes made by A. A. Berle on September 2, 1939, reproduced in the first Hiss Trial, "United States of America vs. Alger Hiss," 3325.

41. The diary entry is reprinted in Berle, *Navigating the Rapids,* 250.

42. Ibid., 598.

43. "Berle Testifies in Chambers Case," *New York Times,* August 31, 1948.

44. Memo, Ladd to director, December 29, 1948, Hiss-Chambers file, FBI, 74-1333-659, 2.
45. November 30 Bentley statement, 12; Bentley, *Out of Bondage,* 111.
46. November 30 Bentley statement, 12; Bentley, *Out of Bondage,* 112.
47. Bentley, *Out of Bondage,* 117.
48. Ibid., 116.
49. Primakov, *Ocherki Istorii Rossiyskoy Vneshney Razvedki.*
50. Elizabeth told this story both in her published memoir and, much more important, in her secret autobiography for the NKGB. Since there was no reason for her to lie about the plea bargain to the Soviets, who presumably knew all about it, she must have believed the story to be true. See Weinstein and Vassiliev, *The Haunted Wood,* 87, and Bentley, *Out of Bondage,* 118–19. The National Archives cannot find any files relating to Golos's plea bargain; so her account is impossible to verify.
51. Bentley, *Out of Bondage,* 119.
52. Bentley described this as a weeks-long "trial" in her autobiography, but in fact it was merely a grand jury investigation. See "Corporation Is Accused as Russ Agent," *Washington Post,* March 14, 1943, and "Soviet Agent Pleads Guilty, Is Fined $500," *Washington Post,* March 15, 1943.
53. Haynes and Klehr, *Venona,* 85.
54. Bentley, *Out of Bondage,* 120.
55. Haynes and Klehr, *Venona,* 96.

CHAPTER THREE

1. Brothman testimony in grand jury records of "United States of America vs. Alger Hiss," July 22, 1947, 851–74. Bentley later said that Brothman had been stealing the blueprints from Republic Steel, but actually they were the property of his own firm, Republic Chemical Machinery Company. For an overview of industrial espionage by the Soviets in the United States before the Cold War, see Sibley, "Soviet Industrial Espionage," 95–107.
2. November 30, 1945, Bentley statement to the FBI, 65-56402-220, 13.
3. Ibid., 14; Bentley, *Out of Bondage,* 130.
4. For more on Bentley's role in leading the FBI to Brothman and Gold, see Radosh and Milton, *The Rosenberg File,* 22, 33–36.
5. Bentley, *Out of Bondage,* 126.
6. Ibid., 125.
7. Ibid., 126.
8. Richard Green to Joseph Rauh, November 15, 1948, Rauh Papers, Library of Congress.

9. Bentley, *Out of Bondage*, 121.

10. See "Trotsky's Guard Discovered Slain," *New York Times*, June 26, 1940.

11. Bentley, *Out of Bondage*, 121.

12. November 30 Bentley statement, 14.

13. Ibid., 15. While it is doubtful that the OGPU issued identity cards for its agents to carry around in their wallets, it is certainly plausible that Elizabeth saw *something* in those files that prompted her to question her lover about his ties to Soviet intelligence.

14. Bentley, *Out of Bondage*, 129.

15. Ibid.

16. November 30 Bentley statement, 15. See also her testimony in grand jury records of "United States of America vs. Alger Hiss," March 30, 1948, 2798, and February 16, 1949, 6293.

17. November 30 Bentley statement, 15.

18. Haynes and Klehr, *Venona*, 151.

19. Bentley, *Out of Bondage*, 140.

20. Letter, Edward Scheidt to director, January 31, 1947, Silvermaster file, FBI, 65-56402-1976.

21. Bentley, *Out of Bondage*, 127, 133.

22. Coy, *The Prices and the Moores*, 154. See also Uesugi, "'Jim Crow Must Go!,'" 7–8.

23. Interview with Mildred Price Coy by Mary Frederickson, April 26, 1976, Southern Oral History Program Collection, 22.

24. Interview with Mary Price Adamson by Mary Frederickson, April 19, 1976, Southern Oral History Program Collection, 67–71.

25. Price took the Fifth Amendment when asked about Communist Party membership. See Mary Price testimony in grand jury records of "United States of America vs. Alger Hiss," December 3, 1947, 2582.

26. Mary Price Adamson interview, 74.

27. Bentley, *Out of Bondage*, 131; description of Mary Price taken from Coy, *The Prices and the Moores*, 317, and photo between pages 288 and 289.

28. Bentley, *Out of Bondage*, 131.

29. U.S. Senate Investigations Subcommittee, *Export Policy and Loyalty*, July 30, 1948, 27. For evidence of Price's spying, see November 30 Bentley statement, 16, and Venona messages 868, New York to Moscow, June 8, 1943, and 1065, New York to Moscow, July 28, 1944, National Security Agency.

30. Bentley, *Out of Bondage*, 131–32.

31. Ibid., 138; November 30 Bentley statement, 16–17; Haynes and Klehr, *Venona*, 113–14.

32. Bentley, *Out of Bondage,* 142.

33. November 30 Bentley statement, 17; Bentley, *Out of Bondage,* 144.

34. Bentley, *Out of Bondage,* 144.

35. Ibid., 145.

36. November 30 Bentley statement, 21; Bentley, *Out of Bondage,* 146.

37. Bentley, *Out of Bondage,* 148.

38. Ibid., 146.

39. Ibid., 147.

40. Andrew and Mitrokhin, *The Sword and the Shield,* 132.

41. Nigel West, *Venona,* 227.

42. Bentley, *Out of Bondage,* 149–51; Haynes and Klehr, *Venona,* 131.

43. Weinstein and Vassiliev, *The Haunted Wood,* 157. Other sources contend that Silvermaster began spying after the Nazi invasion of the USSR in the summer of 1941. That is what Bentley believed; see her grand jury testimony of February 16, 1949, 6294.

44. Bentley, *Out of Bondage,* 152–53.

45. Weinstein and Vassiliev, *The Haunted Wood,* 164.

46. Bentley, *Out of Bondage,* 153; November 30 Bentley statement, 18.

47. Weinstein and Vassiliev, *The Haunted Wood,* 159. There are sixty-one Venona messages that concern Silvermaster. For a list, see Haynes and Klehr, *Venona,* 463 n. 288.

48. Weinstein and Vassiliev, *The Haunted Wood,* 159; Haynes and Klehr, *Venona,* 136.

49. Weinstein and Vassiliev, *The Haunted Wood,* 159–60.

50. Ibid., 160.

51. November 30 Bentley statement, 22.

52. Soviet documents confirm that Adler was indeed a Soviet source; decoded Soviet cables confirm Elizabeth's charges against Coe and the Golds. For her original charges against Adler and the Golds, see November 30 Bentley statement, 26–28. For an examination of Coe and Adler's guilt, see Craig, "Treasonable Doubt," 160–68; Weinstein and Vassiliev, *The Haunted Wood,* 78, 158, 162, 169, 229; Haynes and Klehr, *Venona,* 143–45. For an examination of the Golds' guilt, see Craig, 172–76, Weinstein and Vassiliev, 167; Haynes and Klehr, 134.

53. Bentley, *Out of Bondage,* 165.

54. See Hope Hale Davis, *Great Day Coming,* 133–35; and "Looking Back at My Years in the Party," *New Leader,* February 11, 1980, 18.

55. Bentley, *Out of Bondage,* 166.

56. For examples of the types of information stolen by Silverman, see Ve-

nona messages 1061, 1063 New York to Moscow, July 3, 1943, and 1081 New York to Moscow, July 6, 1943. See also Weinstein, *Perjury,* 189–91.

57. November 30 Bentley statement, 27; Haynes and Klehr, *Venona,* 138.

58. Sandilands, *The Life and Political Economy of Lauchlin Currie,* 372.

59. Letter, Lauchlin Currie to Richard Wels, February 14, 1951, Lauchlin Currie file, Tanenhaus Papers, Hoover Institution.

60. November 30 Bentley statement, 25.

61. For various theories about the meaning of Currie's revelation, see Benson and Warner, *Venona,* xiv; Haynes and Klehr, *Venona,* 47–48; Andrew and Mitrokhin, *The Sword and the Shield,* 130; and Sandilands, "Guilt by Association?," 483–84.

62. NSA report cited in Sandilands, "Guilt by Association?," 485.

63. Roger Sandilands, in ibid., contends that the case against Currie is still unproven. However, the Venona cables and one particular KGB document in Moscow provide strong corroborative evidence that Currie was a conscious source for Silvermaster and Silverman. See Weinstein and Vassiliev, *The Haunted Wood,* 106, and the nine Venona messages mentioning Currie, especially the following: 1317 New York to Moscow, August 10, 1943; 900 New York to Moscow, June 24, 1944; 1463 New York to Moscow, October 14, 1944; and 253 Moscow to New York, March 20, 1945.

64. November 30 Bentley statement, 25.

65. See Craig, "Treasonable Doubt," 520–33; Chambers, *Witness,* 67–68, 429.

66. Craig, "Treasonable Doubt," 560. The two most important Venona messages mentioning White are 1119-1121 New York to Moscow, August 4–5, 1944, and 1634 New York to Moscow, November 20, 1944.

67. Craig, "Treasonable Doubt," 585. For a less sympathetic treatment of White's assistance to the Soviets, see Haynes and Klehr, *Venona,* 141–43.

68. For evidence of Halperin's guilt, see Haynes and Klehr, *Venona,* 100–104; Weinstein and Vassiliev, *The Haunted Wood,* 106, 256; and Kirschner, *Cold War Exile,* 309–24. The twenty-eight Venona messages mentioning Halperin are listed in Haynes and Klehr, *Venona,* 453 n. 131. See, for example, 1437 New York to Moscow, October 10, 1944.

69. November 30 Bentley statement, 32.

70. Bentley, *Out of Bondage,* 263.

71. Memo, Duncan Lee to his children, "The Elizabeth Bentley Matter," September 15, 1983, 20. I wish to thank the Lee family for giving me permission to quote this memo.

72. "Duncan Lee Chronology," courtesy of Eleanore Lee.

73. Lee memo, 25.

74. November 30 Bentley statement, 34–35.

75. Ibid., 36.

76. Ibid., 35; Haynes and Klehr, *Venona,* 105, 408 n; Venona 782 New York to Moscow, May 26, 1943; Venona 887 New York to Moscow, June 9, 1943.

77. Bentley, *Out of Bondage,* 264; Weinstein and Vassiliev, *The Haunted Wood,* 259; Haynes and Klehr, *Venona,* 107; Venona 1325-1326 New York to Moscow, September 15, 1944; Venona 1354 New York to Moscow, September 22, 1944.

78. For their argument, see John Lee's open letter at www.netaxs.com/~leer /duncanlee. For Lee's own defense, see his testimony in the grand jury records of "United States of America vs. Alger Hiss" and his HUAC testimony quoted and cited in Chapter 7.

79. See, for example, the security document discussed above. Halperin and Donald Wheeler would not have access to a document that mentioned suspicions about their loyalty.

80. John Lee letter.

81. Bentley, *Out of Bondage,* 179.

82. Gary May, *Un-American Activities,* 21.

83. Quoted in ibid., 19.

84. November 30 Bentley statement, 48; Bentley, *Out of Bondage,* 179.

85. Bentley, *Out of Bondage,* 180.

86. Ibid.

87. For an insightful discussion of the motivations of the spies, see Isserman, "Disloyalty as a Principle."

88. Abt with Myerson, *Advocate and Activist,* 303.

89. Davis, "Looking Back at My Years in the Party," 13.

90. Quoted in Albright and Kunstel, *Bombshell,* 284.

91. November 30 Bentley statement, 106.

CHAPTER FOUR

1. Memo re: Silvermaster, November 21, 1947, Silvermaster file, FBI, 65-14603-3660; memo re: Silvermaster, November 19, 1947, ibid., 65-14603-3652; Budenz's testimony in the grand jury records of "United States of America vs. Alger Hiss," November 24, 1947, 2429–36.

2. Bentley, *Out of Bondage,* 186–87.

3. November 30, 1945, Bentley statement to the FBI, 65-56402-220, 38.

4. Budenz did indeed know her name. See memo re: Gregory, May 5, 1947, Silvermaster file, 65-14603-3075.

5. November 30 Bentley statement, 39; Haynes and Klehr, *Venona,* 112.

6. Venona 769, 771 New York to Moscow, May 30, 1944, National Security Agency.

7. Haynes and Klehr, *Venona,* 122.

8. November 30 Bentley statement, 91; Weinstein and Vassiliev, *The Haunted Wood,* 92.

9. Weinstein and Vassiliev, *The Haunted Wood,* 92.

10. Ibid., 93.

11. Bentley, *Out of Bondage,* 195.

12. Quoted in Weinstein and Vassiliev, *The Haunted Wood,* 92.

13. Bentley, *Out of Bondage,* 204.

14. November 30 Bentley statement, 91.

15. Bentley, *Out of Bondage,* 191.

16. Elizabeth told the Soviets that Golos needed to get a divorce before he could marry her. See Weinstein and Vassiliev, *The Haunted Wood,* 86. She testified many times, however, that he had no intention of marrying anyone. See, for example, her testimony in "United States vs. William Walter Remington" (1951), 1143.

17. November 8, 1945, Bentley statement to the FBI, Silvermaster file, 100-17493-11, 13.

18. Bentley, *Out of Bondage,* 211–22.

19. Ibid., 226, 245.

20. Ryan, *Earl Browder,* 2.

21. Ibid., 94.

22. For background on Browder, see ibid., passim; Klehr, *The Heyday of American Communism,* 21–25; and Isserman, *Which Side Were You On?,* 4–6.

23. Memo, SAC New Orleans to director, April 7, 1954, Silvermaster file, 65-14603-4596.

24. Bentley, *Out of Bondage,* 226–28.

25. Andrew and Gordievsky, *KGB,* 232.

26. Weinstein and Vassiliev, *The Haunted Wood,* 35–36.

27. November 30 Bentley statement, 73, 75; November 8 Bentley statement, 15.

28. November 8 Bentley statement, 18.

29. Bentley, *Out of Bondage,* 232–34.

30. Weinstein and Vassiliev, *The Haunted Wood,* 95.

31. Abt claimed he met Bentley because of her association with Intourist, not because of espionage. See Abt with Myerson, *Advocate and Activist,*

151. But Abt is mentioned in two Venona messages that support Bentley's version of their meeting. See Venona 588 New York to Moscow, April 29, 1944; and Venona 687 New York to Moscow, May 13, 1944.

32. Bentley, *Out of Bondage*, 237.

33. November 30 Bentley statement, 51; Haynes and Klehr, *Venona*, 117; Bentley, *Out of Bondage*, 239. Elizabeth did not name Magdoff and Fitzgerald in *Out of Bondage*, but she did so in her FBI statement. For the Venona messages on the Perlo group, see numbers 588, 687, and 769, 771, cited above.

34. Hope Hale Davis, *Great Day Coming*, 73.

35. Bentley, *Out of Bondage*, 240; November 30 Bentley statement, 52; Weinstein and Vassiliev, *The Haunted Wood*, 225.

36. Perlo, "Reply to Herbert Aptheker," 26; Haynes and Klehr, *Venona*, 129.

37. Bentley, *Out of Bondage*, 240.

38. Weinstein and Vassiliev, *The Haunted Wood*, 226.

39. Ibid., 231–32 n; Haynes and Klehr, *Venona*, 123.

40. See "Cartels Depicted as Nazi War Tool," *New York Times*, February 4, 1944, and Venona 1015, KGB New York to Moscow, July 22, 1944.

41. Weinstein and Vassiliev, *The Haunted Wood*, 233–34.

42. Memo, Washington field division to director, April 3, 1947, Silvermaster file, 65-56402-2448, 3.

43. "Administrative: The Mr. and Mrs. Victor Perlo Letter," 65-5428, no serial, no date, Harry Dexter White file, FBI, 9; Craig, "Treasonable Doubt," 102.

44. Bentley, *Out of Bondage*, 242.

45. Weinstein and Vassiliev, *The Haunted Wood*, 97.

46. Richard Green to Joseph Rauh, October 28, 1948, Rauh Papers, Library of Congress.

47. Reynolds grand jury testimony, October 19, 1948, 3320, Box 71, Tanenhaus Papers, Hoover Institution.

48. Weinstein and Vassiliev, *The Haunted Wood*, 100.

49. Phone interview with Matusow, July 11, 2001.

50. Interview with Mary Price Adamson by Mary Frederickson, April 19, 1976, Southern Oral History Program Collection, 123.

51. Weinstein and Vassiliev, *The Haunted Wood*, 100. Mary Price's recollection could be dismissed as a nasty lie designed to discredit her accuser. But the Soviet document found by Weinstein and Vassiliev is a contemporary, secret charge of sexual harassment against Elizabeth at the same time that Price alleges a similar experience. As such, it provides strong evidence corroborating Price's account.

52. Ibid., 97–98.

53. Ibid., 97.

54. Ibid., 96. See also Venona 973, New York to Moscow, July 11, 1944.

55. Bentley testimony in grand jury records of "United States of America vs. Alger Hiss," February 16, 1949, 6384.

56. Weinstein and Vassiliev, *The Haunted Wood,* 98.

57. Ibid.

58. Bentley, *Out of Bondage,* 246–47. See also November 30 Bentley statement, 84.

59. Weinstein and Vassiliev, *The Haunted Wood,* 99.

60. Ibid., 259–60.

61. Ishbel Petrie, letter to author, June 12, 2000.

62. Bentley, *Out of Bondage,* 261. See also Bentley grand jury testimony, February 16, 1949, 6386.

63. Petrie to author.

64. Mary Price Adamson interview, 123.

65. Frank Adams, "Hurricane Tears Destructive Path 500 Miles on Coast," *New York Times,* September 15, 1944.

66. Bentley, *Out of Bondage,* 248.

67. Ibid., 249; November 30 Bentley statement, 76.

68. Bentley, *Out of Bondage,* 250.

69. Haynes and Klehr, *Venona,* 267.

70. Bentley, *Out of Bondage,* 273.

71. Weinstein and Vassiliev, *The Haunted Wood,* 108.

72. November 30 Bentley statement, 77; Bentley, *Out of Bondage,* 250.

73. November 8 Bentley statement, 18.

74. Bentley, *Out of Bondage,* 252.

75. Andrew and Mitrokhin, *The Sword and the Shield,* 90.

76. Andrew and Gordievsky, *KGB,* 261.

77. November 8 Bentley statement, 19.

78. Bentley, *Out of Bondage,* 254–55.

79. Ibid.; Weinstein and Vassiliev, *The Haunted Wood,* 99.

80. Bentley, *Out of Bondage,* 267.

81. Ibid., 268.

82. Weinstein and Vassiliev, *The Haunted Wood,* 99.

83. Bentley, *Out of Bondage,* 269.

84. Ibid., 127, 163.

85. November 30 Bentley statement, 58–61.

86. Bentley, *Out of Bondage,* 271.

87. Ibid., 270.

88. For Heller's appearance, see Roger Gleason to SAC New York, August 29, 1945, Silvermaster file, 65-56402-3414.

89. Weinstein and Vassiliev, *The Haunted Wood,* 100.

90. Silvermaster file, 65-56402-3414; Weinstein and Vassiliev, *The Haunted Wood,* 100.

91. Reynolds grand jury testimony, October 19, 1948, 3311.

92. Memo re: Gregory, October 24, 1950, Silvermaster file, 65-14603-4311.

93. Silvermaster file, 65-56402-3414.

94. Ibid.

95. Boardman to director, January 26, 1955, Silvermaster file, 65-56402-4189.

96. Memo re: Peter Frank Heller, November 19, 1945, Silvermaster file, 65-14603-87.

97. November 30 Bentley statement, 85.

98. November 8 Bentley statement, 30.

99. November 30 Bentley statement, 85.

100. Weinstein and Vassiliev, *The Haunted Wood,* 101.

101. U.S. Senate Investigations Subcommittee, *Export Policy and Loyalty,* July 30, 1948, 21.

102. Weinstein and Vassiliev, *The Haunted Wood,* 101.

103. November 30 Bentley statement, 85.

104. Weinstein and Vassiliev, *The Haunted Wood,* 101.

105. Bentley, *Out of Bondage,* 282.

CHAPTER FIVE

1. Bentley, *Out of Bondage,* 284–85.

2. "Japanese Will Sign Surrender Document Aboard American Battleship," *New Haven Register,* August 23, 1945.

3. Bentley, *Out of Bondage,* 286–87.

4. Ibid., 289; memo, SAC New Haven to SAC New York, August 29, 1945, Silvermaster file, FBI, 65-56402-3414.

5. Memo, SAC New Haven to director, July 30, 1955, Bentley file, FBI, 134-435-177, 1.

6. Memo, New York to director, January 31, 1947, Silvermaster file, 65-56402-1976, 6.

7. Memo, SAC New Haven to director, July 30, 1955, Bentley file, 134-435-177, 2.

8. Silvermaster file, 65-56402-3414.

9. Memo, Boardman to director, January 25, 1955, Silvermaster file, 65-56402-4189, 3.

10. Memo, Simon to SAC New York, July 28, 1955, Bentley file, 134-182-101.
11. Gouzenko, *This Was My Choice,* 302.
12. Ibid., 302–7.
13. Ibid., 307–20.
14. Bentley, *Out of Bondage,* 103; Newton, *The Cambridge Spies,* 94–95.
15. Newton, *The Cambridge Spies,* 94.
16. November 30, 1945, Bentley statement to the FBI, 65-56402-220, 60.
17. Bentley, *Out of Bondage,* 290.
18. November 30 Bentley statement, 60–61.
19. Ibid., 86.
20. Ibid.
21. Weinstein and Vassiliev, *The Haunted Wood,* 101–2.
22. Ibid., 102.
23. Ibid.
24. "United States vs. William Walter Remington" (1951), 1298.
25. *New York Times,* October 11, 1945.
26. "Reconversion," *Time,* October 22, 1945, 60.
27. "Daily Worker Editor Renounces Communism for Catholic Faith," *New York Times,* October 11, 1945.
28. "Budenz to Lecture on Communist Peril," *New York Times,* October 13, 1945.
29. Memo, Coyne to Ladd, December 20, 1945, Silvermaster file, 65-56402-133.
30. For a detailed discussion of the FBI's letter to Bentley requesting the appointment, see the 1951 Remington trial, 1328–39.
31. Weinstein and Vassiliev, *The Haunted Wood,* 105.
32. Memo re: Lieutenant Peter Heller, Impersonation, Espionage, November 5, 1945, Silvermaster file, 65-56402-3466, 1–4.
33. Bentley file, 134-182-101.
34. Silvermaster file, 65-56402-3466, 1–4.
35. Memo, SAC Los Angeles to director, July 28, 1955, Bentley file, 134-435-174, 2.
36. Silvermaster file, 65-56402-3466, 4.
37. Weinstein and Vassiliev, *The Haunted Wood,* 103.
38. November 30 Bentley statement, 87.
39. Weinstein and Vassiliev, *The Haunted Wood,* 103.
40. November 30 Bentley statement, 87.
41. Harris testimony in grand jury records of "United States of America vs. Alger Hiss," March 31, 1948, 2804, 2825.

42. Dyson, *Red Harvest*, 104–5.

43. November 30 Bentley statement, 97; Bentley testimony in grand jury records of "United States of America vs. Alger Hiss," April 6, 1948, 2932.

44. November 30 Bentley statement, 102; WFO to director and SAC, November 8, 1945, Silvermaster file, 65-56402-1, 7.

45. November 30 Bentley statement, 97–98; Silvermaster file, 65-56402-1, 7.

46. Memo, SAC New York to director, July 28, 1955, Bentley file, 134-435-173, 2.

47. Phone interview, Edward Buckley, August 9, 2001.

48. Phone interview, Don Jardine, July 13, 2001. Bentley quote from 1951 Remington trial, 1289.

49. Silvermaster file, 65-56402-1, 1.

50. Phone interview.

51. Memo, Simon to Ladd, November 8, 1945, Silvermaster file, 65-56402-8.

52. Phone interview.

53. November 30 Bentley statement, 105.

54. Ibid.

55. Ibid., 106.

56. Memo, SAC New York to director, January 4, 1951, Silvermaster file, 65-56402-3875.

57. November 30 Bentley statement, 12.

58. Ibid., 20, 25, 43.

59. Ibid., 48.

60. Ibid., 27.

61. Memo re: Gregory, November 16, 1945, Silvermaster file, 65-14603-56.

62. Memo re: Gregory, October 6, 1948, Silvermaster file, 65-14603-4145. See also Memo, Ladd to Tamm, November 21, 1945, ibid., 65-56402-54; and memo, Hendon to Tolson, November 19, 1945, ibid., 65-56402-38, 1.

63. Cable, November 21, 1945, Silvermaster file, 65-56402-53.

64. Memo, Ladd to Tamm, November 21, 1945, Silvermaster file, 65-56402-54.

65. Handwritten note, Clark to Hoover, undated; memo, director to attorney general, November 28, 1945; and memo, director to attorney general, November 30, 1945, all in Silvermaster file and numbered 65-56402-94.

66. See, for example, report, December 13, 1945, Silvermaster file, 65-56402-234, 72–75.

67. Memo re: Silvermaster, November 21, 1945, Silvermaster file, 65-14603-181.

68. Memo re: Elizabeth Bentley, November 14, 1945, Silvermaster file, 65-14603-142.

69. Memo re: Silvermaster, April 3, 1946, Silvermaster file, 65-14603-1261.
70. Memo, Ladd to Tamm, November 23, 1945, Silvermaster file, 65-56402-108.
71. Silvermaster file, 65-14603-181.
72. Memo, Ladd to Tamm, November 21, 1945, Silvermaster file, 65-56402-46.
73. Cable, New York to director and SAC, November 21, 1945, Silvermaster file, 65-56402-56.
74. Ibid., 3.
75. Ibid., 1.
76. Weinstein and Vassiliev quote selectively from Gorsky's report of the conversation in *The Haunted Wood,* 103. However, without seeing the complete document, it is impossible to determine if his account supports Elizabeth's version.
77. Memo, Howe to Ladd, November 22, 1945, Silvermaster file, 65-56402-58.
78. Silvermaster file, 65-56402-56.
79. Weinstein and Vassiliev, *The Haunted Wood,* 103.
80. Memo: General Information, January 10, 1946, Silvermaster file, 65-14603-738.
81. Mickey Ladd advised Hoover to brief Stephenson on Bentley. See memo, Ladd to director, November 9, 1945, Silvermaster file, 65-56402-8, 3.
82. Weinstein and Vassiliev, *The Haunted Wood,* 104.
83. Ibid., 106-7.
84. Report re: Gregory, June 11, 1947, Silvermaster file, 65-56402-2608, 3. See also Haynes and Klehr, *Venona,* 151–52.
85. Weinstein and Vassiliev, *The Haunted Wood,* 177.
86. Ibid., 198.
87. Ibid., 217–18.
88. Ibid., 106–7.
89. Ibid., 108.
90. Cable, New York to director and SAC, November 23, 1945, Silvermaster file, 65-56402-66.
91. Teletype, New York to director, November 30, 1945, Silvermaster file, 65-56402-43.
92. Memo, Ladd to Tamm, November 19, 1945, Silvermaster file, 65-56402-37.
93. U.S. Senate Investigations Subcommittee, *Export Policy and Loyalty,* 10.
94. See the daily surveillance logs of Bentley's activities in volume D-3 of the Silvermaster file.

95. Memo, Morgan to Clegg, January 14, 1947, Silvermaster file, 65-56402-2077, 2.

96. Bentley grand jury testimony, February 16, 1949, 6388, 6375.

97. Ibid., 6389.

98. For example, see summaries of her meetings with Caroline Klein and Rae Elson in teletype, New York to director and SAC, November 23, 1945, Silvermaster file, 65-56402-66, and report, "Nathan Gregory Silvermaster," January 7, 1946, Silvermaster file, 65-56402-420, 4–5.

99. Bentley, *Out of Bondage,* 303; report, no date, Silvermaster file, 65-14603-810, 59.

100. Bentley, *Out of Bondage,* 304.

101. Silvermaster file, 65-14603-810, 61.

102. Bentley, *Out of Bondage,* 304.

103. Running memo re: Gregory, March 19, 1947, Silvermaster file, 65-14603-2904.

104. Letter, Scheidt to director, February 12, 1947, Silvermaster file, 65-56402-2407, 2; memo, Ladd to director, January 15, 1947, Silvermaster file, 65-56402-2081, 2.

105. Teletype, Hoover to New York SAC, January 16, 1947, Silvermaster file, 65-56402-1914.

106. Silvermaster file, 65-56402-2081, 2.

107. Teletype, Scheidt to director, January 17, 1947, Silvermaster file, 65-56402-2053.

108. Silvermaster file, 65-56402-2081, 2.

109. Ibid.

110. Ibid., 3.

111. Silvermaster file, 65-56402-2407.

112. Ibid.

113. Reynolds testimony in grand jury records of "United States of America vs. Alger Hiss," October 19, 1948, 3316–17.

114. Ibid., 3317–18.

115. Ibid., 3319.

116. Memo re: Gregory, January 14, 1947, Silvermaster file, 65-14603-2645; memo re: Gregory, December 2, 1947, Silvermaster file, 65-14603-3672.

117. For the suit itself, see court brief, no date, no serial, Silvermaster file, vol. 96. For the discussion of Donegan's role, see letter, Scheidt to director, February 15, 1947, Silvermaster file, 65-56402-2093; Fitch to Ladd, April 17, 1947, ibid., 65-56402-2299; and memo re: Gregory, January 28, 1947, ibid., 65-14603-2698.

118. Memo re: Gregory, November 1, 1950, Silvermaster file, 65-14603-4321; memo, SAC New York to director, May 24, 1947, ibid., 65-56402-2478; "11th Witness Calls Remington Red, U.S. Rests Perjury Case," *New York Herald Tribune,* January 11, 1951; memo re: Gregory, April 8, 1947, Silvermaster file, 65-14603-2972 (office manager); memo re: Gregory, May 29, 1947, Silvermaster file, 65-14603-3146 (no money left).

119. Bentley grand jury testimony, February 16, 1949, 6398.

CHAPTER SIX

1. Fried, *Nightmare in Red,* 63.
2. Harper, *The Politics of Loyalty,* 24, 54 n. 10; and Theoharis, "The Escalation of the Loyalty Program," in Bernstein, ed., *Politics and Policies of the Truman Administration,* 248.
3. Gentry, *J. Edgar Hoover,* 319, 356.
4. Sullivan, *The Bureau,* 38.
5. O'Reilly, *Hoover and the Un-Americans,* 101.
6. Powers, *Secrecy and Power,* 281.
7. Gentry, *J. Edgar Hoover,* 323; Powers, *Secrecy and Power,* 277.
8. See Klehr and Radosh, *The Amerasia Spy Case,* 128–32; Powers, *Secrecy and Power,* 280; and Theoharis and Cox, *The Boss,* 244–46.
9. Memo, Jones to Ladd, January 16, 1947, Silvermaster file, FBI, 65-56402-2296.
10. Memo, Tamm to director, January 23, 1947, Silvermaster file, 65-56402-2007, 2.
11. Memo, Morgan to Clegg, January 14, 1947, Silvermaster file, 65-56402-2077.
12. Memo, Nichols to Tamm, February 14, 1947, Silvermaster file, 65-56402-2166.
13. Silvermaster file, 65-56402-2296, 6.
14. Memo, Hoover to attorney general, January 27, 1947, Silvermaster file, 65-56402-2168, 2.
15. Silvermaster file, 65-56402-2007, 2.
16. Gary May, *Un-American Activities,* 89.
17. Gentry, *J. Edgar Hoover,* 354–55.
18. Silvermaster file, 65-56402-2296, 4.
19. O'Reilly, *Hoover and the Un-Americans,* 105; Gentry, *J. Edgar Hoover,* 357; Pearson, *Diaries,* 58–59.
20. Silvermaster file, 65-56402-2077, 5.
21. For other examples of the FBI's search for a "weak" informer or "weak

sister," see memo re: Gregory, January 9, 1947, Silvermaster file, 65-14603-2610; and memo re: Gregory, January 3, 1947, ibid., 65-14603-2599, 2.

22. See, for example, memo, Ladd to director, April 16, 1947, Silvermaster file, 65-56402-2324; memo, Ladd to director, April 18, 1947, ibid., 65-56402-2340; and memo, SAC Birmingham to director, April 18, 1947, ibid., 65-56402-2449.

23. Memo re: Gregory, May 29, 1947, Silvermaster file, 65-14603-3147.

24. Memo, Ladd to director, March 10, 1947, Silvermaster file, 65-56402-2137.

25. Letter, Scheidt to director, January 9, 1947, Silvermaster file, 65-56402-2031; memo re: Gregory, January 9, 1947, ibid., 65-14603-2610.

26. Memo re: Gregory, February 6, 1947, Silvermaster file, 65-14603-2733; memo re: Gregory, March 27, 1947, ibid., 65-14603-2947.

27. Silvermaster file, 65-14603-2947.

28. Letter, Richard Green to Joe Rauh, October 28, 1948, Rauh Papers, Library of Congress.

29. Memo re: Gregory, March 10, 1947, Silvermaster file, 65-14603-2854; memo re: Gregory, June 4, 1947, ibid., 65-14603-3184.

30. Memo re: Gregory, October 23, 1950, Silvermaster file, 65-14603-4318, 6.

31. Article dated October 20, 1947, in Silvermaster file, 65-56402-2890. See also October 9, 1947, ibid., 65-56402-2944; October 10, 1947, ibid., 65-56402-2962; October 16, 1947, ibid., 65-56402-2945; and November 14, 1947, ibid., 65-56402-2954.

32. Marquis Childs, "Washington Calling," *Washington Post,* November 21, 1947.

33. Memo, Hoover to attorney general, November 25, 1947, Silvermaster file, 65-56402-2960.

34. Memo, Coyne to Ladd, December 9, 1947, Silvermaster file, 65-56402-3005.

35. Memo, SAC New York to director, December 22, 1947, Silvermaster file, 65-56402-3019.

36. Bentley testimony in grand jury records of "United States of America vs. Alger Hiss," February 16, 1949, 6375.

37. Silvermaster file, 65-56402-3019.

38. Weinstein and Vassiliev, *The Haunted Wood,* 108.

39. Silvermaster file, 65-56402-3019, 2.

40. Ibid., 1.

41. Ibid.

42. Ibid., 2.

43. Ibid. See also memo, Jones to Coyne, December 11, 1947, Silvermaster file, 65-56402-3007.

44. Silvermaster file, 65-56402-3019, 2.

45. Memo, Tamm to director, January 9, 1948, Silvermaster file, 65-56402-3032.

46. Memo, Hoover to Tolson, Tamm, Ladd, and Nichols, April 1, 1948, Silvermaster file, 65-56402-3179.

47. Ibid.

48. Ibid.

49. Memo re: Gregory, March 20, 1948, Silvermaster file, 65-14603-3829. See also Belknap, *Cold War Political Justice,* 47–48.

50. Silvermaster file, 65-56402-3179. Emphasis in original.

51. Bentley grand jury testimony, March 30, 1948, 2760.

52. Ibid.

53. Ibid., 2760, 2767.

54. Ibid., 2777.

55. Ibid., 2778.

56. Ibid., 2764.

57. Ibid., 2771–72.

58. Ibid., 2795.

59. See memo re: Gregory, April 5, 1948, Silvermaster file, 65-14603-3847.

60. Bentley grand jury testimony, February 16, 1949, 6399.

61. Cook, *Maverick,* 22.

62. Memo, Coyne to Ladd, February 9, 1948, Silvermaster file, 65-56402-3022X.

63. Memo, SAC New York to director, February 11, 1948, Silvermaster file, 65-56402-3124.

64. Memo, Fletcher to Ladd, April 3, 1948, Silvermaster file, 65-56402-3185.

65. Cook, *Maverick,* 28.

66. Ibid.; memo, director to attorney general, April 3, 1948, Silvermaster file, 65-56402-3182.

67. Notation at bottom of Silvermaster file, 65-56402-3185.

68. Memo, Fletcher to Ladd, April 5, 1948, Silvermaster file, 65-56402-3197; memo re: Gregory, April 5, 1948, ibid., 65-14603-3946.

69. Memo, SAC New York to director, April 21, 1948, Silvermaster file, 65-56402-3223.

70. Telegram, New York to director and SAC, April 20, 1948, Silvermaster file, 65-56402-3230; "World-Telegram Touched Off Spy Expose," *New York World-Telegram,* August 5, 1948.

71. "United States vs. William Walter Remington" (1951), 1306–7.

72. Memo, Fletcher to Ladd, May 7, 1948, Silvermaster file, 65-56402-3243.

73. For background on the pressures on the grand jury, see Ralph de Tole-dano, "The Bentley-Chambers Story," *New Leader,* August 14, 1948.

74. Belknap, *Cold War Political Justice,* 52.

75. Memo, Nichols to Tolson, July 21, 1948, Silvermaster file, 65-56402-3299.

76. Memo, Fletcher to Ladd, July 19, 1948, Silvermaster file, 65-56402-3288.

77. Memo, Fletcher to Ladd, Silvermaster file, July 27, 1948, Silvermaster file, 65-56402-3494, 3.

78. Nelson Frank and Norton Mockridge, "Red Ring Bared by Blond Queen," *New York World-Telegram,* July 21, 1948.

79. Memo re: Gregory, July 22, 1948, Silvermaster file, 65-14603-3915; 1951 Remington trial, 1311; memo re: Gregory, July 24, 1948, Silvermaster file, 65-14603-3927; memo re: Gregory, July 26, 1948, ibid., 65-14603-3929.

80. See the *World-Telegram* for July 21–28, 1948.

81. "World-Telegram Touched Off Spy Expose"; memo re: Gregory, July 29, 1948, Silvermaster file, 65-14603-3939.

82. Memo re: Gregory, July 23, 1948, Silvermaster file, 65-14603-3917.

83. Carr, *The House Committee on Un-American Activities,* 40.

84. Memo, Nichols to Tolson, July 26, 1948, Silvermaster file, 65-56402-3293.

85. The *Times* did publish a death notice, which did not include telling de-tails such as where he died. See *New York Times,* November 28, 1943.

86. "Washington Merry-Go-Round," *Washington Post,* September 26, 1948.

87. Subpoena dated July 21, 1948, HUAC files, NARA.

88. Silvermaster file, 65-56402-3293.

89. Memo, Nichols to Tolson, July 26, 1948, Silvermaster file, 65-56402-3495X.

90. See stories in the *Washington Times Herald,* the *New York Journal-Ameri-can,* and the *New York Sun.*

91. Nelson Frank and Norton Mockridge, "Red Spy Queen Drops Mask," *New York World-Telegram,* July 28, 1948.

92. See, for example, the *Rochester Democrat and Chronicle* of July 27, 1948.

93. "United States of America vs. Abraham Brothman and Miriam Mosko-witz," 487.

94. U.S. Senate Investigations Subcommittee, *Export Policy and Loyalty,* July 30, 1948, 44, 15.

95. Willie Chanler to Joe Rauh, October 16, 1950, Rauh Papers.

96. November 30, 1945, Bentley statement to the FBI, 65-56402-220, 48.

97. U.S. Senate Investigations Subcommittee, *Export Policy and Loyalty,* 32.

98. Goodman, *The Committee,* 24.

99. Ibid., 65.

100. For background on Rankin, see ibid., 167–74.

101. 1948 HUAC hearings, 86, 118; the pagination comes from the transcript in the Silvermaster file, 65-56402-3476.

102. Bentley grand jury testimony, March 30, 1948, 2775.

103. HUAC hearings, 107, 120, 108, 109, 104.

104. Ibid., 122.

105. Ibid., 109.

106. Ibid., 83.

107. Ibid., 24.

108. November 30 Bentley statement, 27.

109. For the FBI's failure to follow up on this, see memo, August 17, 1948, Silvermaster file, 65-56402-3448. For background on the official U.S. briefings to the Soviets in advance of D-Day, see Dallek, *Franklin D. Roosevelt and American Foreign Policy,* 450. Allen Weinstein and Alexander Vassiliev have found evidence in Moscow that Duncan Lee—not Ullmann—reported on March 3, 1944, that "the second front will be opened between mid-May and the beginning of June." Possibly Bentley confused Lee with Ullmann, or possibly they both reported similar guesses. In any event, according to Dallek, the United States gave the Soviets a much more precise date (within three days of May 31) on April 10. The information from Bentley on D-Day, then, could only have served to reassure the Russians that the United States was not going to double-cross them. See *The Haunted Wood,* 258.

110. HUAC hearings, 62. Cigarette: "Investigations," *Time,* August 9, 1948, 16.

111. Memo re: Gregory, August 17, 1948, Silvermaster file, 65-14603-3982. See also memo re: Gregory, August 11, 1948, ibid., 65-14603-3969.

112. HUAC hearings, 139–41.

113. Ibid., 138, 147.

114. For an astute analysis of Bentley's use of traditional gender roles in her writings and testimony, see Wilson, "Elizabeth Bentley and Cold War Representation." Kate Weigand also discusses the role of traditional gender roles in anti-Communist investigations—and comes to conclusions quite different from mine—in her article "The Red Menace, the Feminine Mystique, and the Ohio Un-American Activities Commission."

115. "Blonde Spy Testifies: White House Aide Gave Data" and "Probers Demand Ex-Spy Reveal All," *New York Journal-American,* July 31, 1948.

116. Latham, *The Communist Controversy in Washington,* 160.

117. Liebling, "The Wayward Press," *New Yorker,* August 28, 1948, 42.

118. Alsop, "Miss Bentley's Bondage," *Commonweal,* November 9, 1951, 120.

119. Kempton, *Part of Our Time,* 220 n, 219. Kempton's source was Krugman, "The Interplay of Social and Psychological Factors in Political Deviance," 111.

120. Elaine Tyler May, *Homeward Bound,* 89.

121. Ibid., 90. On the antifeminist backlash after the war, see also Leila J. Rupp, "The Survival of American Feminism: The Women's Movement in the Postwar Period," in Bremner and Reichard, eds., *Reshaping America;* and Rupp and Taylor, *Survival in the Doldrums,* chap. 2. On the crisis in masculinity, see Cuordileone, "'Politics in an Age of Anxiety.'"

122. Hartmann, *The Home Front and Beyond,* 202.

123. See Kaplan, ed., *Women in Film Noir,* 35–54.

124. For example, David Brion Davis sees the image of the wicked woman in nineteenth-century American fiction in part as the result of anxiety over the changing status of women, while Virginia Mae Allen sees the image of the femme fatale in late-nineteenth-century paintings as a reaction to increasing feminist agitation. See Davis, *Homicide in American Fiction,* 201–9, and Allen, *The Femme Fatale,* viii, 20–35.

125. Sayre, "Cold-War Cinema II," *Nation,* March 3, 1979, 245. See also Rosen, *Popcorn Venus,* 147–58.

126. Douglas, *Where the Girls Are,* 47.

127. Ernst and Loth, *Report on the American Communist,* 180.

128. Friends quoted in Smith, *Alger Hiss,* 246–47; Zeligs, *Friendship and Fratricide,* 183; Massing, *This Deception,* 175; and Harvey Bundy, Columbia University Oral History Collection, 309.

129. Nixon, *Six Crises,* 38.

130. Richard Nixon, "Lessons of the Alger Hiss Case," *New York Times,* January 8, 1986.

131. James Daniel, "Mrs. Rosenberg Was Like a Red Spider," *New York World-Telegram and Sun,* January 15, 1953.

132. Bob Considine, "Rosenbergs Worked Hard to Become Red A-Spies," *New York Journal-American,* January 12, 1953; "The Inside Story of Two A-Spies," *New York Journal-American,* January 11, 1953.

133. Eisenhower, *Mandate for Change,* 225.

134. The limited references to Ethel in the Soviet archives are discussed by Weinstein and Vassiliev in *The Haunted Wood,* 217 and 331. Julius's NKGB case officer, Alexander Feklisov, says that Julius worked for him but that Ethel was not an active spy. See Alessandra Stanley, "Ex-KGB Spy Talks of Buying Secrets from Rosenberg," *San Francisco Examiner,* March 16, 1997. Feklisov also repeated this view of Ethel on camera for the Discovery Channel documentary "The Rosenberg File Case Closed" (Dis-

covery Communications, Inc., 1998). On Julius's guilt, see Walter and
Miriam Schneir, "Cryptic Answers," *Nation,* August 14/21, 1995, 152–53.

135. Edward Nellor, "Editor Supplies Red Spy Link," *New York Sun,* July 30,
1948.

136. Quoted in Tanenhaus, *Whittaker Chambers,* 210.

137. Ibid., 219–23.

CHAPTER SEVEN

1. U.S. House Committee on Un-American Activities (HUAC), *Hearings Regarding Communist Espionage in the United States,* August 13, 1948, 879.

2. Ibid., 878.

3. Ibid., 881.

4. "Wallace Laments White," *New York Times,* August 18, 1948.

5. HUAC, *Hearings,* August 13, 1948, 855.

6. Ibid., August 10, 1948, 720, 721. Lee's entire testimony is on 715–25 and
733–59.

7. Remington's testimony can be found in U.S. Senate Investigations Subcommittee, *Export Policy and Loyalty,* 67–112, 165–264.

8. Gary May, *Un-American Activities,* 119.

9. Daniel Lang, "Days of Suspicion," *New Yorker,* May 21, 1949, 39.

10. Memo re: Gregory, July 29, 1948, Silvermaster file, FBI, 65-14603-3934.

11. Memo re: Gregory, August 5, 1948, Silvermaster file, 65-14603-3960.

12. Memo re: Gregory, July 28, 1948, Silvermaster file, 65-14603-3933; memo
re: Gregory, July 30, 1948, ibid., 65-14603-3941; memo re: Gregory, July
29, 1948, ibid., 65-14603-3939; memo, Fletcher to Ladd, August 2, 1948,
ibid., 65-56402-3323; "Smear Foiled, Says Senator," *Rochester Democrat
and Chronicle,* August 29, 1948.

13. Teletype, New Haven to director, December 16, 1948, Bentley file, FBI,
134-435-6. See also 134-435-7 and 134-435-8 in the same file.

14. Memo, Fletcher to Ladd, August 2, 1948, Silvermaster file, 65-56402-
3321.

15. Memo, Fletcher to Laughlin, August 25, 1948, Silvermaster file, 65-56402-
3458.

16. "Link Clothing on Span to Spy Quiz," *San Francisco Call-Bulletin,* August 4, 1948, Silvermaster file, 65-56402-3434.

17. Silvermaster file, 65-14603-3960.

18. Ibid.; "Message Appears to Link Death Leap, Spy for Reds," *Rochester
Democrat and Chronicle,* August 5, 1948.

19. Hamby, *Man of the People,* 453; "Not a Herring but an Octopus," *New
York Sun,* August 6, 1948.

20. "House Spy Probers Accuse Truman of Refusing to Help Protect Security," *Rochester Democrat and Chronicle,* August 29, 1948.

21. "Ferguson Talks of Impeaching Truman," *San Francisco Chronicle,* August 8, 1948.

22. "Communism and Children," *Newsweek,* August 9, 1948, 21.

23. See, for example, "Russian Soldiers Kidnap Yank Official in Berlin as 'Cold War' Continues," *Rochester Democrat and Chronicle,* August 23, 1948.

24. Quoted in Griffith, *The Politics of Fear,* 46.

25. For background on Truman's relationship with Wallace, see Hamby, *Man of the People,* 356.

26. Hamby, *Beyond the New Deal,* 206–8.

27. Hamby, *Man of the People,* 453.

28. Quoted in William W. Remington vs. Elizabeth T. Bentley et al., 4, Rauh Papers, Library of Congress.

29. Green to Rauh, June 9, 1949, Rauh Papers.

30. Rauh to Green, October 7, 1948, Rauh Papers; Rauh affidavit, October 8, 1948, ibid.; Green to Rauh, October 7, 1948, ibid.; Green to Bentley, October 8, 1948, ibid.; Rauh to Green, October 15, 1948, ibid.; Rauh to Green, October 29, 1948, ibid.; Green to Rauh, November 3, 1948, ibid.; Edward F. Ryan to Rauh, November 12, 1948, ibid.

31. "Ex–Spy Queen Bentley Joins Catholic Church," *New York World-Telegram,* November 16, 1948. See also "Miss Bentley, Ex-Spy, Becomes Catholic," *New York Times,* November 16, 1948.

32. Donald F. Crosby, "The Politics of Religion: American Catholics and the Anti-Communist Impulse," in Griffith and Theoharis, *The Specter,* 21–28. See also Crosby's *God, Church, and Flag,* passim.

33. Gentry, *J. Edgar Hoover,* 347.

34. For background on Budenz's conversion, see his memoir, *This Is My Story,* 154–65, 332–49.

35. Lynch, *Selling Catholicism,* 23. For Sheen's description of some of his conversions, see Sheen, *Treasures in Clay,* 251–79.

36. Quoted in Lynch, *Selling Catholicism,* 79.

37. "Elizabeth Bentley Is Happy to Be Herself Once Again," *New York World-Telegram,* December 6, 1948.

38. Gary May, *Un-American Activities,* 122.

39. "She'll Accept Suit Summons, Miss Bentley Asserts Here," *Rochester Democrat and Chronicle,* November 22, 1948.

40. Ibid.

41. Green to Rauh, December 15, 1948, Rauh Papers.

42. "Lecturer Looks for Jury's Call," *New Orleans Times-Picayune,* December 16, 1948.

43. "Miss Bentley Gets Summons in Slander Suit," *New York Herald Tribune,* December 30, 1948.

44. "Ex-Spy 'Queen' Never Grilled in Remington Loyalty Review," *New York Post,* January 10, 1949.

45. Quoted in Gary May, *Un-American Activities,* 127.

46. Teletype, January 26, 1949, Silvermaster file, 65-14603-4199. See also Green to Rauh, October 13, 1948, Rauh Papers.

47. For a lively account of the trial, see Belknap, *Cold War Political Justice,* chap. 4.

48. Bentley testimony in grand jury records of "United States of America vs. Alger Hiss," February 17, 1949, 6423.

49. Ibid., February 16, 1949, 6328.

50. Ibid., 6325.

51. For one account of her lectures, see "Learn about Reds, Ex-Spy Declares," *Huntsville Times,* March 11, 1949, Bentley file, 134-435-10.

52. U.S. Senate Subcommittee on Immigration and Naturalization, *S. 1832,* May 13, 1949, 119. Emphasis added.

53. Report, May 6, 1955, Silvermaster file, 65-56402-4201, 21–22. See also memo, director to SAC New Orleans, December 15, 1954, Bentley file, 134-435-126; and SAC New Orleans to director, January 25, 1955, ibid., 134-435-127. For a timetable of the 1944–45 U.S. bombing of Tokyo, see Schaffer, *Wings of Judgment,* 107–27.

54. Hayden Peake disagrees with me on this point. See Peake, afterword to *Out of Bondage,* 289 n. 135.

55. Complaint form, August 10, 1948, Silvermaster file, 65-14603-4011; "Memorandum of Conversation with Dr. Lombardo," October 4, 1950, Rauh Papers.

56. Joe Rauh to Edwin Rothschild, November 27, 1951, Rauh Papers; Civil Intelligence Report: Albany, NY, January 10, 1951, ibid.; James Allen to Rauh, June 18, 1949, ibid.

57. Green to Rauh, June 13, 1949, Rauh Papers; Green to Rauh, June 9, 1949, ibid.

58. Rauh to Allen, September 23, 1949, Rauh Papers; Rauh to Green, September 23, 1949, ibid.; Gary May, *Un-American Activities,* 138.

59. Letter, January 27, 1949, Mundelein College Records, Women and Leadership Archives, Loyola University of Chicago, Series F.4.1.c, Full Time Lay/Clerical Faculty: Bentley, Elizabeth—Political Science, 1949–50. Hereafter cited as Bentley file, WLA/LUC.

60. See letter dated May 15, 1949, and contract dated May 24, 1949, Bentley file, WLA/LUC.

61. See February 1950 letter to Daughter of Mundelein College, Bentley file, WLA/LUC.

62. See letter dated September 2, 1949, Bentley file, WLA/LUC.

63. "Elizabeth Bentley," October 18, 1950, Rauh Papers.

64. Ibid.

65. Teletype, New York to director and SAC, March 1, 1950, Silvermaster file, 65-56402-3830.

66. See letters dated December 1, 1950, and February 20, 1951, from Sister Mary Josephine to Bentley, Bentley file, WLA/LUC.

67. Gary May, *Un-American Activities,* 143; HUAC, *Hearings,* May 6, 1950, 1850–52; "Remington Settles Slander Suit against Miss Bentley, 2 Others," *New York Herald Tribune,* March 1, 1950.

68. Memo, SAC New York to director, May 3, 1950, Bentley file, 134-435-20; memo, SAC Chicago to director, February 21, 1950, ibid., 134-435-15.

69. Benson and Warner, *Venona,* xii–xxiv; Haynes and Klehr, *Venona,* 23–33.

70. Benson and Warner, *Venona,* xxv–xxvi.

71. Lamphere and Shachtman, *FBI-KGB War,* 141–42.

72. Memo re: Gregory, May 29, 1947, Silvermaster file, 65-14603-3147. See also teletype, New York to director and SAC, May 30, 1947, Silvermaster file, 65-56402-2515, and Brothman testimony in grand jury records of "United States of America vs. Alger Hiss," July 22, 1947, 873.

73. Radosh and Milton, *The Rosenberg File,* 36–47, 81–85; Roberts, *The Brother,* 208–44.

74. Brunini, "Rolling Stone," chap. 14, 9, box 5, folder 24, Brunini Papers, Georgetown University. Brunini's memoir was incomplete when he died.

75. Rauh to Frances Brody, June 23, 1951, Rauh Papers; Civil Intelligence Report: John G. Brunini, January 22, 1951, ibid. See Brunini's brief autobiography in Romig, ed., *The Book of Catholic Authors,* 40–47. On Lady Armstrong, see her obituary in the *New York Times,* May 29, 1953.

76. Brunini, "Rolling Stone," chap. 14, 9.

77. Ibid.

78. Ibid., 11–15.

79. Gary May, *Un-American Activities,* 157.

80. Brunini, "Rolling Stone," chap. 14, 14–15.

81. Gary May, *Un-American Activities,* 159–66.

82. HUAC, *Hearings,* May 6, 1950, 1856, 1859.

83. Gary May, *Un-American Activities,* 167.

84. Phone interview, June 25, 2001.

85. Memo, Ladd to Belmont, October 18, 1950, Bentley file, 134-435, no serial. See also teletype, New York to director, October 16, 1950, ibid., 134-435-28.
86. Ladd to Belmont, October 18, 1950.
87. Memo re: Gregory, October 31, 1950, Silvermaster file, 65-14603-4316.
88. Memo re: Gregory, November 1, 1950, Silvermaster file, 65-14603-4320, 2; memo re: Gregory, September 20, 1950, Silvermaster file, 65-14603-4299.
89. Silvermaster file, 65-14603-4320; 65-14603-4316; memo re: Gregory, October 30, 1950, ibid., 65-14603-4319; memo re: Gregory, October 27, 1950, ibid., 65-14603-4318A.
90. Silvermaster file, 65-14603-4316; teletype, New York to director, November 2, 1950, Bentley file, 134-435-32; teletype, New York to director, October 30, 1950, ibid., 134-435-29; memo, Belmont to Ladd, October 30, 1950, ibid., 134-435-30; memo re: Gregory, November 4, 1950, Silvermaster file, 65-14603-4324.
91. Silvermaster file, 65-14603-4320, 2.
92. Memo re: Gregory, October 23, 1950, Silvermaster file, 65-14603-4318.
93. Phone interview, July 9, 2001.
94. Brothman's business partner, Miriam Moskowitz, stood trial with him on the lesser charges of conspiring to obstruct justice.
95. Zion, *The Autobiography of Roy Cohn,* 66.
96. "Miss Bentley Testifies Brothman Was in Communist Party in '40," *New York Herald Tribune,* November 15, 1950.
97. November 30, 1945, Bentley statement to the FBI, 65-56402-220, 14; "United States of America vs. Abraham Brothman and Miriam Moskowitz," 366.
98. Brothman trial, 438, 421, 398.
99. "Miss Bentley Testifies Brothman Was in Communist Party in '40," *New York Herald Tribune,* November 15, 1950; "Brothman a Spy, Says Miss Bentley," *New York Times,* November 15, 1950.
100. "United States vs. William Walter Remington" (1951), 1076, 1077, 1079.
101. Ibid., 1292, 1339-40, 1243.
102. "Given Secrets by Remington, Bentley Says," *Washington Post,* January 9, 1951; "Thefts of Secrets Laid to Remington," *New York Times,* January 9, 1951; Max Lerner, "Portrait of a Lady," *New York Post,* January 10, 1951.
103. Gary May, *Un-American Activities,* 265.
104. Teletype, August 11, 1950, Silvermaster file, 65-14603-4297. See also memo re: Jules Korchein, ibid., 65-14603-2207.
105. "Julius and Ethel Rosenberg vs. United States," 978.

NOTES TO PAGES 159-64

106. Ibid., 1000, 1002.

107. Ibid., 1001.

108. Ibid., 1008.

109. Ibid., 1655.

110. Memo, Nichols to Tolson, January 24, 1951, Bentley file, 134-435-35.

111. "Capitolized, Televised, and Now Serialized," *Washington News,* April 24, 1951; letter, Daniel D. Mich to Mrs. E. J. Lintner, July 6, 1951; and letter, Mrs. Lintner to J. Edgar Hoover, July 10, 1951; all in Bentley file, 134-435-41.

112. Elizabeth Bentley, "I Joined the Red Underground with the Man I Loved," *McCall's,* June 1951, 60.

113. Ibid., 36. Emphasis added.

114. Bentley, *Out of Bondage,* 198–99.

115. Venona 1065, New York to Moscow, July 28, 1944.

116. See the discussion of this incident in Chapter 4.

117. November 30 Bentley statement, 94.

118. Bentley grand jury testimony, February 16, 1949, 6382.

119. "United States of America vs. William Walter Remington" (1953), 273; memo, SAC New Orleans to director, January 21, 1954, Silvermaster file, 65-14603-4570, 2; White, *Harry Dexter White,* 344–46.

120. Alsop, "Miss Bentley's Bondage," *Commonweal,* November 9, 1951, 120.

121. *New Yorker,* October 20, 1951, 150.

122. George Pancoast remembers Bentley typing for days at a time in the room she rented from his family. Phone interview, June 25, 2001. Devin-Adair no longer has any drafts of *Out of Bondage,* so it is impossible to determine how much of Bentley's original text made it into the book. Undated letter, Roger Lourie to author.

123. Silvermaster file, 65-14603-4316; Gary May, *Un-American Activities,* 235–37.

124. Brunini, "Everyday Murder," box 4, folder 42, Brunini Papers; see also "The Great Lover Loves," box 4, folder 49; Bentley, *Out of Bondage,* 258.

125. Civil Intelligence Report: T. O'Conor Sloane, III, January 22, 1951, Rauh Papers.

126. Donald McDonald, "Wayward Crusader," *Commonweal,* June 8, 1951, 207; Richard Stokes, "Senator Taft on Catholic Schools," *Catholic World* 175 (July 1952): 246.

127. See Jordan with Stokes, *From Major Jordan's Diaries,* 49–65, 126–37.

128. See Craig, "Treasonable Doubt," chap. 5.

129. Richard Stokes, "The Quarter-Billion Occupation Mark Swindle," *Freeman,* November 17, 1952, 121.

130. Bentley, *Out of Bondage,* 241.

131. Memo, Hennrich to Belmont, October 23, 1953, Bentley file, 134-435-84.

132. Craig, "Treasonable Doubt," 245. Like many officials, White did not fore-see the disastrous consequences of the decision to share the plates. But there is no evidence that he acted on Soviet orders.

CHAPTER EIGHT

1. Memo, SAC New York to director, September 29, 1951, Bentley file, FBI, 134-435-45; "Elizabeth Bentley Living in Madison," *New Haven Register,* October 16, 1951, in Bentley file, 134-435-48.

2. "Elizabeth Bentley Living in Madison."

3. Memo, SAC New York to director, May 16, 1952, Bentley file, 134-435-58.

4. Memo re: Gregory, May 7, 1952, Silvermaster file, FBI, 65-14603-4413A; memo, Belmont to Ladd, May 13, 1952, Bentley file, 134-435-56. On Wright's tendency to brag, see memo, Spencer to SAC New York, June 14, 1954, Silvermaster file, 65-14603-4609.

5. Bentley file, 134-435-58.

6. Memo, SAC New Haven to SAC New York, September 6, 1951, Silver-master file, 65-14603-4379.

7. Memo, SAC New York to director, January 4, 1951, Bentley file, 134-435, no serial.

8. Gary May, *Un-American Activities,* 271–74.

9. Memo, Belmont to Ladd, January 17, 1952, Silvermaster file, 65-56402-3945, 4. See also letter, Godfrey Schmidt to Myles Lane, November 16, 1951, in the U.S. Attorney's file on Remington, NARA, New York, N.Y.

10. Silvermaster file, 65-56402-3945.

11. See release and receipt dated March 1952, Silvermaster file, 65-56402-3956.

12. Memo, William Johnson to SAC New York, March 21, 1952, Silvermaster file, 65-14603-4411; memo re: Elizabeth Bentley, March 21, 1952, ibid., 65-14603-4410.

13. Bentley file, 134-435-58; memo re: Gregory, May 14, 1952, Silvermaster file, 65-14603-4418.

14. Bentley file, 134-435-58.

15. Ibid.; memo re: Gregory, May 12, 1952, Silvermaster file, 65-14603-4416.

16. Memo, Cleveland to Belmont, May 8, 1952, Bentley file, 134-435, no serial.

17. Von Hoffman, *Citizen Cohn,* 89–90, 265–77, 307–8, 325–27.

18. Memo re: Gregory, May 13, 1952, Silvermaster file, 65-14603-4417.

19. Ibid.; Silvermaster file, 65-14603-4413A.

20. Silvermaster file, 65-14603-4417.

21. Memo, Belmont to Ladd, May 15, 1952, Bentley file, 134-435-57.

22. Bentley file, 134-435-58, 4.

23. Letter, John Wright to Hoover, March 9, 1953, Bentley file, no serial.

24. U.S. Senate Subcommittee to Investigate the Administration of the Internal Security Act (SISS), *The Institute of Pacific Relations,* August 14, 1951, 439.

25. Ibid., May 29, 1952, 4778.

26. Memo, Belmont to Ladd, November 23, 1953, Bentley file, 134-435, no serial.

27. Phone interview, July 11, 2001.

28. Letter, Matthews to Bentley, March 1, 1954; letter, Bentley to Matthews, March 4, 1954, Matthews Papers, Perkins Library, Duke University.

29. Memo, SAC New York to director, July 10, 1952, Silvermaster file, 65-14603-4429.

30. Memo re: Gregory, July 8, 1952, Silvermaster file, 65-14603-4428.

31. SAC New York to director, July 10, 1952, Bentley file, 134-435-59, 3.

32. SAC New York to director, July 16, 1952, Bentley file, 134-435-59, and July 16, 1952, 134-435-60.

33. Belmont to Ladd, August 29, 1952, Bentley file, 134-435-61; SAC New York to director, September 4, 1952, Bentley file, 134-435-63.

34. Teletype, New Haven to director, August 29, 1952, Bentley file, 134-435-62.

35. Bentley file, 134-435-61.

36. Bentley file, 134-435-63; memo, SAC New Haven to director, November 17, 1952, Bentley file, 134-435-71.

37. Bentley file, 134-435-71.

38. SAC New York to director, September 26, 1952, Bentley file, 134-435-66; Hennrich to Belmont, September 22, 1952, ibid., 134-435-65.

39. Bentley file, 134-435-66, 5–6.

40. Ibid., 6, 9.

41. Ibid., 7.

42. Ibid., 2.

43. Ibid., 8.

44. Memo re: Elizabeth Bentley, September 29, 1952, Bentley file, 134-182-6; memo, Belmont to Ladd, September 26, 1952, ibid., 134-435-67.

45. Bentley file, 134-435-67, 2.

46. Ibid.

47. SAC New York to director, October 8, 1952, Bentley file, 134-182-7.

48. Memo, Branigan to Belmont, October 15, 1952, Bentley file, 134-435-70.

49. Memo, director to SAC New York, October 22, 1952, Bentley file, 134-435-69.

50. Memo by Lester Gallaher, October 29, 1952, Bentley file, 134-182-8; memo, Kennelly to Keele, November 17, 1952, ibid., 134-182, no serial.

51. Memo, SAC New York to director, March 24, 1955, Bentley file, 134-182-66, 2–3.

52. Memo, director to Tompkins, March 8, 1955, Bentley file, 134-435, no serial, 2. On Matusow, see Schrecker, *Many Are the Crimes,* 311–13, 344–47.

53. SISS, *Strategy and Tactics of World Communism,* 88. The description of the dinner is taken from Matusow's testimony on pages 46, 55, 88–89, 101–3. See also Matusow, *False Witness,* 154.

54. Teletype, February 22, 1955, Bentley file, 134-435-130. Bentley remembered Ruth Matthews attending the "luncheon" with Matusow, but this appears to have been a different occasion.

55. SISS, *Strategy and Tactics of World Communism,* 55.

56. Memo, Hoover to Tompkins, March 4, 1955, Bentley file, 134-435-134.

57. Report, March 9, 1955, Bentley file, 134-182-74, 6.

58. Bentley file, 134-182-66, 4.

59. SISS, *Strategy and Tactics of World Communism,* 89.

60. Phone interview, July 11, 2001.

61. Bentley file, 134-182-74, 9.

62. 1953 Remington trial, 276, 281, 284, 282, 279.

63. Memo, SAC New York to director, January 16, 1953, Bentley file, 134-435-72; director to SAC New York, February 3, 1953, ibid., 134-435-72.

64. Phone interview, Harvey Matusow, July 11, 2001.

65. Memo, SAC New York to director, February 5, 1953, Bentley file, 134-435, no serial; emails from Sheila Kurtz to author, March 26 and 27, 2001.

66. Phone interview, July 11, 2001.

67. Ibid.

68. Airtel, February 25, 1953, Bentley file, 134-435-73. Emphasis added.

69. Richard L. Stokes, "The Quarter-Billion Occupation Mark Swindle," *Freeman,* November 17, 1952, 121, 123–24. Elizabeth had always told the FBI she was not sure why Gorsky had given her the money.

70. U.S. Senate Subcommittee on Government Operations Abroad, *Transfer of Occupation Currency Plates,* 28, 30, 32.

71. Memo, Hennrich to Belmont, October 23, 1953, Bentley file, 134-435-84.

72. See Craig, "Treasonable Doubt," chap. 5.

73. Ibid., 439–49.
74. SISS, *Interlocking Subversion in Government Departments,* November 17, 1953, 1145.
75. Memo, Belmont to Ladd, December 8, 1953, Bentley file, 134-435-88.
76. Memo, Jones to Nichols, December 7, 1953, Bentley file, 134-435-89, 1–4. Hoover's remarks are written at the bottom.
77. *Meet the Press* transcript, White House Central Files, Eisenhower Library.
78. Ibid.; Bentley file, 134-435-89.
79. "Ex–Spy Queen Tells Own Story," *Daily Mirror,* December 13, 1953.
80. Memo, SAC New York to director, December 16, 1953, Bentley file, 134-435-92.
81. "First A-Bomb Tip Given to Ring by Aide of 'Wild Bill,'" *Daily Mirror,* December 15, 1953.
82. Bentley file, 134-435-92.
83. Teletype, New York to director and SAC, December 22, 1953, Bentley file, 134-435-93.
84. SAC New York to director, December 22, 1953, Bentley file, 134-435-94, 2.
85. Memo, Branigan to Belmont, January 6, 1954, Bentley file, 134-435-97, 3.
86. Report, May 6, 1955, Silvermaster file, 65-56402-4201 (hereafter Taylor Report), 2.
87. "Taylor Is under Loyalty Probe," *Washington Daily News,* November 20, 1953.
88. See Nigel West, *Venona,* 307.
89. Memo, SAC New Orleans to director, May 7, 1954, Bentley file, 134-435-112; teletype, FBI New Orleans to director, February 2, 1954, ibid., 134-435, no serial; memo, Judge Edwin Hunter to Mr. Hamilton, April 12, 1954, ibid., 134-435-105.
90. Memo, Belmont to Boardman, April 16, 1954, Bentley file, 134-435-105.
91. Hunter to Hamilton, Bentley file, 134-435-105.
92. Memo, SAC New Orleans to director, May 10, 1954, Bentley file, 134-435-108.
93. Memo, SAC New Orleans to director, April 23, 1954, Bentley file, 134-435-107.
94. Memo, Belmont to Ladd, February 4, 1954, Bentley file, 134-435-100.
95. Memo, SAC New York to director, April 10, 1953, Bentley file, 134-435-76.
96. Teletype, New Orleans to director, May 8, 1954, Bentley file, 134-435-109, 1–2.
97. Bentley file, 134-435-112, 3; 134-435-109, 2.
98. The affidavit is reprinted in White, *Harry Dexter White,* 344–46.
99. Memo, Gallaher to SAC New York, June 17, 1954, Bentley file, 134-182-50.

100. Bottles: email communication to author from Sheila Kurtz.

101. Gary May, *Un-American Activities*, 7–9, 307–10.

102. Teletype, November 24, 1954, Bentley file, 134-435-125.

103. Alfred E. Kahn, "The Story behind This Book," in Matusow, *False Witness*, 8–9.

104. SISS, *Strategy and Tactics of World Communism*, 42.

105. Teletype, FBI New Orleans to director, February 22, 1955, Bentley file, 134-435-130; memo, Belmont to Boardman, February 25, 1955, ibid., 134-435-122.

106. Jack Danahy says that he and Tom Spencer took Bentley's confessions in stride but that Kelly would sometimes say in amazement, "Holy Jesus, this woman slept around!" Phone interview, Jack Danahy, July 9, 2001.

107. Memo, Belmont to Boardman, February 23, 1955, Bentley file, 134-435, no serial.

108. Bentley file, 134-182-66, 5.

109. Taylor Report, 6.

110. Ibid., 32.

111. Peake, afterword to *Out of Bondage*, 237–47. Quote on 247.

112. Taylor Report, 3.

113. Ibid., 33.

114. Ibid., 28.

115. Memo, SAC New Haven to director, June 23, 1955, Bentley file, 134-435-157.

116. Memo, director to attorney general, June 27, 1955, Bentley file, 134-435-157; memo, Nichols to Tolson, June 9, 1955, ibid., 134-435-154; teletype, New York to director, June 10, 1955, ibid., 134-435-149; memo, Belmont to Boardman, June 24, 1955, ibid., 134-435-157.

117. See, for example, Bentley file, 134-435-157, and memo, Belmont to Boardman, June 8, 1955, ibid., 134-435-151, 1–2.

118. Director to attorney general, 134-435-157.

119. Memo, Nichols to Tolson, September 1, 1955, Bentley file, 134-435-186; memo, Nichols to Tolson, June 29, 1955, ibid., 134-435-166.

120. Memo, SAC New Haven to director, June 27, 1955, Bentley file, 134-435-169.

121. Memo, SAC New Haven to director, July 9, 1955, Bentley file, 134-435-168.

122. Memo, director to SAC New Haven, July 17, 1955, Bentley file, 134-435-168.

123. "Testimony in Loyalty Case Eyed," Baton Rouge *State Times*, January 13, 1956, in Bentley file, 134-435-210, 2.

124. "Vindication for William Taylor," *Nation,* January 28, 1956, 63.

125. "Testimony in Loyalty Case Eyed."

126. Memo, SAC New Orleans to director, January 16, 1956, Bentley file, 134-435-210, 1.

127. Memo, SAC New Orleans to director, June 5, 1956, Bentley file, 134-435-213.

128. Email to author from Sheila Kurtz.

129. Phone interview, John Turrill, August 2, 2001.

130. Memo, SAC New Haven to director, October 3, 1956, Bentley file, 134-435-216.

131. Email from Nancy Applegate, January 16, 1998.

132. Letter to Mrs. Erb, May 13, 1957, Bentley file, 134-435-217.

133. Ibid.

134. Memo, SAC New York to director, July 8, 1957, Bentley file, 134-435-218.

135. Memo, SAC New Haven to director, March 25, 1958, Bentley file, 134-435-220.

136. Memo, SAC New Haven to director, May 29, 1958, Bentley file, 134-435-222, 1.

137. Ibid.

138. Ibid., 2.

139. Memo, SAC New Haven to director, April 30, 1959, Bentley file, 134-435-226.

140. Memo, Branigan to Belmont, August 13, 1959, Bentley file, 134-435-228.

141. Letter, Bentley to Hoover, August 10, 1959, Bentley file, 134-435-229.

142. Letter, Hoover to Bentley, August 13, 1950, Bentley file, 134-435-229.

143. Letter, Bentley to Hoover, November 11, 1959, Bentley file, 134-435, no serial.

144. Letter, Hoover to Bentley, November 19, 1959, Bentley file, 134-435-231.

145. Memo, director to SAC New Haven, December 6, 1960, Bentley file, 134-435, no serial.

146. Memo, SAC New Haven to director, July 11, 1960, Bentley file, 134-435, no serial.

EPILOGUE

1. Letter, Bentley to Hoover, May 31, 1961, Bentley file, 134-435-232.

2. Letter, Bentley to Sokolsky, March 14, 1960, Sokolsky Papers, Hoover Institution.

3. Postcard, Bentley to Matthews, July 1961, Matthews Papers, Perkins Library, Duke University.

4. Letter, Bentley to Sokolsky, December 23, 1959, Sokolsky Papers.

5. Bentley death certificate, New Haven Vital Statistics.

6. Airtel, SAC New Haven to director and SAC New York, December 3, 1963, Bentley file, 134-435-234; memo, Branigan to Sullivan, December 3, 1963, Bentley file, 134-435-235; phone interview, John Turrill, August 2, 2001.

7. *National Review,* July 29, 1961, and December 17, 1963; "Death of the Witness," *Time,* July 21, 1961; "Milestones," *Time,* December 13, 1963.

8. See, for example, "Other Deaths," *Newsweek,* December 16, 1963; "Elizabeth Bentley Is Dead at 55; Soviet Spy Later Aided U.S.," *New York Times,* December 4, 1963; "Elizabeth Bentley, Red Spy Turned Informer," *New York Herald Tribune,* December 4, 1963.

9. "Milestones"; "Elizabeth Bentley Is Dead at 55."

10. Oliver Pilat, "Elizabeth Bentley—An Epilogue," *New York Post,* December 8, 1963.

11. Phone interview, John Turrill, August 2, 2001.

12. Phone interview, July 27, 2001.

Selected Bibliography

PRIMARY SOURCES

Archives
Abilene, Kansas
   Eisenhower Library
      White House Central Files
Chicago, Illinois
   Loyola University of Chicago
      Women and Leadership Archives, Mundelein College Records
College Park, Maryland
   National Archives and Records Administration (NARA)
      Bureau of Investigation Reports
Durham, North Carolina
   Perkins Library, Duke University
      J. B. Matthews Papers
Florence, Italy
   Archives, Università di Firenze
Fort Meade, Maryland
   National Security Agency
      Venona Documents
         www.nsa.gov/docs/venona/venona_docs.html
New York, New York
   National Archives and Records Administration (NARA)
      U.S. Attorney file of William Walter Remington
Rome, Italy
   Archivio centrale dello Stato, Roma
      Ministero dell'Interno, Direzione generale pubblica sicurezza,
         Divisione affari generali e riservati
      Ministero dell'Interno, Polizia politica, fascicoli personali
Stanford, California
   Hoover Institution on War, Revolution, and Peace

George Sokolsky Papers
Herbert Solow Papers
Sam Tanenhaus Papers
Washington, D.C.
Federal Bureau of Investigation (FBI)
Files of Elizabeth Bentley, Hiss-Chambers, Victor Perlo,
William Walter Remington, Julius and Ethel Rosenberg,
Nathan Gregory Silvermaster, Harry Dexter White
Georgetown University
John Gilland Brunini Papers
Library of Congress
Joseph Rauh Papers
RGASPI Archives
National Archives, Center for Legislative Archives
Records, House Committee on Un-American Activities

Court Records

"United States vs. William Walter Remington," 1951, file #22045, National
Archives and Records Administration, New York.

"United States of America vs. William Walter Remington," 1953, file #22039,
National Archives and Records Administration, New York.

"United States of America vs. Abraham Brothman and Miriam Moskowitz,"
1950, file #C136-289, National Archives and Records Administration,
New York.

"Julius and Ethel Rosenberg vs. United States." New York: National
Committee to Secure Justice in the Rosenberg Case, 1952.

"United States of America vs. Alger Hiss," grand jury records, available at
the National Archives and Records Administration and in the Sam
Tanenhaus Papers at the Hoover Institution on War, Revolution, and
Peace.

Government Publications

U.S. House. Committee on Un-American Activities. *Hearings Regarding
Communism in the United States Government.* 81st Cong. 2d sess.
Washington, D.C., 1950.

U.S. House. Committee on Un-American Activities. *Hearings Regarding
Communist Espionage in the United States.* 80th Cong. 2d sess.
Washington, D.C., 1948.

U.S. Senate. Investigations Subcommittee of the Committee on
Expenditures in the Executive Departments. *Export Policy and Loyalty.*
80th Cong. 2d sess. Washington, D.C., 1948.

U.S. Senate. Subcommittee on Government Operations Abroad of the Committee on Government Operations. *Transfer of Occupation Currency Plates—Espionage Phase.* 83d Cong. 1st sess. Washington, D.C., 1953.

U.S. Senate. Subcommittee on Immigration and Naturalization of the Committee on the Judiciary. *S. 1832.* 81st Cong. 1st sess. Washington, D.C., 1949.

U.S. Senate. Subcommittee to Investigate the Administration of the Internal Security Act and Other Internal Security Laws of the Committee on the Judiciary. *The Institute of Pacific Relations.* 82d Cong. 2d sess. Washington, D.C., 1951–52.

U.S. Senate. Subcommittee to Investigate the Administration of the Internal Security Act and Other Internal Security Laws of the Committee on the Judiciary. *Interlocking Subversion in Government Departments.* 83d Cong. 1st sess. Washington, D.C., 1953.

U.S. Senate. Subcommittee to Investigate the Administration of the Internal Security Act and Other Internal Security Laws of the Committee on the Judiciary. *Strategy and Tactics of World Communism: The Significance of the Matusow Case.* 84th Cong. 1st sess. Washington, D.C., 1955.

Oral Histories

Columbia University Oral History Collection
  Harvey Bundy
Southern Oral History Program Collection, Southern Historical Collection, Wilson Library, University of North Carolina at Chapel Hill
  Mary Price Adamson
  Mildred Coy

SECONDARY SOURCES: BOOKS, ARTICLES, AND DISSERTATIONS

Abt, John, with Michael Myerson. *Advocate and Activist: Memoirs of an American Communist Lawyer.* Urbana: University of Illinois Press, 1993.

Albright, Joseph, and Marcia Kunstel. *Bombshell: The Secret Story of America's Unknown Atomic Spy Conspiracy.* New York: Times Books, 1997.

Allen, Virginia M. *The Femme Fatale: A Study of the Early Development of the Concept in Mid-Nineteenth Century Poetry and Painting.* Ann Arbor: University Microfilms International, 1979.

Andrew, Christopher, and Oleg Gordievsky. *KGB: The Inside Story of Its Foreign Operations from Lenin to Gorbachev.* London: Hodder & Stoughton, 1990.

Andrew, Christopher, and Vasili Mitrokhin. *The Sword and the Shield: The*

Mitrokhin Archive and the Secret History of the KGB. New York: Basic, 1999.

Belknap, Michal. *Cold War Political Justice: The Smith Act, the Communist Party, and American Civil Liberties*. Westport, Conn.: Greenwood, 1977.

Bellamy, Edward. *Looking Backward*. New York: Random House, 1982.

Benson, Robert Louis, and Michael Warner, eds. *Venona: Soviet Espionage and the American Response, 1939–1957*. Washington, D.C.: National Security Agency, 1996.

Bentley, Elizabeth. "Il Bel Gherardino." Master's thesis, Columbia University, 1935.

———. *Out of Bondage*. New York: Devin-Adair, 1951.

Bentley, Joanne. *Hallie Flanagan: A Life in the American Theatre*. New York: Knopf, 1988.

Berle, A. A. *Navigating the Rapids: 1918–1971*. New York: Harcourt Brace Jovanovich, 1973.

Bernstein, Barton, ed. *Politics and Policies of the Truman Administration*. Chicago: Quadrangle Books, 1970.

Blum, John M., Edmund S. Morgan, Willie Lee Rose, Arthur M. Schlesinger Jr., Kenneth M. Stampp, and C. Vann Woodward. *The National Experience*. Part 2, 3d ed. New York: Harcourt Brace Jovanovich, 1973.

Boughton, James M. "The Case against Harry Dexter White: Still Not Proven." *History of Political Economy* 33, no. 2 (Summer 2001): 219–39.

Boyer, Paul S., Clifford E. Clark Jr., Joseph F. Kett, Neal Salisbury, Harvard Sitkoff, and Nancy Woloch. *The Enduring Vision: A History of the American People*. 2d ed. Lexington, Mass.: D. C. Heath, 1993.

Bremner, Robert H., and Gary W. Reichard, eds. *Reshaping America: Society and Institutions, 1945–1960*. Columbus: Ohio State University Press, 1982.

Brennan, Sheila. "Popular Images of American Women in the 1950s and Their Impact on Ethel Rosenberg's Trial and Conviction." *Women's Rights Law Reporter* 14, no. 1 (Winter 1992): 43–63.

Brinkley, Alan. *The Unfinished Nation: A Concise History of the American People*. New York: McGraw-Hill, 1993.

Brown, Michael E., et al., eds. *New Studies in the Politics and Culture of U.S. Communism*. New York: Monthly Review Press, 1993.

Budenz, Louis. *Men without Faces: The Communist Conspiracy in the U.S.A.* New York: Harper & Brothers, 1948.

———. *This Is My Story*. New York: McGraw-Hill, 1947.

Budenz, Margaret R. *Streets*. Huntington, Ind.: Our Sunday Visitor, 1979.

Carr, Robert K. *The House Committee on Un-American Activities, 1945–1950.* Ithaca: Cornell University Press, 1952.

Caute, David. *The Great Fear: The Anti-Communist Purge under Truman and Eisenhower.* New York: Simon and Schuster, 1978.

Cave Brown, Anthony, and Charles B. MacDonald. *On a Field of Red: The Communist International and the Coming of World War II.* New York: Putnam, 1981.

Chambers, Whittaker. *Witness.* New York: Random House, 1952.

Cohen, Robert. *When the Old Left Was Young: Student Radicals and America's First Mass Student Movement, 1929–1941.* New York: Oxford University Press, 1993.

Cook, Fred. *Maverick: Fifty Years of Investigative Reporting.* New York: Putnam, 1984.

——. *The Unfinished Story of Alger Hiss.* New York: William Morrow, 1958.

Coy, Harold. *The Prices and the Moores: James Valentine Price and Pattie Moore Price of Rockingham County, North Carolina: Their Antecedents and Their Children.* Oakland, Calif.: Thomas Moore Price, 1944.

Craig, Bruce. "Treasonable Doubt: The Harry Dexter White Case, 1948–1953." Ph.D. diss., American University, 1999.

Crosby, Donald. *God, Church, and Flag: Senator Joseph R. McCarthy and the Catholic Church, 1950–1957.* Chapel Hill: University of North Carolina Press, 1978.

Culver, John C., and John Hyde. *American Dreamer: The Life and Times of Henry A. Wallace.* New York: Norton, 2000.

Cuordileone, K. A. "'Politics in an Age of Anxiety': Cold War Political Culture and the Crisis in American Masculinity, 1949–1960." *Journal of American History* 87, no. 2 (September 2000): 515–45.

Dallek, Robert. *Franklin D. Roosevelt and American Foreign Policy.* New York: Oxford University Press, 1979.

Davis, David Brion. *Homicide in American Fiction, 1978–1860: A Study in Social Values.* Ithaca: Cornell University Press, 1957.

Davis, Hope Hale. *Great Day Coming: A Memoir of the 1930s.* South Royalton, Vt.: Steerforth Press, 1994.

Devine, Thomas. "The Eclipse of Progressivism: Henry A. Wallace and the 1948 Presidential Election." Ph.D. diss., University of North Carolina, Chapel Hill, 2000.

Diggins, John P. *Mussolini and Fascism: The View from America.* Princeton: Princeton University Press, 1972.

Divine, Robert A., T. H. Breen, George M. Fredrickson, and R. Hal Williams. *America, Past and Present.* Glenview, Ill.: Scott, Foresman, 1984.

Dixler, Elsa. "The Woman Question: Women and the American Communist Party, 1929–1941." Ph.D. diss., Yale University, 1975.

Douglas, Susan J. *Where the Girls Are: Growing Up Female with the Mass Media.* New York: Times Books, 1994.

Dyson, Lowell. *Red Harvest: The Communist Party and American Farmers.* Lincoln: University of Nebraska Press, 1982.

Eisenhower, Dwight D. *Mandate for Change, 1953–1956.* Garden City, N.Y.: Doubleday, 1963.

Ernst, Morris L., and David Loth. *Report on the American Communist.* New York: Henry Holt, 1952.

Faragher, John Mack, Mari Jo Buhle, Daniel Czitrom, and Susan H. Armitage. *Out of Many: A History of the American People.* 2d ed. Upper Saddle River, N.J.: Prentice Hall, 1997.

Fass, Paula. *The Damned and the Beautiful: American Youth in the 1920s.* New York: Oxford University Press, 1977.

Fried, Richard. *Nightmare in Red: The McCarthy Era in Perspective.* New York: Oxford University Press, 1990.

Gallagher, Dorothy. *All the Right Enemies: The Life and Murder of Carlo Tresca.* New Brunswick, N.J.: Rutgers University Press, 1988.

Garber, Marjorie, and Rebecca L. Walkowitz, eds. *Secret Agents: The Rosenberg Case, McCarthyism, and Fifties America.* New York: Routledge, 1995.

Garraty, John A., and Robert A. McCaughey. *The American Nation: A History of the United States since 1865.* 6th ed. New York: Harper and Row, 1987.

Gentry, Curt. *J. Edgar Hoover: The Man and the Secrets.* New York: Penguin, 1992.

Gitlow, Benjamin. *The Whole of Their Lives: Communism in America—A Personal History and Intimate Portrayal of Its Leaders.* New York: Charles Scribner's Sons, 1948.

Goodman, Walter. *The Committee: The Extraordinary Career of the House Committee on Un-American Activities.* New York: Farrar, Straus and Giroux, 1968.

Gornick, Vivian. *The Romance of American Communism.* New York: Basic, 1977.

Gosse, Van. "'To Organize in Every Neighborhood, in Every Home': The Gender Politics of American Communists between the Wars." *Radical History Review* 50 (Spring 1991): 109–41.

Gouzenko, Igor. *This Was My Choice.* London: Eyre & Spottiswoode, 1948.

Griffith, Robert. *The Politics of Fear: Joseph R. McCarthy and the Senate.* 2d ed. Amherst: University of Massachusetts Press, 1987.

SELECTED BIBLIOGRAPHY

Griffith, Robert, and Athan Theoharis, eds. *The Specter: Original Essays on the Cold War and the Origins of McCarthyism.* New York: Franklin Watts, 1974.

Hamby, Alonzo. *Beyond the New Deal: Harry S. Truman and American Liberalism.* New York: Columbia University Press, 1973.

———. *Man of the People: A Life of Harry S. Truman.* New York: Oxford University Press, 1995.

Harper, Alan D. *The Politics of Loyalty: The White House and the Communist Issue, 1946–1952.* Westport, Conn.: Greenwood, 1969.

Hartmann, Susan M. *The Home Front and Beyond: American Women in the 1940s.* Boston: Twayne, 1982.

Haynes, John Earl, and Harvey Klehr. *The American Communist Movement: Storming Heaven Itself.* New York: Twayne, 1992.

———. *Venona: Decoding Soviet Espionage in America.* New Haven: Yale University Press, 1999.

Healey, Dorothy, and Maurice Isserman. *Dorothy Healey Remembers: A Life in the American Communist Party.* New York: Oxford University Press, 1990.

Henretta, James A., W. Elliot Brownlee, David Brody, and Susan Ware. *America's History.* Chicago: Dorsey Press, 1987.

Hiss, Alger. *In the Court of Public Opinion.* New York: Knopf, 1957.

———. *Recollections of a Life.* New York: Henry Holt, 1988.

Hiss, Tony. *Laughing Last.* Boston: Houghton Mifflin, 1977.

———. *The View from Alger's Window: A Son's Memoir.* New York: Knopf, 1999.

Horowitz, Daniel. *Betty Friedan and the Making of the Feminine Mystique.* Amherst: University of Massachusetts Press, 1998.

Isserman, Maurice. "Disloyalty as a Principle: Why Communists Spied." *Foreign Service Journal* 77, no. 10 (October 2000): 29–38.

———. *Which Side Were You On?: The American Communist Party during the Second World War.* Middletown, Conn.: Wesleyan University Press, 1982.

Jordan, George Racey, with Richard L. Stokes. *From Major Jordan's Diaries.* New York: Harcourt, Brace, 1952.

Jordan, Winthrop D., and Leon F. Litwack. *The United States.* 7th ed. Englewood Cliffs, N.J.: Prentice Hall, 1991.

Jowitt, Earl. *The Strange Case of Alger Hiss.* Garden City, N.Y.: Doubleday, 1953.

Kaplan, E. Ann, ed. *Women in Film Noir.* London: BFI Publishing, 1980.

Kazin, Alfred. *Starting Out in the Thirties.* Boston: Little, Brown, 1965.

Kelley, Robin D. G. *Hammer and Hoe: Alabama Communists during the Great Depression.* Chapel Hill: University of North Carolina Press, 1990.

Kempton, Murray. *Part of Our Time: Some Ruins and Monuments of the Thirties.* New York: Simon and Schuster, 1955.

Kirschner, Don S. *Cold War Exile: The Unclosed Case of Maurice Halperin.* Columbia: University of Missouri Press, 1995.

Klehr, Harvey. *The Heyday of American Communism: The Depression Decade.* New York: Basic, 1984.

Klehr, Harvey, John Earl Haynes, and Fridrikh Firsov. *The Secret World of American Communism.* New Haven: Yale University Press, 1995.

Klehr, Harvey, and Ronald Radosh. *The Amerasia Spy Case: Prelude to McCarthyism.* Chapel Hill: University of North Carolina Press, 1996.

Krugman, Herbert E. "The Interplay of Social and Psychological Factors in Political Deviance." Ph.D. diss., Columbia University, 1952.

Krutnik, Frank. *In a Lonely Street: Film Noir, Genre, Masculinity.* London and New York: Routledge, 1991.

Lamphere, Robert, and Tom Shachtman. *The FBI-KGB War: A Special Agent's Story.* New York: Random House, 1986.

Latham, Earl. *The Communist Controversy in Washington: From the New Deal to McCarthy.* Cambridge: Harvard University Press, 1966.

Levitt, Morton, and Michael Levitt. *A Tissue of Lies: Nixon vs. Hiss.* New York: McGraw-Hill, 1979.

Lieberman, Robbie. *My Song Is My Weapon: People's Songs, American Communism, and the Politics of Culture.* Urbana: University of Illinois Press, 1989.

Lowenthal, John. "Venona and Alger Hiss." *Intelligence and National Security* 15, no. 3 (Autumn 2000): 98–130.

Lynch, Christopher Owen. *Selling Catholicism: Bishop Sheen and the Power of Television.* Lexington: University Press of Kentucky, 1998.

Massing, Hede. *This Deception.* New York: Duell, Sloane and Pearce, 1951.

Matusow, Harvey. *False Witness.* New York: Cameron and Kahn, 1955.

May, Elaine Tyler. *Homeward Bound: American Families in the Cold War Era.* New York: Basic, 1988.

May, Gary. *Un-American Activities: The Trials of William Remington.* New York: Oxford University Press, 1994.

Nash, Gary B., and Julie Roy Jeffrey, eds. *The American People: Creating a Nation and a Society.* New York: Harper and Row, 1986.

Newman, Robert P. *Owen Lattimore and the "Loss" of China.* Berkeley: University of California Press, 1992.

Newton, Verne W. *The Cambridge Spies: The Untold Story of Maclean, Philby, and Burgess in America.* Lanham, Md.: Madison, 1991.

Nixon, Richard. *Six Crises.* Garden City, N.Y.: Doubleday, 1962.

Norton, Mary Beth, David M. Katzman, Paul D. Escott, Howard P. Chudacoff, Thomas G. Paterson, and William M. Tuttle Jr. *A People and a Nation: A History of the United States.* 2d ed. Boston: Houghton Mifflin, 1986.

O'Reilly, Kenneth. *Hoover and the Un-Americans: The FBI, HUAC, and the Red Menace.* Philadelphia: Temple University Press, 1983.

Ottanelli, Fraser. *The Communist Party of the United States: From the Depression to World War II.* New Brunswick, N.J.: Rutgers University Press, 1991.

Packer, Herbert. *Ex-Communist Witnesses: Four Studies in Fact Finding.* Stanford: Stanford University Press, 1962.

Peake, Hayden. Afterword to *Out of Bondage,* by Elizabeth Bentley. New York: Ivy Books, 1988.

Pearson, Drew. *Diaries, 1949–1959.* New York: Holt, Rinehart and Winston, 1974.

Perlo, Victor. "Reply to Herbert Aptheker." *Political Affairs* 71 (June 1992): 25–29.

Philipson, Ilene. *Ethel Rosenberg: Beyond the Myths.* New York: Franklin Watts, 1988.

Powers, Richard Gid. *Not without Honor: The History of American Anticommunism.* New York: Free Press, 1995.

———. *Secrecy and Power: The Life of J. Edgar Hoover.* New York: Free Press, 1987.

Primakov, Y. M., ed. *Ocherki Istorii Rossiyskoy Vneshney Razvedki.* Vol. 3. Moscow: International Relations, 1997.

Radosh, Ronald, and Joyce Milton. *The Rosenberg File: The Search for the Truth.* 2d ed. New Haven: Yale University Press, 1997.

Reale Università degli Studi di Firenze. *Annuario per l'Anno Accademico 1933–1934.* Florence: StabGrafico C. Ruffilli, 1934.

Roberts, Sam. *The Brother: The Untold Story of Atomic Spy David Greenglass and How He Sent His Sister, Ethel Rosenberg, to the Electric Chair.* New York: Random House, 2001.

Romerstein, Herbert, and Eric Breindel. *The Venona Secrets: Exposing Soviet Espionage and America's Traitors.* Washington, D.C.: Regnery, 2000.

Romig, Walter, ed. *The Book of Catholic Authors.* 4th series. Freeport, N.Y.: Books for Libraries Press, 1971.

Rosen, Marjorie. *Popcorn Venus: Women, Movies and the American Dream.* New York: Coward, McCann & Geoghegan, 1973.

Rupp, Leila, and Verta Taylor. *Survival in the Doldrums: The American Women's Rights Movement, 1945 to the 1960s.* New York: Oxford University Press, 1987.

Ryan, James G. *Earl Browder: The Failure of American Communism.* Tuscaloosa: University of Alabama Press, 1997.

Sandilands, Roger. "Guilt by Association?: Lauchlin Currie's Alleged Involvement with Washington Economists in Soviet Espionage." *History of Political Economy* 32, no. 3 (Fall 2000): 473–515.

———. *The Life and Political Economy of Lauchlin Currie: New Dealer, Presidential Adviser, and Development Economist.* Durham: Duke University Press, 1990.

Schaffer, Ronald. *Wings of Judgment: American Bombing in World War II.* New York: Oxford University Press, 1985.

Schneir, Walter, and Miriam Schneir. *Invitation to an Inquest: Reopening the Rosenberg "Atom Spy" Case.* Baltimore: Penguin, 1965.

Schrecker, Ellen. *Many Are the Crimes: McCarthyism in America.* Boston: Little, Brown, 1998.

Sheen, Fulton J. *Treasures in Clay: The Autobiography of Fulton J. Sheen.* Garden City, N.Y.: Doubleday, 1980.

Sibley, Katherine A. S. "Soviet Industrial Espionage against American Military Technology and the U.S. Response, 1930–1945." *Intelligence and National Security* 14, no. 2 (Summer 1999): 94–123.

Smith, John Chabot. *Alger Hiss: The True Story.* New York: Holt, Rinehart and Winston, 1976.

Solomon, Barbara Miller. *In the Company of Educated Women: A History of Women and Higher Education in America.* New Haven: Yale University Press, 1985.

Stokes, Richard. "Senator Taft on Catholic Schools." *Catholic World* 175 (July 1952): 246.

Sullivan, William, with Bill Brown. *The Bureau: My Thirty Years in Hoover's FBI.* New York: Norton, 1979.

Tanenhaus, Sam. *Whittaker Chambers.* New York: Random House, 1997.

Theoharis, Athan G., ed. *Beyond the Hiss Case: The FBI, Congress, and the Cold War.* Philadelphia: Temple University Press, 1982.

Theoharis, Athan G., and John Stuart Cox. *The Boss: J. Edgar Hoover and the Great American Inquisition.* Philadelphia: Temple University Press, 1988.

Thernstrom, Stephan. *A History of the American People.* Vol. 2, 2d ed. San Diego: Harcourt Brace Jovanovich, 1984.

Trimberger, Ellen. "Women in the Old and New Left: The Evolution of a Politics of Personal Life." *Feminist Studies* 5 (Fall 1979): 432–61.

Uesugi, Sayoko. "'Jim Crow Must Go!': Women's Activism, the Cold War, and the Making of the Progressive Party in North Carolina, 1945–1948." Master's thesis, University of North Carolina, Chapel Hill, 1997.

von Hoffman, Nicholas. *Citizen Cohn.* New York: Doubleday, 1988.

Warnock, Timothy. "Associate Justice Tom C. Clark: Advocate of Judicial Reform." Ph.D. diss., University of Georgia, 1972.

Wechsler, James. *Age of Suspicion.* New York: Random House, 1953.

Weigand, Kate. *Red Feminism: American Communism and the Making of Women's Liberation.* Baltimore: Johns Hopkins University Press, 2001.

———. "The Red Menace, the Feminine Mystique, and the Ohio Un-American Activities Commission: Gender and Anti-Communism in Ohio, 1951–1954." *Journal of Women's History* 3, no. 3 (Winter 1992): 70–94.

Weinstein, Allen. *Perjury: The Hiss-Chambers Case.* New York: Random House, 1978.

Weinstein, Allen, and Alexander Vassiliev. *The Haunted Wood: Soviet Espionage in America—The Stalin Era.* New York: Random House, 1999.

West, Nigel. *Venona: The Greatest Secret of the Cold War.* London: HarperCollins, 1999.

West, Rebecca. *The New Meaning of Treason.* New York: Viking, 1964.

White, Nathan I. *Harry Dexter White: Loyal American.* Waban, Mass.: Bessie (White) Bloom, 1956.

Wilson, Veronica A. "Elizabeth Bentley and Cold War Representation: Some Masks Not Dropped." *Intelligence and National Security* 14, no. 2 (Summer 1999): 49–69.

Zeligs, Meyer A. *Friendship and Fratricide: An Analysis of Whittaker Chambers and Alger Hiss.* New York: Viking, 1967.

Zion, Sidney. *The Autobiography of Roy Cohn.* Secaucus, N.J.: Lyle Stuart, 1988.

Index

62; and Bentley's espionage, 43,
63, 64, 65, 68–69, 70, 71; and
Silvermaster, 45; and Soviet es-
pionage in United States, 63, 70;
and Katz, 73; Bentley names as
spy, 96; and U.S. Service and
Shipping Corporation, 99
Browder, William, 96
Brown, F., 18–19, 23
Brownell, Herbert, 187, 196
Brunini, John Gilland, 156–58, 159,
163, 168–69, 178
Buck, Tim, 27
Buckley, Edward, 97, 98, 99, 100
Budenz, Louis, 57–58, 95, 96, 97,
113, 121, 146–48, 150, 176, 188
Budenz, Margaret, 146, 174

Calomiris, Angela, 150
Canada, 27, 91–92
Canadian Communist Party, 27
Carl. *See* Chambers, Whittaker
Carr, Robert, x
Casa Italiana, 14
Casella, Mario, 7, 153
Casper, Joe, 179
Cathedral School of St. Mary,
197–98
Catherine. *See* Lowry, Helen
Catholic Church, 95, 146–48, 156–
57, 168, 169, 173, 197
Cave Brown, Anthony, 21, 23
Central Intelligence Agency, 115
Chambers, Jay Vivian. *See* Cham-
bers, Whittaker
Chambers, Whittaker: as male de-
fector, x; personal characteristics
of, 28–29; and Hiss, 29, 31, 101,
137, 138–39, 142, 149–50; and
Stalinist purges, 29–30; evidence

collected by, 30, 31, 92; defection
of, 30–32; and FBI, 31–32; and
Silverman, 48; and White, 50,
100, 138, 140; and Akhmerov, 63;
and concealed enemy, 114; and
HUAC, 138; Bentley's charges
about wealth of, 176; and Bent-
ley's defense of informants, 188;
death of, 203
Chanler, William, 163
Childs, Marquis, 119–20
China, 48
China Aid Council, 51–52
CIO-PAC, 65
Civil rights movement, 131
Clark, Tom, 103, 115, 116, 118, 120,
142
Coady, Edward, 90–91
Coe, Frank, 47, 214 (n. 52)
Cohn, Roy, 175–86 passim, 196
Cold War, 129, 132, 136, 137, 138,
139, 144, 150, 203
College of the Sacred Heart, 185,
191, 193, 196, 197
Columbia Spectator, 14, 26
Columbia University, 5, 8, 9, 13–14,
28–29, 131, 152, 193
Communist International, 164
Communist Party of the United
States of America (CPUSA): and
Flanagan, 4; Bentley's involve-
ment with, 4, 9–10, 13, 15, 16–17,
18, 23, 24, 25, 27, 69, 89, 126; and
Fuhr, 9–10; Workers School of,
10, 15; and anti-Communist activism, 10–11; transitional period
of, 10–11; attractions of, 11–12;
and gender relations, 12, 135; and
sense of history, 13; underground
of, 15–16, 22, 23, 24, 29, 41, 48,

ley as double agent, 103–5, 106, 107–11; and atomic espionage case, 106, 118, 155–56, 164; and Tenney, 108–11; and suspicion of U.S. government subversion, 115; and grand jury investigation, 118, 119, 120–23; and Bentley's autobiography, 120–21, 124, 125, 168; and Frank, 127; and HUAC, 128; and Catholicism, 146, 147; and Venona project, 155; investigation of Bentley's past by, 161; Bentley's blackmailing of, 174, 178–81, 183, 192, 196, 199, 201, 204; and Wright's relationship with Bentley, 175, 176; and Cohn's protection of Bentley, 175–76; payments to Bentley by, 178–79, 181, 184, 185; and Matusow, 182; and Remington's trial, 184; and occupation currency scandal, 186; Bentley's praise for, 188, 189; and subpoena from Dejean, 191; Bentley withdraws from working with, 199–200; periodic consultation with Bentley, 202

Federal Theater Project, 4

Feklisov, Alexander, 106

Ferguson, Homer, 127, 129, 138, 142, 143, 149, 151

Ferguson Committee, 127, 129–30, 138, 142, 151

Fitin, Pavel, 68

Fitzgerald, Edward, 65, 66

Flanagan, Hallie, 4

Florentine, Joseph, 119

Ford, Henry, II, 147

Foreign Economic Administration, 47

Foxcroft school, 5

Frank, Jerome, 165

Frank, Nelson, 123–29, 132, 134, 142, 157

Frank, William, 125

Fuchs, Klaus, 37, 155, 156

Fuhr, Lini Moerkrik (Lee), 8–10

Gallaher, Lester, 181, 192

Gardner, Meredith, 155

Garrity, Devin A., 157

Gender roles: and Bentley's image, x, 134–36, 203, 204; and male ex-Communists, x, 176; and Bentley's youth, 3; and CPUSA, 12, 135; and World War II, 135–36; and societal changes, 136, 137–38, 230 (n. 124); and Bentley's autobiography, 169

Gitlow, Benjamin, 17

Gold, Bela, 47, 214 (n. 52)

Gold, Harry, 37, 73, 118, 155, 156, 158, 164

Gold, Sonia, 47, 214 (n. 52)

Golos, Celia, 23, 60

Golos, Jacob: and Bentley as spy, 18, 24–27, 28, 35, 36, 37, 39, 40–46, 51, 52, 54, 56, 57–58, 59, 60, 64, 72; and Soviet espionage, 18–19, 21, 22, 26, 33–35, 39–40, 41, 43–44, 57–60, 63, 213 (n. 13); and first meeting with Bentley, 18–19, 22, 23–24; Bentley's personal relationship with, 18–19, 22, 23–26, 28, 38–39, 60–62, 162, 164–65, 166, 203; and FBI, 20–21, 30, 35, 40–41, 94; and CPUSA, 20–23, 34; and Browder, 22, 34, 43, 62, 63; possible execution of,

30; and antifascism, 32; Bentley's discovery of identity of, 32–33; plea bargain of, 34, 212 (n. 50); and Brothman, 36, 162; and Reynolds, 37–38; health of, 41, 57, 60–61; and Price, 42, 43, 59; and Silvermaster, 45, 59, 214 (n. 43); and Rosenberg, 56, 57, 101, 164; death of, 61–62, 63, 64; and Bentley's visit to New York FBI office, 96; and Bentley's FBI statement, 101, 107; and Stripling, 128; and Remington, 163

Golos, Milton, 23
Goodman, Walter, x, 130–31
Gorbachev, Mikhail, 66
Gornick, Vivian, 13
Gorsky, Anatoly: Bentley's meetings with, 73–76, 79, 93–94, 195; and Bentley as Soviet spy, 73–78, 93–94, 95, 97, 98, 101, 108; and Katz, 77–78; and Budenz, 95; and bribe money for Bentley, 97, 101, 119, 133, 173–74, 186; and Bentley's FBI statement, 99; and Bentley as double agent, 104–5, 108; and Bentley's defection, 106–7, 125
Gouzenko, Igor, 91–93, 105, 108
Government Operations Committee, 186
Green, Richard G., 145–46, 148, 149, 152
Greenglass, David, 37, 106, 156, 164
Greinke, Bill. *See* Akhmerov, Iskhak Abdulovich
Gromov, Anatoli. *See* Gorsky, Anatoly
Groopman, Samuel, 176, 180

GRU (Soviet military intelligence), 29
Gruppo Universitate Fascisti, 6

Hall, Theodore, 55
Halperin, Maurice, 50–51, 52, 54, 99, 102, 106
Hamby, Alonzo, 144
Harris, Lem, 37, 98, 99
Hartmann, Susan, 135–36
Haynes, John Earl, 34, 59
Heller, Peter F., 76–78, 90–91, 94, 95–96, 97, 104, 119, 163, 173
Herndon, Angelo, 14
Hickey, Edward, 179
Hiss, Alger: and Bentley, ix, 100–101, 103, 177, 203; and Chambers, 29, 31, 101, 137, 138–39, 142, 149–50; perjury conviction of, 156
Hiss, Donald, 31
Hiss, Priscilla, 103, 137
Hitler, Adolf, 28, 31, 32, 43, 55
Hollywood blacklist, 150
Hoover, Herbert, 27
Hoover, J. Edgar: Bentley as informant of, x, 89; Bentley's admiration for, xi, 188; and Soviet espionage, 58–59; and Bentley's FBI statement, 102, 103; and Hiss, 103; and Bentley's Soviet defection, 105; and Tenney, 109; and Republican Party, 114–15; and Truman, 114–17; and Bentley's grand jury investigation, 120, 121, 122; and Bentley's life story, 124; and Frank, 127; and Catholicism, 146; and Rosenberg case, 156; and protection of Bentley, 180, 181, 191; and Bentley's

payments, 184; and Senate Internal Security Subcommittee, 187; and Bentley's truthfulness, 187, 189, 200, 204; and Bentley's tax problems, 196; Bentley withdraws from working for, 199, 200; Bentley's correspondence with, 200–201, 202

House Un-American Activities Committee (HUAC): and Flanagan, 4; and Golos, 39; and Hoover, 116–17; and Clark, 118; and Frank, 127; and Bentley's subpoena, 128; Bentley's testimony for, 130–33, 140, 143, 144, 158, 190; and Chambers, 138; and Remington, 141, 142, 145; and Taylor, 190

Howard, Roy, 123

Hull, Cordell, 46

Institute of Pacific Relations, 177

Internal Revenue Service, 195–96

International Monetary Fund, 49, 190

International Organizations Employee Loyalty Board, 190, 194, 196

Intourist, 111

Italian fascism, 5, 6–7, 9, 13–14, 24–25, 26

Italian Library of Information, 18, 24, 26

Jack. *See* Katz, Joseph

Jardine, Don, 99, 100

Jenner, William, 187

John (Soviet agent), 44–45

Jones, F. L., 116

Jordan, George Racey, 169, 170

Justice Department: and anti-Communist activism, 10; and Golos, 33–34; and U.S. Service and Shipping Corporation, 111; and Bentley's espionage case, 114, 116; and *Amerasia* case, 115; and Bentley's grand jury investigation, 118, 119–23, 125; and Smith Act indictments, 122, 125; and Brunini, 159; and Brothman trial, 161–62; and Bentley's subpoena from Dejean, 191; and Bentley's tax problems, 196

Katz, Joseph, 72–73, 77–78, 99, 106–7, 120

Kelly, Joseph, 101, 119, 124, 142, 194

Kempton, Murray, 135

Keynes, John Maynard, 48

KGB. *See* NKGB

Kilgore, Harley, 65

King, Mackenzie, 92

Klehr, Harvey, 34, 59

Kleinman, William, 162

Koral, Alexander, 106

Kramer, Charlie, 65, 66, 100, 102, 106, 138, 141

Krivitsky, Walter, 30, 31

Ladd, Mickey, 109–10, 133

Lane, Myles, 176

Lasky, Victor, 160

Latham, Earl, 134

Lattimore, Owen, 177, 178

League for Industrial Democracy, 4

Lee, Duncan, 51–53, 71, 99, 102, 107, 141–42, 229 (n. 109)

Lee, Ishbel, 71, 141

Lend-Lease, 46, 169

Lenin, Vladimir Ilyich, 22, 29, 122

Remington, Ann, 53–54, 158
Remington, William: background of, 53–54; as Bentley's source, 54, 59, 66, 102; Bentley's testimony against, 130, 170, 183, 184, 203; and HUAC, 141, 142, 145; Loyalty Review Board hearing of, 145, 148–49; and suit against Bentley, 145, 149, 152, 153, 154, 163; FBI's perjury evidence against, 157–58; perjury indictment of, 158, 159, 161, 173; and detectives following Bentley, 160; trials of, 162–64, 173, 175, 179, 180, 181, 183, 184; Bentley's accusations against, 178, 183, 189, 190; death of, 193, 203
Republican Party, 114–15, 116, 129, 143, 144, 145, 177, 182, 186
Reynolds, John Hazard, 37–38, 67, 77, 93, 111–12, 146
Richardson, Seth, 149
Riggs, Robert, 188
Rogers, Pauline, 15, 17
Rogers, William, 196
Roosevelt, Franklin D., 31, 46, 48, 66, 144
Rosenberg, Ethel, 37, 137, 158, 159, 164, 165, 203, 230 (n. 134)
Rosenberg, Julius: Bentley's testimony and, 37, 159, 164, 165, 203; and Golos, 56, 57, 101, 164; and Greenglass, 106, 156; and FBI, 106, 158; conviction of, 175; Bentley's refusal to identify, 178
Rushmore, Howard, 160
Russian War Relief, 51

Sayre, Nora, 136
Scott, Byron N., 192, 196–97

Senate Immigration and Naturalization Subcommittee, 151
Senate Internal Security Subcommittee, 177, 187, 190, 193
Senate Subcommittee on War Mobilization, 65
Sheen, Fulton J., 95, 146, 147, 148, 153
Sherman, Roger, 1, 4
Silverman, George, 48, 49, 66, 99, 102, 126, 141, 215 (n. 63)
Silvermaster, Helen, 45, 46, 47, 72, 99, 102, 103, 106
Silvermaster, Nathan Gregory: background of, 45; and Soviet espionage, 45, 49–50, 214 (n. 43); and Golos, 45, 59, 214 (n. 43); and Taylor, 47–48, 189–90; and Currie, 48–49, 50, 133, 215 (n. 63); and FBI, 49, 102, 103; as Stalinist, 54; and Akhmerov, 67, 68, 72; and Bentley's FBI statement, 99; and Bentley's defection, 106; and Bentley's HUAC testimony, 133; and HUAC, 141; lack of documentary evidence on, 150; and Bentley's truthfulness, 189
Silvermaster group, 45–50, 55, 63, 68–69, 72
Sloane, Thomas, 169
Smith, Mr. (Russian agent), 17
Smith Act indictments, ix, 122, 125, 144, 150
Sobell, Morton, 164
Sokolsky, George, 160, 196, 202
Soviet Union: as model, 12–13; and Nazi-Soviet Pact, 28, 31, 32, 40, 58; and plots against Stalin, 29–30; and Price sisters, 42; Nazi